TRIMBLERIGG

A Book of Revelation

*

'O, let him pass! he hates him,
That would upon the rack of this tough world
Stretch him out longer.'

JONATHAN TRIMBLERIGG
From a drawing by
Edmond X. Kapp

TRIMBLERIGG
A Book of Revelation
by
Laurence Housman

*

With a
frontispiece from a recent portrait
by Kapp

Jonathan Cape Ltd
Eleven Gower Street London

Republished 1971
Scholarly Press, Inc., 22929 Industrial Drive East
St. Clair Shores, Michigan 48080

FIRST   PUBLISHED   IN   MCMXXIV
MADE & PRINTED IN GREAT BRITAIN
BY BUTLER & TANNER LTD
FROME   AND
LONDON

Library of Congress Catalog Card Number: 75-145094
ISBN 0-403-01032-2

4/72

Contents

5

CONTENTS

CONTENTS

CONTENTS

Editorial

THE TRIBAL DEITY TO WHOM MR. TRIMBLERIGG OWED his origin would, I think, have shown a better sense of the eternal fitness of things had he chosen for his amanuensis one whose theological antecedents were more within his keeping and jurisdiction than my own. But when he visited me with the attack of verbal inspiration which I was powerless to throw off in any other form than that which here follows, he seems rather to have assumed an intellectual agreement which certainly does not exist, and to have ignored as unimportant a divergence of view which I now wish to place on record. For, to put it plainly, I do not worship the god of Mr. Trimblerigg; and had these pages been a complete expression of my own feelings, they would have borne hostile witness not so much against Mr. Trimblerigg, as against his deity.

When nations declare war, or when gods deliver judgment against criminals who are so largely of their own making, — fastening in self-justification on some flagrant instance of wrong-doing which, for those who do not wish to reflect, puts the culprit wholly out of court, — they would do well to select their official historians from minds too abject and submissive to form views of their own; and of course verbal inspiration, as in the case of Balaam, is one way of getting the thing done. But whereas, in that historical instance, it was the ass and not the prophet who kicked last, in this instance, having delivered my message, I claim the right to exonerate myself in a foreword which is entirely my own. And so here, in this place — before he makes revelation or utters prophecy — Balaam speaks his own mind.

I do not think that Mr. Trimblerigg's deity has dealt

fairly by him. To me he seems chargeable with the same exploitive elasticity as that which he exposes in Mr. Trimblerigg, whom he first cockered up in his own conceit by a course of tribal theology, and then callously abandoned to its logical consequences when tribal theology went suddenly out of fashion. For Mr. Trimblerigg was emphatically a product of that self-worship of the tribe or clan, on which divine Individualism has so long fattened itself. He was brought up to believe himself one of a chosen sect of a chosen people, and to judge from a theocratic standpoint the ways, doings, and morals of other sects, communities, principalities, and powers. He could not remotely conceive, without being false to his deity, that his own was not immeasurably the best religion in the world, his god a god of perfect balance and proportion, and himself a chosen vessel of the Lord. In that character he was always anointing himself with fresh oil, which, losing its balance, ran far further than it ought to have done. But if, in consequence, he became an oleaginous character, whose mainly was the blame?

I cannot acquit the deity in whose tenets he had been trained. Having been brought up to read history as a pre-eminent dispensation of mercies and favours to his own race, with a slight push of miracle at the back of it — is it any wonder that, when he applied his gospel to propaganda for the interests of that same race, or went out a missionary to the heathen, it was with a conscientious conviction that a little compulsion was necessary for the saving of souls?

And so, in that shadiest episode of all his career, presented to us by his deity in such an unfavourable light, when the poor benighted heathen began painting Mr.

Trimblerigg's fellow-missionaries black and tan, and other horrible colours to indicate their hearty dislike for a blended gospel of free salvation in Christ and duty and allegiance to the Puto-Congo Rubber shareholders; when they did that, he – quite naturally – invoked the law of the Mosaic dispensation, and did the same to them: and defended himself for these gospel-reprisals by saying that it would have been very unreasonable not to protect Christian missionaries by the only method which savages could understand as a stepping-stone to the methods of Christianity.

The picture as presented is true: that was Mr. Trimblerigg all over. He had a lively notion that Christianity could be induced by pagan methods. But has his deity the right to cast either the first or the last stone at him? If he seemed to be always carrying the New Testament in his coat-tail pocket and making it his foundation for occasions of sitting down and doing nothing, while, up and doing, it was the law of Moses with which he stuffed his breast: and if, when he wanted to thump the big drum (as he so often did), he thumped the Old Testament, he was only doing with more momentary conviction and verve and personal magnetism what the larger tribalism of his day had been doing all along; and his tribal deity never seems to have had the slightest qualms in allowing Mr. Trimblerigg to regard himself as a Christian.

Yet all the time the deity himself knew better, as this record abundantly shows; for having made Mr. Trimblerigg partly but not entirely in his own image, he then used him as a plaything, an object of curiosity; and committing him to that creed of racial aggrandisement of which he himself was beginning to tire, thereby reduced him to ridicule, made a fool of him, exalted him to the likeness and similitude of a god, and then – let him go. And though, in the ensuing pages, he has helped himself freely to my opinions, as though they were his own, I do not feel that they were honestly adopted. For a god who tires of his handiwork is still responsible for it, however disillusioned; and when, employing me as his mouthpiece, Mr. Trimblerigg's maker mocks at the tribal religions which have brought the world so near to ruin, he remains nevertheless a deity tribal in character, albeit a disgruntled one. And if he has manœuvred this record in order to wash his hands of responsibility, it comes, I fear, too late; the source is too suspect to be regarded as impartial, and he himself very much more of a Mr. Trimblerigg than he seems to be aware.

And so my business here is to express an utter disbelief (which I hope readers will bear in mind) that Mr. Trimblerigg's deity was one about whom it is possible to entertain the larger hope, even in the faint degree suggested by Tennyson, – or that he was anything except a tribal survival to whom Mr. Trimblerigg and others gave names which did not properly belong to him.

What finally laid Mr. Trimblerigg by the heels was the fact that having picked up this god as he went along (finding him favourable to the main chance) it was the main chance – idealized as 'the larger hope' – which he really worshipped without knowing it. Upon the strength of that inspiration environment intoxicated him, and he drew his spiritual life from the atmosphere around him. Then he was like a bottle of seltzer, which at the first touch of the outer air begins almost explosively to expand; whereas, for the bulk of us, we unbottle to it like still wine without sound or foam, accepting it as the natural element for which we were born. To Mr. Trimblerigg, on the other hand, it came as a thing direct from God: at the first touch of the herd-instinct he bubbled, and felt himself divine. And in the rush of pentecostal tongues amid which he lost his head, he forgot that atmosphere and environment are but small local conditions, and that, outside these, vacuum and interstellar space hold the true balances of Heaven more surely and correctively than do the brief and shifting lives of men.

This spiritual adventurer, with his alert vision so curiously reduced in scale to seize the opportunities of day and hour, missed the march of time from listening too acutely to the ticks of the clock. And if he offers us an example for our better learning, it is mainly as showing what belittling results the herd-instinct and tribal-deism may produce in a mercurial and magnetic temperament, — making him imagine himself something quite other from what he really is, and his god a person far removed from that category in which he has been placed.

My own interpretation of this 'Revelation,' which has made me its involuntary mouthpiece, is that it shows the beginning – but the beginning only – of mental change in a god who has become tired of deceiving himself about the work of his creation; and that it has begun to dawn upon his mind – though he denies it in words – that, in making Mr. Trimblerigg, he has made another little mistake, and that his creation was really stuffed as full of them as a plum-pudding is stuffed with plums. And I have a hope that when tribal deity becomes properly apologetic for its many misshapings of a divided world, humanity will begin to come by its own, and acquire a theology which is not an

13

organized hypocrisy for the bolstering up of nationalities and peoples.

For here we have a world full of mistakes, which is governed, according to the theologians, by a God who makes none. And what between predestination and free-will, and grace abounding mixed up with original sin, and orthodoxy and heterodoxy at such universal clash throughout the world that not one honest soul in a million has an even chance of being really right, – when that is the spectacle presented to us in the life of the human race, it becomes something of a mockery to minds of intelligence to be told that their gods have never made mistakes.

Those who have been blessed with good parents, do not like them less because of certain failings and limitations which go to the shaping of their characters; and when, arrived at the age of discretion, they have to withstand their failings and recognize their limitations, they do so with a certain amount of deference and with undiminished affection; but they do not, if they are wise, or if they have the well-being of their parents really at heart, – they do not let it be thought that they regard them either as immaculate or infallible.

I have come to the conclusion that a like duty towards its tribal deities belongs to the human race; and that man has made many mistakes simply by regarding these tribal emanations as immune from error, all-seeing, all-wise, all-loving – which they certainly are not. And I believe that Mr. Trimblerigg would have been a very much better and more useful man if he could have conceived his tribal deity as one liable to error like himself. The terrible Nemesis which seized the soul of Mr. Trimblerigg and hurled it to destruction was a very limited and one-sided conception of what was good and right, embodied in the form of a personal deity who could do no wrong.

So here, as I read it, we have the revelation of the detriment done to a human soul by an embodied belief in itself under cover of a religious creed. And the record of that process has been handed over to me, I suppose, because the tribal deity responsible for the results has got a little tired of the abject flattery of his worshippers, and a little doubtful whether that relation between the human and the divine is really the right one. He is suffering in fact, as I read him, from a slight attack of creative indigestion, and is anxious to get rid of certain by-products which his system cannot properly assimilate: he is anxious, amongst other things, to get rid of responsibility for Mr. Trimble-rigg. But the responsibility is there; and I allow myself this foreword in order to declare it in spite of the things which hereafter I am made to say.

'You cannot unscramble eggs,' is a dictum as applicable to gods as to mortals. And if people would remember that in their prayers, prayers would be less foolish and fatuous than they often are.

You cannot unscramble eggs. And so, having scrambled Mr. Trimblerigg in the making, his god was attempting a vain thing in trying to unscramble him; and when Mr. Trimblerigg went on his knees and prayed, as he occasionally did, to be unscrambled, he was only scrambling himself yet more in the fry-pan of his tribal theology.

And indeed, when I look at him, I have to admire what a scramble of a man he was! — how the yolk and the white of it, the good and the evil, the thick and the thin of his character did mix, 'yea, meet and mingle,' as he would have said himself when his platform sense of poetry got the better of him. And so, in the exercise of those contradictory agilities of soul and brain which made him so mixed yet so divided a character, he skipped through life like a flea to Abraham's bosom, and there — after so many an *alias* hastily assumed and as hastily discarded — lies waiting to answer to his true name when true names are called.

What kind of a name, one wonders, did he finally make for himself in the Book of Life? In that desperate saving of his own face which constitutes his career, he put out of countenance many that were his betters; but it was himself that, in the process, he put out of countenance most of all. Yet in the end revelation came to him; and when, in that ghastly moment of self-discovery, he stood fully charged with the truth, who shall say what miraculous, what fundamental change it may not have wrought in him? When he followed the upward rope which led him so expeditiously Elsewhere, it may have been with the equipment of a new self capable of much better and more honest things that he finally entered Heaven. I cannot believe that such a genius for self-adaptation has incontinently missed its mark. But, in that forward aim, it may well be that he and his tribal deity have parted company; for it is to be noted that, at the last gasp, the god loses sight — does not know what has become of him: thinks, perhaps, that he has gone irretrievably and abysmally — Down. I, on the contrary, have a suspicion and a hope that his tendency may have been — UP.

L. H.

CHAPTER ONE

Deus Loquitur

OF COURSE WHEN I MADE MR. TRIMBLERIGG, THOUGH I had shaped him – I will not say to my liking, but at least to my satisfaction – I did not foresee how he would turn out. It is not my custom to look ahead. I can, to be sure, do so when I please: but that makes the *dénouement* so dull. I prefer, therefore – and have now made it a rule – that my creations shall, in what they do, come upon me as a surprise – pleasant or the reverse. For since I have given them free-will, let me also have the benefit of it: let them make their own plans, their own careers, – attributing to me, if they must, those features of both for which they do not feel themselves responsible; and let me (in the moment when they think to have fulfilled themselves) experience that small stimulus of novelty which the infinite variety and individuality of my creatures is always capable of providing.

For it is this spice of novelty alone which keeps me from being unutterably disinterested in the workings of what theologians are pleased to call 'the moral purpose of the universe.'

So it was that, having shaped Mr. Trimblerigg to my satisfaction, I let him go. And as, with his future in his own very confident hands, he went, I did not for the moment trouble to look after him.

When I say that I shaped him to my satisfaction, I am speaking merely as a craftsman. I knew that I had made a very clever man. As to liking him, that had nothing to do with craftsmanship, but would depend entirely on what he did with himself – how he appealed to me as a

17   B

student of life, when – laying aside my rôle of maker, I became merely the observer.

It is always an interesting experiment whether I shall be drawn to my creations before they become drawn to me. Sometimes I find that they interest me enormously, even while denying me with their last breath. But the unrequited affections of a god have always an element of comedy; for though, in the spiritual direction, one's creations may take a way of their own, they are never as quit of us as they suppose; and when they know it least they come back to us for inspection and renovation. Even the soul that thinks itself lost is not so lost as to leave one unaware of its condition; though it may have ceased to call, its address is still known.

In Mr. Trimblerigg's case it was all the other way – from the moment that he discovered me he never let me alone; though I had cast him forth like bread upon the waters, not expecting to see him again for many days, he came back to me early, and from that time on gave me the advantage of his intimate and varying acquaintance to the very end.

I wonder to myself sometimes whether I tried him as much as he tried me, and whether he managed to like me up to the last. This at least I found – that by the time he was five years old, whether I liked him or not, Mr. Trimblerigg liked me; and the reason for his liking was simple – he found me useful.

For one day, having done something which deserved, or was supposed to deserve punishment, he lied about it, and was discovered. The discovery came to his ears before he was actually taxed with it. The small world on which he stood became suddenly an abyss; lifting up his feet he fled for refuge to his own chamber, and was about to hide in the cupboard, when he heard the awful tread of judgment ascending the stairs. Being clever (for which I admit I was responsible) he realized how temporary a refuge the cupboard must necessarily be; what he needed was the eternal; and so, throwing himself on his knees he began praying to me – aloud. And in his prayer he told the truth, volubly, abundantly, and without making any excuse for himself. 'I have told a lie,' he cried, 'O God, I have told a lie!'

The agony of his prayer was heard, not so much by me as by the elder for whose entry he had so accurately timed it. And who, looking upon that youthful and ingenuous countenance, could doubt the sincerity of his grief? His lips quivered, his eyes streamed tears, his nails dug into his tender flesh, leaving marks. At that sight, at those sounds, the paternal heart was deeply moved; the birch was laid aside; elder and younger knelt together and prayed for quite a long time, with great fervour, fixity, and unanimity of purpose, that henceforth young Mr. Trimblerigg should be a good boy, and never never again be caught telling a lie.

That prayer unfortunately was not entirely answered – though between us we did our best. In the years that followed Mr. Trimblerigg lied often and well, but was very seldom caught, and still more seldom punished.

The only really important outcome of that incident was that Mr. Trimblerigg found he liked me; I had been useful to him. And yet I had done, I protest, absolutely nothing – except making him clever. It was not through my providential intervention that he liked me, but through his own. The prayer of faith had saved him from a whipping; it was a lesson he never forgot.

And so, from that day on, he made me his general help and stay; and on every occasion of doubt, difficulty, or distress, was able, by coming to me, to convince himself that he meant well. Never in my whole world's existence have I come upon anybody who was able to answer his own prayers about himself, and about other people, with such conviction, avidity, and enthusiasm as Mr. Trimblerigg. And why should I complain? It made him a great power in the world, without my having to lift a finger, or turn a hair, or do anything, in fact, except wink an eye, or seem to.

The virtuous incentives of family life, though only provided on a small scale, were not lacking for the development of Mr. Trimblerigg's character. He had three uncles, two aunts, a great-uncle and a grandfather – all fairly contiguous, the family being of the indigenous not of the migratory kind – besides a father, a mother and a sister, with whom contact was continuous and unescapable. Even in their naming the children had been linked for lovely and pleasant relationship in after life; for when the Trimblerigg first-born, whom its parents confidently expected to be a son, turned into a daughter – adapting the forechosen name to suit her sex, they called her Davidina; and when, nearly two years later, our own Mr. Trimblerigg struggled out into the world, nearly killing his mother in the process, the destined name Jonathan was there waiting for him.

And so, very early in his career, Mr. Trimblerigg's sister Davidina became the whetstone of his virtues – its operation summed up in the word 'emulation.' Nature would perhaps have brought it about in any case, even if the parental plan had not inculcated and forced it home; but when it became clear to Mr. and Mrs. Trimblerigg senior that no more children were to be theirs, they conceived the idea of blending the business with the moral instincts, and in the training of their two offspring making virtue competitive.

No wonder then, that, as their moral sense dawned, the germ of mutual suspicion and hatred grew lodged in their souls. This, however, did not prevent them, when self-interest prompted, from being also allies, as the following may show.

The parental idea of making virtue competitive had taken one of its earlier forms – for economic reasons, I fancy – in the matter of pocket-money; and the weekly penny was tendered not as a right nor even as a reward for good average behaviour, but as a prize to be wrestled for, gain by the one involving loss by the other – a device that had the incidental advantage of halving the tax on the pocket which provided it.

The fact that Davidina won it far more frequently and easily than he did, set Mr. Trimblerigg his first problem in goodness run as a means to profit. He accordingly invited his sister to an arrangement whereby, irrespective of conduct, they should go shares; and when this accommodating olive-branch was scornfully rejected, he became so offensively good for three weeks on end that Davidina, left penniless, capitulated on terms, and, in order to get a remnant of her money's worth, bargained that they should be good – or at least each better than the other – in alternate weeks, this being a more tolerable arrangement to her careful soul than that brother Jonathan, with no

effort at all, ever secondary in virtue, should share equally
the pennies which she had earned.

For a while the plan worked well; Mr. Trimblerigg by
calculated effort bettered his sister in the alternate weeks,
got the penny and shared it grudgingly but honourably –
while Davidina, remaining merely herself, received it in
the natural course when Jonathan reverted to his more
normal standard.

But there came a day when Mr. Trimblerigg had privily
done certain things about which his elders knew less than
did Davidina, and so got wrongfully the penny he had not
earned. Davidina demanded it; on the denial of her claim
they fought, and between them the penny got lost. The
next week, though Davidina earned it, Mr. Trimblerigg
claimed it, arguing that as last week's penny had been lost
to him through her, this week's should be his. Davidina
thought differently; and putting the penny for safety in
her mouth, in the resulting struggle by accident swallowed
it.

After that the alliance was over. Thenceforth Jonathan
had a permanent and lively incentive for becoming good;
and in the competition that ensued Davidina was decisively
worsted. Goodness became for Mr. Trimblerigg a matter
of calculation, habit, resolute will, and in the long series
of defeats which followed, Davidina might, had she
chosen, have found satisfaction in the large part she
played toward the reshaping of her brother's character.

So decisive was the change that it became apparent to
the world, and was reckoned as proof of that conversion
to grace which was necessary for full church-membership
in the sect where he belonged. And so, at an unusually
early age, Jonathan was baptized into the congregation of

the Free United Evangelicals. That incident decided his career; he became destined for the ministry.

Thus out of evil comes good.

When the matter was first decided Mr. Trimblerigg himself knew nothing about it. It was the elders of the family, the parents, grandparents, uncles and aunts – sitting together in conclave for the adjustment of ways to narrow means, who foresaw the convenience of the call which in due time came to him.

Mr. Trimblerigg himself was then making other plans of his own. A sense of his abilities had begun to stir his mind to the prospects of life. He had become conscious that a career was awaiting him – or, to put it more accurately, several careers – of which he had only to choose. One day, in a weak moment of expansiveness, when Davidina by a histrionic show of sisterly sympathy had led him on, he confided to her the sparkling alternatives which he had in mind. And she, when her first admiration had become tempered with criticism, passed word of them carefully on to the ears of his Uncle Jonah. Jonah, who was anti-romantic by temperament, made it his duty to strip these pretensions bare before the eyes of the assembled family – doing it no doubt for his nephew's good.

'Jonathan is thinking,' said he, 'that he would like to be Prime Minister; and well he might be if he had the ability to be consistent in his principles. Seems also he'd like to be President to the Free Church Conference; but for that he needs to be spiritual and one that speaks nothing but the truth. Failing that he's for being Lord Chief Justice and Master of the Rolls; but Jonathan hasn't the judicial mind. And to be Field-Marshal rising from the ranks (which is another flea he has in his bonnet) God in His great mercy hasn't given him sufficient inches to meet the military requirements. You'll do well, Jonathan; for you're quick in the turnover, and your convictions don't trouble you; and you've a wonderful courage for thinking yourself right when all the evidence is against you. But what you'll do if you're wise is find a master who'll let you hide behind his back and be clever for him in the ways that don't show; one who'll take over all the responsibility for your mistakes, for the sake of all the times when you've guessed right. Given he's got the patience to put up with you, you'll be worth it to him, and a credit to your family. But there's a deal of practice you've to get before you can do the thing well. Don't spread yourself.'

But Uncle Jonah, being an undertaker by trade, had narrow and confining views; and the shadow of his daily occupation, entailing a too-frequent wearing of black, caused him to set foot on life sombrely, especially on life that was young. This also was said before the time when nephew Jonathan had become conspicuously good.

With his higher aspirations thus blown upon, Mr. Trimblerigg, after watering Davidina's pet fern with strong tea which it did not like, diverted his invention to more practical ends, and for a time wished to be a conjurer, having read accounts of the wonders performed at the Egyptian Hall, London, by Messrs. Maskelyne & Cooke. But as ill-luck would have it, his first sight of conjuring came to him at a village fair; and there, while others stared and were amazed, he with his sharp eyes saw how everything was done, and found the entertainment dull. Now had he only been interested and stirred to emulation thus early, I am quite convinced that Mr. Trimblerigg

JONATHAN TRIMBLERIGG
(aged 7) with his Mother & Sister
Davidina

could have become a conjurer such as the world has never seen. If his parents could only have afforded to take him to London, and to the Egyptian Hall, the world's history might have been different. It was not to be.

Mr. Trimblerigg's attention was first attracted to the career his elders designed for him, not so much by the habitual goodness with which the rivalry of Davidina had imbued his character, as by his observation of the sensation caused in his native village by the missionizing efforts of a certain boy-preacher, then known to fame as 'The Infant Samuel Samuel,' whose call, beginning at his baptism in that strange invocative reduplication of the family name imposed by his godparents, went on till it suddenly passed in silence to an obscurity from which the veil has never been lifted. What happened then nobody knows, or nobody chooses to tell. But between the ages of seven and fifteen, while sustained by the call, Samuel Samuel never saw a vacant seat, or an uncrowded aisle, or had sitting under him a congregation unrent by sobs in the hundreds of chapels to which the spirit bore him.

When Mr. Trimblerigg heard him, Samuel Samuel at the age of ten was still in the zenith of his powers; and it has been credibly reported that, in the mining villages which he passed through, publicans went bankrupt and committed suicide because of him, and pit-ponies, their ears robbed of the familiar expletives to which they had been trained, no longer obeyed orders; and that alongside of these manifestations of grace, the illegitimate birth-rates went up and struck a record; till, six months later, things settled back and became the same; birth-rates went down, pit-ponies obeyed a restored vocabulary, and ruined publicans were vindicated in the prosperity of their successors.

But these things only happened after; and when Mr. Trimblerigg heard the cry of the Infant Samuel Samuel, he discerned a kindred spirit, and saw a way opening before his feet, under a light which thereafter continued to shine. And so at the age of twelve the designs which Mr. Trimblerigg's elders had on him, and the designs which he had on himself, coalesced and became one; and even Davidina, borne down by the sense of the majority, had to accept the fact that her brother Jonathan had received a call.

Thus early did the conversion of souls enter into the life and calculations of Mr. Trimblerigg. A striking justification of his chosen calling followed immediately, when, without in the least intending it, he converted an almost lost soul in a single day – the soul of an Uncle, James Hubback by name, the only uncle upon his mother's side left over from a large family – who while still clinging to the outward respectability of a Free Church minister, had taken secretly to drink.

Mr. Trimblerigg had been born and brought up in a household where the idea that spirits were anything to drink had never been allowed to enter his head. He only knew of spirit as of something that would catch fire and boil a kettle, or embrace death in a bottle and preserve it from decay. These aspects of its beneficence he had gathered first in the back kitchen of his own home, and secondly in the natural history department of the County Museum, to which as a Sunday-school treat he had been taken. Returning therefrom, he had been bitten for a short while with a desire to catch, kill, and preserve frogs,

26

bats, beetles, snakes, and other low forms of existence, and make a museum of his own – his originality at that time being mainly imitative. To this end he clamoured to his mother to release his saved pennies which she held in safe keeping for him, in order that he might buy spirit for collecting purposes; and so pestered her that at last she promised that if for a beginning he could find an adder, he should have a bottle of spirit to keep it in.

Close upon that his Uncle James arrived for a stay made sadly indefinite by the low water in which he found himself. He still wore his clerical garb but was without cure of souls: Bethel and he had become separated, and his family in consequence was not pleased with him. Nevertheless as a foretaste of reformation he wore a blue ribbon, and was prevented thereby from letting himself be seen on licensed premises; while a totally abstaining household, and a village with only one inn which had been warned not to serve him, and no shop that sold liquor, seemed to provide a safe environment for convalescence.

It is at this point that Mr. Trimblerigg steps in. One day, taking down a book from the shelf in the little study, he discovered behind it a small square bottle of spirits: he did not have to taste or smell it – the label 'old brandy' was enough; and supposing in his innocence the word 'old' to indicate that it had passed its best use, at once his volatile mind was seized with the notion that here was a mother's surprise waiting for him, and that he had only to provide the adder for the bottle and its contents to become his. And so with that calculating larkishness which made him do audacious things that when done had to be swallowed, he determined to give his mother a surprise in return.

Going off in search of his adder and failing to get it him-self, he gave another boy a penny for finding him a dead one. An hour later the adder was inside the brandy bottle behind the books; and an hour after that his Uncle James had achieved complete and lifelong conversion to total abstinence.

The *dénouement* presented itself to Mr. Trimblerigg at first with a shock of disappointment in the form of smashed glass, and his dead adder lying in a spent pool of brandy on the study floor; and only gradually did it dawn upon him after a cautious survey of the domestic situation that this was not as he had at first feared his mother's angry rejection of the surprise he had prepared for her: on the contrary she was pleased with him. His uncle, he learned, was upstairs lying down, without appetite either for tea or supper. Mr. Trimblerigg heard him moaning in the night, and he came down to breakfast the next day a changed character. Within a year he had secured rein-statement in the ministry, and was become a shining light on the temperance platform, telling with great fervour anecdotes which give hope. There was, however, one story of a drunkard's reformation which he never told: perhaps because, on after-reflection, though he had ac-cepted their testimony against him, he could not really believe his eyes, perhaps because there are certain experi-ences which remain too deep and sacred and mysterious ever to be told.

But to Mr. Trimblerigg the glory of what he had done was in a while made plain. More than ever it showed him destined for the ministry: it also gave colour to his future ministrations, opening his mind in the direction of a cer-tain school of thought in which presently he became an

adept. 'The Kingdom of Heaven is taken by tricks,' became the subconscious foundation of his belief; and when
he entered the pulpit at the age of twenty-one, he was by
calculative instinct that curious combination of the tipster,
the thimblerigger, and the prophet, the man of vision and
the man of lies, which drew to itself the adoration of one
half and the detestation of the other half of the Free
United Evangelical Connection, eventually dividing that
great body into two unequal portions, and driving its soul
into a limbo of spiritual frustration and ineffectiveness till
it found itself again under new names.

The Early Worm

THOUGH MR. TRIMBLERIGG HAD NOT AT THE TIME TAKEN the advice of his Uncle Jonah in very good part, he did eventually accept a large part of it – good or otherwise – in the shaping of his career. His wish to become a great functionary of State gradually faded away, giving place to others. But his intention to be President of the Free Church Conference remained and grew strong. And to that end – spirituality being required – he accepted faithfully Uncle Jonah's last bit of advice, and seeking a master behind whose back he could hide and be clever in ways that didn't show – have responsibility taken for his mistakes, and get adequate recognition for the many things which he did right – seeking for such a master, he found him to his own satisfaction in the oldest of old ways; and never from that day on did the suspicion enter his head, that the master whom he chose under so devout an *alias* was himself.

If, in the process, he received a call, so did I; and it was at this stage of his career that I began to watch him with real interest. His calls became frequent; and though there was not always an apparent answer there was always an attentive ear.

It may well be that when human nature appears, to those whose business is to understand it, most unexpected and incalculable, is the very time when it is or ought to be most instructive to eyes which are open. And certainly at this preliminary period – before I got accustomed to him – Mr. Trimblerigg did make me open my eyes wider and wider, till he got me to the point when nothing that he did surprised me. But that was not because I became able to anticipate his reactions to any given circumstance or tight hole in which he might find himself: but merely that experience of him caused me to give up all rules based on the law of averages: he was a law by himself. What at first baffled me was the passionate sincerity with which he was always able to deceive himself – doing it mainly, I admit, by invoking my assistance: that is to say, by prayer.

To see him fall upon his knees and start busily lighting his own little lamp for guidance through the perils immediately surrounding him – while firmly convinced all the time that the lamp was not his lighting but mine – gave me what I can only describe as an extraordinary sense of helplessness. The passionate fervour of his prayer to whatever end he desired, put him more utterly beyond reach of instruction than a conscious plunge into sin. Against that there might have been a natural reaction; but against the spiritual avidity with which he set to work saving his own skin day by day, no reaction was possible. The day-spring from on high visited him with a light-heeled nimbleness which cleared not only all obstacles of a material kind but all qualms of conscience as well. In the holy of holies of his inmost being self-interest sat rapturously enshrined; there lay its ark of the covenant, and over it the twin cherubim of faith and hope stretched their protecting wings. Mr. Trimblerigg might bow himself in single spirit when first his prayer began; but always, before it ended, his spirits had got the better of him, and he would rise from his knees as beautifully unrepentant as a puppy that has dodged a whipping, his face radiant with happiness, having found an answer to his prayer awaiting him in the direction to which from the first it had been set, much as your Arctic explorer finds the North Pole by a faithful following of his nose after having first pointed it to the north.

I date my completed understanding of Mr. Trimblerigg, and of the use he had made of me, to the day when – faced with an exposure which would have gone far to reduce his ministerial career to a nullity – he put up a prayer which (had I been a mere mortal) would have made me jump out of my skin. I will not skin him retributively by quoting him in full, but the gist of it all was that, much to his perplexity he found himself suffering from a strange temptation, out of keeping with his whole character, and threatening destruction to that life of energetic usefulness in the service of others which he was striving to lead. And so he prayed to be kept ('kept' was the very word) – 'humble, and honest, and honourable.' It was no change that he desired; but only a continuance in that narrow and straight path of acquired virtue down which (since the truth must be told) he had hitherto danced his way more like a cat on hot bricks, than the happily-banded pilgrim he believed himself to be. 'Kept' was the word; and as I heard him I thought of it in all its meanings – and wondered which. I thought of how dead game 'keeps' up to a point, and is better in flavour for the keeping; but how, after that point is reached, the keeping defeats itself, and the game is game no longer, but mere offal. Was it in that sense that he wished to be 'kept'? For certainly I had found him good game, quick in the uptake, and brisk on the wing.

It is difficult in this record to remain consecutive. Those who would follow with accuracy the career of Mr. Trimblerigg, must jump to and fro with the original – one of whom it has to be said that though he denied himself

32

many times (even in the face of the clearest evidence) he denied himself nothing that held out any prospect of keeping his fortunes on the move; and the stitch in time with which he so often and so nimbly saved himself ran in no straight line of machine-made regularity, but rather in a series of diversions this way and that, stepping sideways and back preparatory to the next forward leap; and in this feather-stitching along life's road he covered more ground, and far more ornamentally, than do those who go merely upon their convictions, holding to one opinion and doing only one thing at a time.

Yet it would be wrong to say that he was ever false to his convictions, for these he seldom knew. Enough that so long as they lasted his intuitions were sacred to him; and as it is the very essence of intuitions that at any moment they may change, his changeableness had about it a sort of truth, of consistency, to which slower minds cannot attain.

But why call it 'intuition'; why not 'vision'? Well, if a camera of powerful lens and stocked with highly sensitive films may be said to have vision, vision he had in abundance. Adjusting his focus to the chosen point of view, he clicked the switch of his receptivity, snapt a picture, wound it off upon its wheel, and was ready for another. In the space of a few minutes he had as many pictures stored as he had a mind for. 'Vision'? You may grant it him, if you will, so long as you remember that that was the process. I would rather be inclined to call it 'optics'; and I see his career now rather as a series of optical delusions, through every one of which he remained quite convinced that he was right, and that the truth had come to him by way of revelation. An early example will serve.

The small hill-side village in which Mr. Trimblerigg

first learned to escape the limitations of ordinary life was a place where things seldom happened; and there were times in his early upbringing when he found himself at a loose end, a rose wasting its sweetness to the desert air; there was nothing doing in the neighbourhood on which he could decisively set his mark. This was to live in vain; and often he searched through his small world of ideas to find inspiration. Should he run away from home, and be found wandering with his memory a blank? Should he be kidnapped by gipsies and escape in nothing but his shirt? Should a sheep fall into the stone quarry so that he might rescue it, or a lamb get lost in the snow during the lambing-season, that he might go out, and find, and return bearing it in his bosom? Or should he go forth and become famous as a boy-missionary, preaching to the heathen in an unknown tongue? These were all possibilities, only the last suggested any difficulty.

Whenever in doubt, adopting the method of old Uncle Trimblerigg, he turned to the Scriptures: he did not search them, for that would have been self-willed and presumptuous; he merely opened them, putting a blind finger to the spot where divine guidance awaited him. It was in this way that Uncle Trimblerigg had become rich; forty years ago he had invested his savings in house property all through having set thumb to the text, 'I have builded an house to Thy name.' And without searching the Scriptures further he had built twenty of them. At a later date, slate-quarrying having started in the district, their value was doubled.

So one day, in a like faith, our own Mr. Trimblerigg committed himself to the same experiment. His first point on opening drew a startling reply, 'Get thee behind me,

Satan, for thou savourest not the things which be of God, but the things which be of men.' Very right and proper, of course: Satan thus safely disposed of, he tried again. 'Remember Lot's wife,' failed for the moment to convey any meaning; he knew that it could not refer to him: it seemed rather to indicate that his Bible had not yet given him its thorough attention. To warm it to its task he lifted it as a heave-offering, administered to it the oath, as he had seen done in a police court, kissed it, and set it down again. This time it answered sharply, but still not to the point: 'Ye generation of vipers, who hath warned you to flee from the wrath to come?' Evidently the Lord was trying him. He turned from the New Testament to the old: perhaps it was only the old he should have consulted, for he had an idea that this was an Old Testament method. That would account for the delay.

The Old Testament made a better response to his appeal. 'The zeal of Thy House hath eaten me up,' suggested something at any rate, but did not make the way quite clear; 'Down with it, down with it, even unto the ground!' was practical in its bearing upon the Lord's House, but puzzling; 'Behold how great a matter a little fire kindleth' gave him the light he sought.

For at that time Bethesda, the chapel of the Free Evangelicals, had fallen lamentably into disrepair, and since Uncle Trimblerigg, the only man of substance in the district, had retired from the innovation of hymn-singing to a stricter Bethel of his own, there seemed little chance of raising the necessary funds for demolition and restoration. And so decay went on, while still, from old habit, the chapel continued to be insured.

Now whether we call it 'vision' or 'optical illusion,' there can be no doubt that, thus aided by Scripture, Mr. Trimblerigg visualized rapidly and clearly the means to an end which so many desired. And so it came about one Saturday night, while frost held the village water-supply firmly in its grip, and the road running up from the valley slipped with ice, that Bethesda, through a supposed leakage in her heating apparatus, caught fire; and only the fact that Mr. Trimblerigg fetched the fire-engine from the town four miles away, saved it from utter destruction. He had been sent into the town by his mother to do errands, when at the foot of the hill he suddenly remembered Lot's wife, and looking back saw the chapel windows gustily ablaze, and interpreting the peradventure aright had sped on with the news. The miraculous arrival of the fire engine with him on it, only half an hour after the villagers' discovery of an already well-established insurance claim in swift operation, had caused an immense sensation and some inquiry.

But Mr. Trimblerigg had a case on which no suspicion could rest; that the fire was fought expeditiously, though under difficulties, was largely owing to him, and the subsequent inquiries of the insurance office agent who came to inspect the damage were only of a formal kind. Every effort had been made, and a half-saved chapel was the result; but its previous dilapidation made it easier to rebuild than to restore, and when a new Bethesda rose from the ruins of the old, the insurance company paid for it.

It was two days after the happy catastrophe, that Davidina remarked (when, to be sure, he was taking them to light the lamp in another room), 'I wish you wouldn't always go taking away the matches!'

'I'm bringing them back,' said Jonathan correctively.

'You didn't the last time,' Davidina retorted. And at the word and the tone of her voice, Jonathan trepidated and fled.

Was it 'vision' that made him do so, or only optical illusion on the mental plane? For as far as I have been able to probe into Davidina's mind, which is not always clear to me, she knew nothing. It was merely her way: the hunting instinct was strong in her, and he her spiritual quarry: never in all their born days together was she to let him go.

Of course Mr. Trimblerigg did not go on doing things like that. It was an act of crude callow youth, done at a time when the romantic instinct takes unbalanced forms; yet in a way it was representative of him, and helped me to a larger insight into his character and motives. For here was Mr. Trimblerigg, thus early, genuinely anxious to have guidance from above for the exploitation of his superabundant energies; and when, at first showing, the guidance seemed rather to head him off from being energetic at all, he persisted till his faith in himself found ratification, and thereafter went his way with the assurance that what he decided to do must almost necessarily be right.

Mr. Trimblerigg did not in after days actually set fire to anything in order that he might come running to the rescue when rescue was too late; but he did inflame many a situation seven times more than it was wont to be inflamed, setting people by the ears, and causing many an uprooting in places where no replanting could avail. And when he had got matters thus thoroughly involved, he would apply thereto his marvellous powers of accommodation and persuasion, and, if some sort of peace and order did thereafter emerge, regard himself quite genuinely as the deliverer.

At a later date his zeal for the Lord's House broke up the Free United Evangelicals into separate groups of an unimportant size, which when they seemed about to disappear wholly from view, he reunited again; and having for the moment redoubled what was left, regarded his work as good, though in the religious world the Free Evangelicals had forfeited thenceforth their old priority of place, a circumstance from which (when convinced of its permanence) he made his personal escape by embracing second Adventism. And though doubtless he carried his Free Evangelism with him into the field of modern prophecy, the Free Evangelicals within their own four walls knew him no more. Very effectively he had burnt them out, and in their case no insurance policy provided for the rebuilding: in that seat of the mighty, probed by the beams of a new day, only the elderly grey ashes remained of men whose word once gave light.

CHAPTER THREE

Trial and Error

AT A VERY EARLY STAGE IN HIS CAREER, BEFORE HIS theological training had overtly begun, the moral consciousness of Mr. Trimblerigg was far more accurately summed up in the words, 'Thou, Davidina, seest me,' than in the more generally accepted text which shone with symbolic rays from an illuminated scroll hung over his bed. That text with its angel faces and gold edgings did not pierce the joints of his harness, to the discovery of vulnerable spots, with the same sharp efficiency as did the dark watchful eye of Davidina.

As he entered into his 'teens with the instinct for spiritual adventure growing strong, he had an uncomfortable sense of transparency where Davidina was concerned – or rather where she was not concerned but chose to intrude – which made him cease to feel a self-contained person. If there was anyone in the world who knew him – not as he wished to be known, but as in his more disconcerted moments he sometimes suspected himself to be – it was Davidina. Under the fixture of her eye he lost confidence; its calm quizzical gaze tripped his thoughts, and checked the flow of his words: initiative and invention went out of him.

The result was truly grievous, for though he could do without self-respect for quite long intervals, self-complacency was the necessary basis for every action. Davidina deprived him of that.

Her power was horrible; she could do it in a momentary look, in a single word; it seemed to be her mission in life, whenever he whitewashed the window of his soul for better privacy, to scratch a hole and look through.

39

When, for instance, he first experimented in kissing outside the routine of family life, Davidina seemed by instinct to know of it. Secretively, in the presence of their elders, she held him with her eye, pursed her lips, and made the kissing sound; then, before he could compose a countenance suitable to meet the charge, her glance shot off and left him. For Davidina was a sleek adept in giving that flick of the eye which does not wait for the repartee; though on other occasions, when her eye definitely challenged him, there was no bearing it down; it stabbed, it stuck, it went in, and came at his back.

It was in these wordless encounters that she beat him worst; till Mr. Trimblerigg, conscious of his inferiority, went and practised at the glass a gesture which he hoped thereby to make more effective – a lifting of the nose, a slight closing of the eyelids, a polished putting-off of the hands, deprecatory but bland; and a smile to show that he was not hurt. But the first time he used it upon her was also the last.

'Did you practise that in the glass?' said Davidina; and the gesture died the death.

Truly at that time of her life he wanted her to die, and slightly damped her shoes on the inside after they had been cleaned, that they might help her to do so. But it was no good; without saying anything, she damped his also, rather more emphatically, so that there could be no mistake; whereas his damping was so delicately done that she ought not to have found it out.

The most afflictive thing about these encounters was his constant failure to score a victory; only once, in the affair of the pocket-money already narrated, had he succeeded in holding his own. Perhaps it was all for the good of his soul; for in matters of finance his sense of probity remained in after years somewhat defective; victory over Davidina in that respect had apparently done him no good. But in other directions she continued to do her best to save his soul; and though he was now committed to the ministry, and was himself to become a soul-saving apparatus, he did not like her way of doing it; temperamentally (and was there ever a character more largely composed of temperament?) he would much rather have gone his own way and been damned, than saved by Davidina on the lines she chose. She stung him like a gad-fly in his weakest spots, till the unerring accuracy of her aim filled him with a superstitious dread; and though never once uttered in words, 'Thou, Davidina, seest me,' was the motive force which thus early drove him so deeply and deviously into subterfuge that it became an infection of his blood. And though against her it availed little, in other directions, pricked to it by her incessant skill, he had a quite phenomenal success, and was – up to a point – the nimblest being that ever skipped from cover to open and from open to cover, till, in the development of speed, he ceased to distinguish which was which; and what he told would tell with the most complete conviction that, if it told to his advantage, it must be truth; and then, on occasion, would avail himself of the truth to such dazzling effect that, lost in the blaze of his rectitude, he forgot those other occasions when he had been truer to himself.

Of Davidina's inspired pin-pricks here is an example, notable for the early date of its delivery, when they were at the respective ages of twelve and eleven. Brother and

sister had fallen out in guessing at an event as to which
with probability all the other way, Davidina proved to be
right. Not believing this to be a guess, 'You *knew*!' he
cried indignantly.

'I didn't,' she replied smoothly, 'I only knew better.'

This was superfluous: it enabled Mr. Trimblerigg to get
in with a retort. 'Even very conceited people,' he said,
'do sometimes manage to guess right.'

Davidina recovered her ground. 'I'm not as conceited as
you,' she replied, 'I never think myself good.' It was the
sticking-out of her tongue, and adding 'so there'! which
gave the barb to those words.

At the earliest opportunity Mr. Trimblerigg retired to
consider them. It was evident that Davidina had penetrated another of his secrets; she had discovered that he
thought himself good. Many years after, when asked by
an American reporter what it felt like to be the greatest
man in the world, he replied that it made him feel shy,
and then was ready to bite his tongue out for having so
aimed at modesty and missed. He saw twenty reporters
writing down the words, 'It makes me feel shy'; and within
twelve hours it was all over the world – a mistake which
he couldn't explain away. That was to be one of the
worst moments of his life; and this was another, that
Davidina should have unearthed so hidden and central a
truth. He was deeply annoyed, partly with her for having
discovered it, much more with himself for having let it
appear.

Yet his cogitations brought him in the end to a conclusion which had in it a measure of comfort. 'After all,' he
said to himself, 'I *am* good sometimes.'

It was that 'sometimes,' and the consciousness of it, that

in the future was to work havoc with his soul. He did know desperately well that he was good sometimes; and the fervour of it used to spread so far beyond the appointed limit that he ceased to know where his goodness began, and where it left off. As from an oasis in the wilderness exhales fragrance from the blossom of the rose, regaling the dusty nostrils of sand-bound travellers, as into its airy horizon ascends mirage from waters, and palm-trees, and temples, that are real *somewhere* – but not in the place where they so phenomenally display themselves – so from parts of him excellent, into other parts less excellent, went the sense that he was 'somehow good'; and he never perceived, in spite of the very genuine interest he took in himself that what made him more interesting than anyone else was the extraordinary division of his character into two parts, a good and a bad, so dexterously allied that they functioned together as one, endowing him with that curious gift of sincerity to each mood while it lasted, which kept him ever true to himself and the main chance, even as the bits of glass in a kaleidoscope always shape to patterns, however varied, having the same fixed centre – a haphazard orderliness which no amount of shaking can destroy.

As has been hinted already, a time unavoidable for youth came in Mr. Trimblerigg's life when kisses began to have an attraction for him: in his case it came rather early, and the attraction grew strong. But so also grew his fear of them – or perhaps it would be more true to say his fear lest Davidina should get wind of them. Davidina had an unlovable scorn for kisses, which she paraded to the world; she kissed nobody except her parents, and them only from a sense of duty, and became

known, in a country-side where kisses were easily
come by, as the girl from whom nobody could get a
kiss.

Few tried; the first who did so had been made a warning
for others.

It is likely enough – since moral emblems have their
contrary effect – that the impregnable barrier set up by
Davidina was responsible for the thing becoming so much
a vogue in other quarters; and Lizzie Seebohm, the pretti-
est small wench of the village, in pure derision of Davidina's aloofness, and under her very eyes, made open sale of
her kisses at a price which, starting from chocolates, rose
to a penny and thence to twopence.

For this amiable weakness she got from Davidina the
nickname of 'Tuppenny,' and in view of the feud which
thence arose, Mr. Trimblerigg was instinctively advised
of danger to his peace of mind if he put himself on Tuppenny's list. And so it came about that, whatever his
natural inclinations in the matter, he saved his pocket-
money and did not apply for her favours.

In this Lizzie Seebohm saw the influence of Davidina;
for which reason and sheer spitefulness, Mr. Trimblerigg
became her quarry.

So one day a communication reached him, artfully told
by the small maiden commissioned thereto as a breach of
confidence. She had heard Lizzie say that Jonathan might
have a kiss of her not merely for nothing; she would give
twopence to get it. A sense that he was really attractive
made him fail to see deep enough, and when the offer
rose to sixpence he succumbed.

Within an hour – Lizzie Seebohm had seen to it –
Davidina got the news. Her wrath and sense of humilia-

tion were deep; in the great battle of life which lay ahead
for the possession of her brother's soul, she had lost a
point, and that to an opponent whom she regarded as insignificant. It was not a case for silence. Davidina descended upon him before the sixpence in his pocket had
had time to get warm. 'You've been kissing Tuppenny!'
she cried.

'Who says?' he demanded, scared at discovery so swift.
Then, bettering his defence: 'Tuppenny, indeed! she's not
worth it. I haven't given her tuppence; I haven't given
her a penny. I haven't given her anything, so there! If
she says I have, she's a liar.'

This seemed almost conclusive; Davidina's faith in the
report wavered. But whenever Jonathan was voluble she
distrusted him; so now.

'It isn't her word I'm going by,' she said. 'Somebody saw
you.'

Mr. Trimblerigg's mind made an alert movement — very
characteristic. He was not ashamed of what he had done;
he only didn't like being caught.

'You said Tuppenny,' he retorted. 'And I say — I didn't
give her tuppence.'

Davidina pressed him along the track, as he meant her
to. 'Then what did you give her?'

'I didn't give her anything; I've told you so already. She
gave me sixpence.'

His tone was triumphant, for now, in his own time and
in his own way, he had made a clean breast of it. Davidina's face was a study.

'Sold again!' he said, watching the effect; and curiously
he did not mean himself, or his virtue, or anything else
belonging to him; he meant Davidina. Having got ahead

of her with the facts, he considered himself top-dog for
that once at least.

But within a few hours of that avowal an amazing thing
happened. It happened during the night; for when he
went to bed the sixpence was in his trouser pocket, and
when he got up in the morning it was gone; nor did he
dare to tax Davidina with the theft.

In chapel, the next Sunday, when the plate came round
for foreign missions, Davidina with ostentation put sixpence into it. Is it to be wondered that, before the week
was over, he had got sixpence back from somewhere, and
took care that Davidina should see him spending it.
Davidina meant well, I am sure; but it is to be questioned
whether her method of clipping his wings was the right
one. He became tangential to the orbit of her spells; they
touched, but they did not contain him.

Meanwhile, without Davidina's aid, even without her
approval, Mr. Trimblerigg's call to the ministry was becoming more assured. And the question mainly was
whether, in that family of cramped means, money could
be found in the years lying immediately ahead to provide
the necessary training. It meant two years spent mainly
away from home at the Free Evangelical Training College;
two years of escape from Davidina for whole months at a
time; it meant leaving home a boy and coming back very
nearly a man. Even had the ministry not appealed to him,
it would have been worth it for the peculiar attraction of
those circumstances.

Whether this could become practically possible depended
mainly upon old Uncle Trimblerigg – Uncle Trimblerigg whose investments in house property had been
inspired by holy scripture, but whose theological tenets

46

were of a kind for which up-to-date Free Evangelicalism no longer provided the college or the training. Nor did he believe that either college or training were necessary for the preaching of the Word. He had done it himself for fifty years, merely by opening the book where it wished to be opened and pondering what was thus presented. The verbal inspiration of Scripture, not merely in its writing but in its presentation to the sense of the true believer, was the very foundation of his faith. The sect of 'the True Believers' had of late years sadly diminished; for as all True Believers believed that while they believed truly they could never make a mistake in their interpretations of Scripture, it became as time went on dangerous for them to meet often or to exchange pulpits, since, where one was found differing from another, mutual excommunication of necessity followed and they walked no more in each other's ways. Only at their great annual congress did they meet to reaffirm the foundation of their faith and thunder with a united voice the Word which did not change.

Thus it came about that dotted over the country were many chapels of True Believers cut off from friendly intercourse with any other by mutual interdict; and the hillside chapel of Uncle Trimblerigg – built by himself for a congregation of some twenty families all told, his tenants, or his dependents in the building trade – was one of them.

So among the True Believers there was small prospect of a career for the budding Mr. Trimblerigg; and yet it was upon the financial aid and favour of one of them that he depended for theological training in a direction which they disapproved.

TRIMBLERIGG

It speaks well for the sanguine temperament and courage of our own Mr. Trimblerigg that the prospect did not dismay him, or even, in the event, present much difficulty.

48

CHAPTER FOUR

The Beard of the Prophet

UNCLE PHINEAS, THE UNCLE OF MR. TRIMBLERIGG'S
father, lived at an elevation, both physical and spiritual, among the stone quarries a-top of the village. His
house and the chapel where he ministered stood adjoining, both of his own building; and in the days when
Jonathan knew him he was seldom seen leaving the one
except to go to the other. For he was now very old, and
having made his money and retired from business, he had
only one interest left in life, the preaching of the strict
tenets of True Belief to the small congregation which
had trickled under him for the last fifty years.

The True Believers had a worship which was all their
own; they flocked by themselves, never going elsewhere,
though others sometimes came to them. No instrument
of music was allowed within their dwelling, nor did they
sing – anything that could be called a tune. When their
voices were lifted in praise they bleated upon a single note,
which now and again they changed, going higher and
higher, and when they could go no higher they stopped.

To our own Mr. Trimblerigg this form of worship was
terrible; he liked music and he liked tunes; diversity
attracted him; and here, by every possible device, diversity
was ruled out. But the importance of Uncle Phineas,
both present and prospective, obliged certain members of
the Trimblerigg family to ascend once at least every Sunday, to hear him preach and pray, and though none of
them professed an exclusive conversion to the teaching of
the True Believers, they kept an open mind about it, and
listened respectfully to all that Uncle Phineas had to
say.

D

Lay-preaching and the ministry of the Word ran strong in the Trimblerigg family, also in that of the Hubbacks, to which on his mother's side Jonathan belonged; and had he cared to divide himself spiritually among his relations there were five sects from which to choose – a division of creeds which did not amount to much, except in the case of the True Believers. Grandfather Hubback, between whom and Uncle Phineas there was theological war, ministered to the Free Evangelicals at the Bethesda which Jonathan had helped to renovate; Uncle James was a Primitive Brother; Uncle Jonah a First Resurrectionist; his Sunday exercise – the practising of the Last Trump – a welcome relief perhaps, from his weekday occupation of undertaker. Mr. Trimblerigg, during his childhood, had sat under all of them; the difference being that under his Uncle Phineas he had been made to sit. Then came the question of his own call to the ministry, and the further question as to ways and means. It was from then on that Mr. Trimblerigg went more constantly and willingly to hear the doctrine of the True Believers, and began to display towards it something wider than an open mind. At the age of fifteen he had got into the habit of going to see and hear his uncle on weekdays as well, and very quietly he would endure for hours together while the old man expounded his unchangeable theology.

Everything about Uncle Phineas was long, including his discourses. He had a long head, a long nose, a long upper lip and a long chin. To these his beard served as a corrective; long also, it stuck out at right angles from his face, till with the weight of its projection it began to droop; at that point he trimmed it hard and square, making no compromise, and if none admired it except its owner, it was at least in charaćter. With such a beard you could not kiss people, and Phineas Trimblerigg was not of a mind to kiss anybody. In spite of old age, it retained a hue which suggested a too hasty breakfast of under-boiled egg; while trying to become grey it remained reminiscently golden.

And the beard symbolized the man; square, blunt and upright, patriarchal in mind and charaćter, he lived in a golden age of the past — the age of romantic theology before science had come to disturb it. His only Tree of Knowledge was the Bible, and this not only in matters of doćtrine; it was his tree of genealogy and history as well. From its topmost branch he surveyed a world six thousand years old, of six days making, and all the wonders that followed, — the Flood, the Tower whose height had threatened Heaven, and the plagues, pestilences and famines, loosed by an outraged Deity on a stubborn but chosen people, and the sun and the moon which stood still to assist in tribal slaughter, and the special vehicles provided for prophets, .at one time a chariot of fire, at another a great fish, at another a talking ass, — all these things gave him no mental trouble whatever; but joy rather, and confidence, and an abiding faith. He believed them literally, and had required that his family should believe them too. And truly he could say that, in one way or another, he had to begin with made them all God-fearing. If in the process five had died young, and one run away to sea and got drowned, and another fallen into evil courses from which he had not returned alive, so that Phineas in his old age was left childless — all this had but made him more patriarchal in outlook than ever, turning his attention upon nephews and nieces of the second generation, especially

5I

upon one; which, indeed, is the reason why here he becomes an important character.

Fortified by fifty years of prudent investment based upon revelation, and with a comfortable balance at his bank, he cast his other cares upon the Lord; lived frugally, gave a just tithe of all he possessed to the foreign and home missions of the True Believers, drank no wine or strong drink – except tea, denounced the smoking of tobacco, but took it as snuff, believed firmly in Hell, war, and corporal punishment for men, women and children alike, was still an elected, though a non-attending, member of all local bodies, but in the parliamentary election (regarding it as the evil thing) would take no part. To him life, in the main, meant theology.

At the now sharply dividing ways he stood with old Pastor Hubback (or rather against him) a leading and a rival light among the local Free Churches; and because he had money to give and to leave he was still a power in the district as well as in his own family. This was the oracle to which Mr. Trimblerigg, in his fifteenth year, began to give up his half-holidays.

Uncle Phineas was always at home; he had legs which never allowed him to get farther than his own gate, except once a week to the Tabernacle of True Belief, of which he was minister and owner. The larger chapel in the village lower down had not known him for thirty years when the youthful Jonathan first became aware of his importance, and began under parental direction to pay a weekly call at 'Pisgah,' and there learn from the old patriarch things about himself and others, including God, to which he listened with an air of great respect and interest.

Jonathan's way with him was wily but simple: he would

ask a great number of intelligent questions, and receiving unintelligent answers would appear satisfied. Now and then, upon his birthday, or when revivalism was in the air, the old man would give him sixpence, sometimes even a shilling, advising him to bestow it upon the foreign missions of the stricter Evangelicals, especially those to the native races of Central Africa and America, where the undiluted truth of the Word had still necessarily to be taught. For those primitive minds the taint of modernism had no effect; Heaven had so shaped them to the divine purpose that nothing short of literal True Belief could touch their hearts and soften their understandings. And the old man would talk wondrously to Jonathan of how, in the evil days to come, these black races were destined to become the repository of the true faith and reconvert the world to the purer doctrine.

Uncle Phineas was on the look-out for punishment on a world-wide scale, and had he lived to see it, the War of Versailles would have gladdened his heart. For he wanted all the Nations to be punished, including his own, – a point on which Mr. Trimblerigg ventured privately to differ from him; being in that matter a Free Evangelical, and preferring Heaven to Hell. Uncle Phineas preferred Hell; punishment was owing, and the imaginary infliction of it was what in the main attracted him to religion.

Punishment: first and foremost for man's breaking of the Sabbath; then followed in order drink, horse-racing, gambling, the increase of divorces, modernism, and the higher criticism, with all its resultant forms of infidelity, the agitation for Women's Suffrage, and finally the impious attempt of Labour to depose Capital.

All these things were of the Devil and must be fought;

and in the discussion of them Jonathan began – not to be
in a difficulty because some of them made an appeal to his
dawning intelligence, but to become agile. Luckily for
him Uncle Phineas's information was very nearly as narrow as his intelligence, and Mr. Trimblerigg was able to
jump to and fro across his sedentary and parochial mind
with small fear of discovery. But the repeated interviews
made him brisk, supple, and conversationally adaptable;
and once when the old man remarked half-approvingly,
'Aye, Jonathan, you've got eyes in your head, but don't
let 'em out by the back door,' he had a momentary qualm
lest behind that observation dangerous knowledge might
lurk.

But it was only his uncle's constitutional disapproval of
a mind that could move; and of Jonathan's outside doings
and opinions he had at that time heard nothing to rouse
suspicion. But clearly when Mr. Trimblerigg was called
to the ministry and began to preach there would be a
difficulty; for what would go down at Bethesda among the
Free Evangelicals, where his obvious career was awaiting
him, would not do up at Horeb, the chapel on the hill;
and it was well within the bounds of possibility that owing
to his family connections Mr. Trimblerigg might find it
advantageous to preach at both.

That, however, was a problem still lying some few years
away; meanwhile Uncle Phineas might very reasonably
die; and it was just about this time that I heard Mr.
Trimblerigg beginning to pray for peace to the old man
in his declining years, that he might not be kept unduly on
the rack of this tough world after so good a life.

And indeed it was a life in which he had accomplished
much; for a man of his small beginnings he had become of

notable substance, and his income derived from quarries and the houses he had built for his workers was reckoned to amount to anything from six to eight hundred a year, of which, in spite of generous gifts to foreign missions, he did not spend one-half.

His expectant relatives did not talk among themselves about the matter where, of necessity, interests were divided; but they thought much, and occasionally they had their fears.

'I shouldn't wonder,' said Jonathan's father one day, 'if when Uncle dies it isn't found that he had an unsound mind.'

It was to obviate such a calamity that Jonathan was sent to pay his weekly visit, and that one or another of the family, at least once every Sunday, went up to Horeb to pray.

Quite early in his examination of the tenets of True Belief, anxious that she should keep him in countenance, Mr. Trimblerigg asked Davidina what she thought of them.

'My belief is,' said Davidina, 'that we can all believe what we want to believe; and if you only believe it enough, it comes true – for you, at any rate. You can believe every word of the Bible is true, or that every word of it is false; and either way, you can live up to it. The True Believers are right there, anyway. And if,' she added, 'you've got nothing else to believe, you can believe in yourself: and you can smile at yourself in the glass, and look at your teeth, and think they are milestones on the road to Heaven, till they all drop out. Believing's easy; it's choosing what you mean to believe that matters. I believe the kettle's boiling over.'

55

She went, leaving Mr. Trimblerigg to his medita-
tions, also to a doubt whether she had taken him quite
seriously.

With his Uncle Phineas it was all the other way; they
were nothing if not serious together; but it often puzzled
his ingenuous mind how his uncle managed to believe all
the things he did.

One day: 'Uncle Phineas,' he said, 'how did you come to
be a True Believer?'

'When I felt the need of conversion as a young man,'
replied Uncle Phineas, 'I started reading the Scriptures.
Every day, before I opened the book, I said, "Lord, help
me to believe!" And by the time I'd read 'em three times
through, I believed every word.'

'I've only read them twice yet,' said Jonathan in meek
admission, but glad to get hold of the excuse.

'Read 'em again,' said his uncle.

'And all the genealogies, too, Uncle?' he inquired, for all
the world as though he felt genuinely committed to the
task if the other should say 'yes.'

'Why would you leave them out?' queried his uncle.
'It's the sowing of the seed. When you sow a field, you've
not to care about this grain or that, picking and choosing:
it's the sowing that matters. Sow your mind with the seed
of the Word, and don't leave gaps. You never know how
you may come to need it hereafter. "Abram begat Isaac;
and Isaac married Rebecca, and begat Jacob:" – that was
the text the Lord showed me when He would have me
choose a wife, whose name was Rebecca.' He fetched a
sigh. 'And I did,' he said. 'She was a poor weak wife to
me, and the children took after her; so now not one of
them is left. It was the Lord's will.'

'But if you had married some one else, wouldn't it have been the Lord's will too?' inquired Jonathan.

'That we won't discuss,' said his uncle. 'I shouldn't have chosen without first looking to Scripture. There was only one Rebecca in the village, and I hadn't thought of her till then. 'Twas a marvellous showing, and she on a bed of sickness at the time.'

Mr. Trimblerigg was properly impressed; but he doubted whether he would choose his own wife that way, even should he become a True Believer. So, not to linger on doubtful ground, he changed the subject and began to ask about missionaries; having a wish to see the world, they attracted him.

'If I become a True Believer,' he said, 'I shan't stay and preach in one place; I shall go out and preach everywhere.'

'You'll do as the Lord tells you,' said his uncle. 'It's no good one that's not a True Believer talking of what he'll do when he becomes one.'

'No, Uncle,' said Jonathan meekly, still out to do business; 'but living at home makes it very hard for me. I'm much nearer to being a True Believer than Mother is, or Father, or Davidina. Davidina says you can believe anything if you'll only make yourself. She says she could make herself believe that the Bible was all false, if she were to try.'

'Has she tried, does she mean?' inquired Uncle Phineas grimly.

'I don't know,' replied Jonathan ingenuously. 'It would be very wicked if anyone did try, wouldn't it?'

'It would,' said his uncle. 'I've known men struck down dead for less. I knew a man once who tore a leaf out of his Bible to light his pipe with, and he was struck by lightning

57

for it the same day. Yet his sin was only against one leaf, one chapter. How much greater the sin if you sin against the whole of it. She thought that, did she? When you go home, send Davidina up to me: I'll talk to her.'

Then Mr. Trimblerigg had a divided mind; for his fear of Davidina was not less but rather more than his fear of Uncle Phineas. Indeed he only feared Uncle Phineas for what he might fail to do for him in the near future, but Davidina he feared for what she was, here and now.

'I think, perhaps, Davidina only meant — anybody who was wicked enough. But please don't tell Davidina that I said anything!'

'Heh?' cried Uncle Phineas, his eye suspicious: 'That so? We'll see.'

He got up, went slowly to his Bible and opened it and without looking put down his thumb.

'Listen to this, Jonathan,' he said; and in solemn tone and with long pauses, he read:

' "She put her hand to the nail . . . and her right hand to the workman's hammer . . . and with the hammer she smote Sisera, she smote off his head . . . when she had pierced and stricken through his temples." . . . You hear that, Jonathan?'

'Yes, Uncle,' he replied, not yet understanding the application of the text.

'You see, Jonathan,' said his uncle, 'Davidina was getting at you.'

Being a True Believer's interpretation, it was not open to discussion, not for Jonathan at any rate. Uncle Phineas was a mighty hunter of the Scriptures before the Lord: the true interpretation never escaped him.

It was a curious and unexplained fact that Davidina was

a great favourite of Uncle Phineas, so far as one so entirely without affection could be said to have favourites. Davidina was far from being a True Believer, yet he trusted her; and he did not yet quite trust Jonathan. But he saw well enough that Jonathan had in him the makings of a prophet and of a preacher; if only he could trust him, he would help him to go far. But the testing process took time.

So, day by day, Mr. Trimblerigg laboured to win his trust, and often, after long hours of boredom in his uncle's company, success seemed near; for intellectually he was now growing fast, and to the cultivation of an agile brain added the cultivation of a wily tongue, and even where his future career did not depend upon it he loved to sustain an argument.

But he never got the better of Uncle Phineas; for when Phineas could not answer him, the Book did. He began to loathe the Book – that particular copy of it, I mean – and to make faces at it behind his uncle's back. But a day came when he loved it like a brother.

At the right time for the forwarding of his plans, Mr. Trimblerigg professed a desire for larger book-learning; he wanted to study theology, and that not from one point of view alone. Ready to satisfy him, up to a point, Uncle Phineas plied him with books containing the true doctrine, some he would make him sit down and read aloud upon the spot while he expounded them; others he let him take away to study and return, questioning him closely thereafter to discover how well he had read them. They were all good books – good in the moral sense, that is to say – books written to inculcate the principles of True Belief; but all, from the contemporary point of view utterly useless, and all deadly dull.

One day Mr. Trimblerigg asked his uncle, 'Where all the other books were – the bad ones, which taught false doctrine.'

Why did he want to know? inquired Uncle Phineas.

'I want to read them,' said Jonathan greatly daring. 'If one doesn't read them, how is one to know how to answer them? I want to read them because they deceive people.'

'Not True Believers,' said his uncle.

'No,' replied Jonathan, 'but people who might become True Believers.'

'They should read their Bibles. There you find the answer to everything.'

'Yes. So I did; I did it last night as I was going to bed: I opened it, just as you do, Uncle, and there it was – written: the thing I was wanting to know.'

'What was it?'

'It was this, Uncle: "Oh, that mine adversary had written a book. Surely I would take it upon my shoulder and bind it as a crown unto me." '

'That doesn't say read it,' objected his uncle.

'No, but it means it. It means that if wicked books are written we've got to do with them, we've not just got to let them alone.'

'We'll see,' replied the other; 'we'll ask the Lord to show us.' He got the Book and opened it. 'There, Jonathan, listen to this:

' "What profiteth the graven image that the maker thereof hath graven it; the molten image, the teacher of lies, that the maker of his work trusteth therein to make dumb idols" . . . God's answered you, Jonathan.'

'But that's about the man who wrote it,' objected Jonathan. 'He trusts in his work, but I don't; he's not going to make a dumb idol of me.'

'You're running your head into danger, Jonathan. If you are not a True Believer, the Book may be only a trap set for you by the Devil. He can quote Scripture when it suits him, as well as any.'

'But I prayed first,' said Jonathan. 'And I'm trying to become a True Believer.'

'When you've become a True Believer, we'll talk about it,' said his uncle.

After that for a whole week his uncle saw no more of him. Then one day, waking up from his afternoon nap, the old man found Jonathan sitting and looking at him.

It was quite five minutes since Jonathan had crept in, and during that time he had not been idle. He had gone to the Book, and arranged a marker, and three and four times he had opened and without looking had put his finger to the exact place; just a finger's length from the bottom on the right-hand side, it was easy to find. Then, sitting far away from the Book, he had waited for his uncle to wake.

He did not allow the haze of sleep to disperse before he made his announcement.

'Uncle,' he said, 'I've become a True Believer. I've had a call: God has shown me the way.'

'How do you know you're a True Believer?' questioned the old man cautiously.

'I've His Word for it. Every time I open the Book it speaks to me – so plain, that at first it frightened me. Then I felt a great joy and a light filling me. And everything in the world is different to what it was.'

61

'Aye,' replied his uncle, 'that sounds the real thing. What has He called you to do?'

'To go out and preach, Uncle. And He's told me I'm to go to college.'

'How has He told you that?' inquired Phineas, sceptical again.

'I asked Him to show me what I was to do, where I was to go; I opened the Book and put my finger on the page; and there – college was the very word!'

'You tell me that you found the word "college" in the Bible?' inquired his uncle incredulously.

'It was found for me,' said Jonathan: 'Hilkiah the priest, and Achbor, and Shaphan, went unto Huldah the prophetess, the wife of Shallum ; and she dwelt in Jerusalem in the college; and they communed with her.'

So, by the mouth of his nephew, Phineas stood corrected in his knowledge of the Scriptures. But he did not quite yield yet. 'Fetch me the Book, Jonathan,' he said.

'No, Uncle,' replied his nephew, 'the Lord is calling to me now, not to you. This is my affair.'

And so saying he opened the Book, drew out the marker, and set his finger upon the page. Then he brought it across to his uncle. 'You read it, Uncle,' he said; and his uncle read: 'Arise, go unto Nineveh, that great city, and preach unto it the preaching that I bid thee.'

Mr. Trimblerigg did not wait for his uncle to speak, he grasped his nettle tight. 'Will you take the responsibility now, Uncle, of telling me that the Lord has not called me; and that I have not plainly heard His Word?'

Uncle Phineas could not quite do that. All he said was: 'Nineveh? Nineveh might mean anything.'

'Yes,' said Mr. Trimblerigg, 'it might; but it doesn't.

If the Lord is calling me – and you can't say that He isn't – will He not also make me sure what the call means?'

'We will ask Him again, Jonathan.'

'We will not,' said Jonathan. 'That would be sin, for it would be tempting Him, trying to make Him think that we have not heard Him already – in our hearts.'

'Spoken like a True Believer,' said Uncle Phineas, convinced at last. 'Jonathan, you shall go.'

Very earnestly that night did Mr. Trimblerigg return thanks that I had opened the eyes of his Uncle Phineas and made him see light. And all the while that he prayed, how helpless he made me feel! Lost in the delight of the end, he forgot the means: and never once did it occur to him that he was really giving thanks to himself.

The Moving Spirit

So MR. TRIMBLERIGG WENT TO COLLEGE TO LEARN TRI-bal divinity as falsely taught by the Free Evangelicals; and his Uncle Phineas paid for it.

He went there as a True Believer; and his fellow-students viewed with wonder so coming-on a disposition confined to so strait and narrow an interpretation of things spiritual. For at that time a great wave of Liberalism had entered the larger bodies of the Free Church Movement, and the Free Evangelicals led the way. They had even gone so far as to admit women students to their University and to its theological studies, though not of course to the ministry; and because of this and similar tendencies, the wider and easier interpretation of Scripture concerned them greatly.

In this large and tolerant atmosphere, where modernism was beginning to lift its head, Mr. Trimblerigg stood all alone. It was a challenge that delighted him. He had no illusions as to the lack of a future outlook afforded by adherence to the strict tenets of True Belief: but he had the sense to realize that what a student believes, or thinks he believes, in his teens under the unavoidable influence of the parental upbringing, matters nothing to his future career. Only when he comes to man's estate, and the full and free possession of his faculties do his opinions and pronouncements begin to measure his qualification for advancement. In the meantime he could sharpen his wits, acquire knowledge, and develop his resources for dialectic and for oratory just as well by maintaining the improbable side of the argument as the probable; what better test indeed for his powers? Convictions could come later,

what he wanted now was training; and though as yet un-
convinced himself, he might on the way convince others,
if only a few, even of the truth of tenets which he meant
presently to discard.

There were three hundred students at the college, fifty
of them women, and he himself the only 'True Believer,'
with the additional drawback that in most of the points
distinguishing his branch of the Free Church body from
others he did not truly believe. Yet he never doubted that
in free debate he could profess a belief that would sound
plausible, and put up at least an attractive fight even
though eventual defeat awaited him.

But though his calculating mind gave a silver lining to
the cloud which hung over him, it was, I maintain, an act
of courage when he stepped so buoyantly into the arena to
face a three-years' process of defeat, and by defeat to learn
the ways of victory. And though presently the buffetings
which he had to endure were tremendous, he was able in
letters, and in conversation when he went home, to convey
to his uncle the impression that True Belief was not only
holding its own, but winning its way in the strongholds of
infidelity. Had he not already made converts, for proof?
Three of the students, two male, one female, had become
True Believers.

One day he brought them over and exhibited them to his
uncle, and when his uncle had examined them thoroughly
in their new-found faith his trust in Mr. Trimblerigg
became almost complete. But still not quite. Uncle
Phineas was a cautious character, and not for nothing had
caution, assisted by revelation, been his companion for
eighty-four years.

It was at this time that he re-made his will, re-made it in

a curious way and let the family know of it. He executed two wills on the same day with the same witnesses; and laying both by, waited for time to decide which of the two should survive him.

'I have great hopes of you, Jonathan,' he said. 'I'm watching you, often when you don't think; and when I'm not quite clear in my own mind the Book tells me.'

That was Uncle Phineas's strong point in his reading of character: the Book could not lead him astray. It was upon that point that Mr. Trimblerigg felt himself most vulnerable. He might trace and traverse to stand in his uncle's good graces, he might abundantly deserve his confidence and all that should go with it or follow from it after his death; but nothing that he could do would prevent the Book opening in the wrong place at the last critical moment, or prevent Phineas from believing that whatever it then told him was true.

And so though Mr. Trimblerigg did in those three years by all his contemporary acts if not by his calculations, deserve that his uncle should think well of him, he could never be quite sure.

During his second year he heard from Davidina that she had fallen out of her uncle's favour, — an event which, having the two wills in mind he did not disapprove; but when he heard later that a hitherto unconsidered great-niece had appeared upon the scene and was keeping house for his uncle, his mind grew troubled. This was a cousin whom he had never seen, named Caroline; the circumstance that she had lately become an orphan made her available as a house-companion for one who, needing an arm to lean on, did not yet require a nurse. She was older than Jonathan by three years, and had managed from her mother's side to be of fair complexion.

Davidina nicknamed her 'the dream-cow'; and when Mr. Trimblerigg saw her for the first time on his return home during vacation he had to admit that the name suited. She was a large creamy creature, slightly mottled with edges of pink; vague, equable, good-tempered, taking things as they came; rather stupid to talk to, but not uncomely to look upon.

As he gazed on her at their first meeting, Mr. Trimblerigg's calculating mind got ahead of him before he could prevent; and 'Shall I have to marry her?' was the thought which suddenly presented itself. With equal suddenness came another, 'If I do, what will Isabel Sparling say? There'll be trouble.'

Isabel Sparling was the woman student whom he had converted to True Belief; and the conversion had been of an emotional character.

She was an ardent believer in the ministry of women, and having the prophetess of Scripture upon her side – Huldah the prophetess who dwelt in the college at Jerusalem for one, as Mr. Trimblerigg was quick to remember – had no difficulty in persuading him that the ministry of women was compatible with 'True Belief.'

Mr. Trimblerigg had seized on it, indeed, with avidity as a forward point for him to score in discussions which forced him generally to take the reactionary line. There was also among True Believers a more obvious opening for women than elsewhere. The ministry of the connection was diminishing together with its funds; and there does come a point, in spiritual work as well as industry, when what cannot support a man will support a

woman. In exchange, therefore, for the allegiance of a
new convert for theological debates which left him so often
in a minority of one, Mr. Trimblerigg blithely gave in his
adherence to the ministry of women; and in the College
debate on the subject, which took place in his second year,
they won an unexpected victory, all but three of the
women students, and more than a third of the men students
voting in the affirmative.

It is symptomatic, however, that of this particular victory
over the powers of evil Mr. Trimblerigg said not a word
to his Uncle Phineas. It was a point over which he apprehended that True Believers of the older school might
differ from the new. Uncle Phineas, sedentary in a small
hill-side village and a chapel of which he himself was the
proprietor, was scarcely in a position to appreciate the
claim of women to spiritual equality; in the field of politics
Mr. Trimblerigg knew that he was decisively against
them; nor was Cousin Caroline, his house-companion, the
sort of person to suggest a quiver of revolt.

And so, while pledged to Isabel Sparling and her fellow-
aspirants to become their champion when membership
of the Synod should give him a voice, Mr. Trimblerigg
for the present allowed the question to sleep. In his own
time and in his own way he would make it his policy, but
not probably so long as his Uncle Phineas was alive, and
his own financial future unassured. He must first himself become a minister.

It was during his third vacation that Uncle Phineas
showed faith, by an overt sign, in his future qualification
for the calling. Jonathan was invited, at the next Wednesday meeting, to put up a prayer, and give an address. The
invitation was made on the Sunday, giving him half a

week's notice; and announcement was made to the congregation.

Local interest in the preaching ability of Mr. Trimblerigg had already been roused. Word had come down from College that in the debates he had become a shining light, and there was regret among the Free Evangelicals that the burning oratory of which he gave promise should become the exclusive possession of the narrowest and most disunited connection in the union of the Free Churches. In the course of the next two days many told him that they were coming to hear him.

This helped to make the occasion important; for if he could fill the chapel and continue filling it on future occasions, Uncle Phineas's recognition of his vocation would become more assured. Mr. Trimblerigg was now eighteen, his uncle was eighty-six; and he could not regard as unpropitious this timing by Providence of their respective lives. Two or three more years in the propaganda of True Belief would not unduly hold up a career for which wider spheres were waiting. Suppose he could, for a couple of years or so, kindle True Believers into new life, make himself indispensable: and then –!

He began to see why possibly he had been called to devote himself temporarily to so narrow a field of service. If he could come bringing his sheaves with him, he would count in the Evangelical world more than if he had merely started as one among many, with no spiritual adventure to single him from the crowd.

Thus his sanguine mind addressed itself to Wednesday's meeting and the possibilities which lay beyond.

It would be doing him an injustice to say that, in regarding the occasion as propitious, he did not also regard it as a solemn one. He made preparation for it – I might indeed say that we made preparation for it together – with frequency and assiduity; and what I was supposed to hear for the first time on Wednesday evening, I heard in various stages of development more times than a few, during the two days preceding. Davidina, it appeared, heard it also: not, I think, by a wilful listening at keyholes, but with a general awareness that rehearsals were taking place. She paid him the compliment of coming to hear 'how he got on', which was her matter of fact way of putting it. All the rest of the family did the same: the meeting was well attended.

Mr. Trimblerigg, in spite, or perhaps because, of previous rehearsal, managed to deliver himself with a great air of spontaneity. He got to the point when he knew that he was making a success of it, and was then sufficiently moved and uplifted to launch out into parentheses which were not only unpremeditated but quite happily expressed.

People pray in different ways; some moan, some become tremulous, some voluble, some halting and inarticulate, some repeat themselves many times as though they suspected one of inattention to their requests. There are very few who say what they want to say in the fewest possible words. I wish they did.

Mr. Trimblerigg was not one of the few; but his prayer had undeniable merit; it was quick, spirited, cheerful, a little shrill and high-flown in a few of its passages, and in its peroration there was a touch of poetry. He said yea, several times instead of yes; a trick which later grew into a habit whenever poetry was his aim; but in spite of small drawbacks it was a highly creditable performance well-pleasing to both of us; and that it was so Mr. Trimblerigg knew as well as I or anyone else.

At the porch-gathering afterwards many praised him; Uncle Phineas had said little, not praising him at all, but Jonathan had been told that he might take Wednesday meeting till further notice. Cousin Caroline had looked at him with her mild dewy eyes, saying nothing but meaning much, as much, at least, as so indeterminate a character could mean. Only Davidina, impenetrable of look, gave him no inkling of what was in her mind.

On the way home, in order to show a proper attitude of detachment from praise for a gift that was spiritual, and perhaps also indifference to her blighting silence, Mr. Trimblerigg inquired airily what they were going to have for supper; whereupon Davidina replied in a dry indifferent tone: 'Same as we've just had in chapel, bubble-and-squeak warmed up again.'

It was the sort of thing to which there was no answer; it was true, yet it was so unjust; no doubt she intended it for his soul's.health, but can anything so cruel be also sanitary? 'Bubble-and-squeak,' he could not fail to see, in caricature, the likeness to his ebullient enthusiasm which had so moved and uplifted the hearts of his hearers, his own also; and as he let the wound go home he felt (without counting) how many times he could have killed her!

And yet, if I can see truly into Davidina's mind, all that she meant was that Jonathan's prayers would be made much better by his not preparing them.

I am not sure that she was right; I have heard both; and I do not think that there was much to choose. Prepared and unprepared alike they always moved his audiences more than they moved me.

71

A Closed Incident

A WEEK LATER HE VERY NEARLY DID KILL HER.
The good which men imagine, and the diminished
version of it which, when it actually takes place, has so
little recognizable likeness to the thing desired, found ex-
emplification in this event. For though Mr. Trimblerigg
had often wished Davidina out of life, it was a serious
shock to him when by sheer accident he one day pushed
her into the water, and was forced for a considerable while
to believe that she was drowned.

It happened late one evening, on the edge of night,
as brother and sister were returning from a shopping
expedition, upon which, rather against his will, he
had been forced to accompany her to help carry parcels.
Taking the short way back, they came by a wood to the
home fields at a point where a deep flowing stream was
crossed by a narrow footbridge. There had been rain;
the plank was slippery, the stream in flood; it was
getting dark. Mr. Trimblerigg thought that he was
carrying more than his share of the parcels, and the
unappreciative companionship of Davidina had made
him cross. Embarked upon the plank Davidina suddenly stopped to change over her parcels so as to get help
of the hand-rail; and Mr. Trimblerigg coming close
behind gave her an impatient nudge harder than he
knew.

With an exasperated scream Davidina missing the hand-
rail toppled and swung sideways. With quaint heroism
she threw him her parcels as she descended streamwards.
Two of them Mr. Trimblerigg managed to field; the third
made the lethal plunge after her, and being of lighter sub-

stance jaunted gaily along the swift current into which she had wholly disappeared.

For a few ghastly seconds that seemed like the threshold of eternity, Mr. Trimblerigg, encumbered with his parcels, stood fixed. The thought flashed that here and now he had done something that he could not help, for he remembered that he did not swim; and though it was a pure accident, he had a swift apprehension that this would be a difficult and also a humiliating matter to explain truthfully. It was a very serious drawback for any young man at the beginning of his ministerial career to push his sister into the water and then have her drown; stated in the mildest terms it showed incompetence; and Mr. Trimblerigg had already begun to pride himself more than most on his efficiency in an emergency.

Luckily, however, nobody had actually seen him give the push; so, if the worst came to the worst, the story would be his own to tell. In the meantime he could but do his best to put matters right. 'I'm really awfully sorry!' he said to himself.

While these or similar thoughts were dividing his swift mind in the couple of seconds that had ensued, there was no reappearance of Davidina. Although the fact that he could not swim made direct action difficult, to attempt her rescue was a debt of honour which did not brook delay. Fleet-footed he crossed the plank, deposited his parcels, and began to race down-stream. If he could not actually rescue her, he must at least keep her in sight and give her all the encouragement in his power. Sight of the floating parcel bobbing against a willow bough seemed to suggest her present whereabouts.

Casting off his coat as he stumbled along the bank to

73

outpace the current, he clutched at an overhanging bough and plunged boldly in. His feet touched bottom: he came up again and crying, 'Davidina, where are you?' felt about him in all directions with his disengaged hand for the life which had so unexpectedly become dear to him. He encountered the parcel, captured it as a small proof of his efficiency and threw it to land. The stream seemed otherwise quite unoccupied. He called again but got no answer.

In order to be thorough, he took another plunge higher up and two others lower down where boughs offered suitable assistance. Each time his feet touched bottom and his hand found emptiness. Had it then struck him to venture further and try walking across the stream, it might have puzzled him how so capable a person as Davidina should have managed to get drowned. But this he did not do; he continued to call upon her in loud appealing tones, and to repeat his dip, approximating to total immersion, at various points up and down stream.

He could not but feel that these scattered attempts were of a somewhat desultory and speculative character, and that the drowning Davidina, could she have known of them, would not have been satisfied. But Davidina's standard was always an exacting one, and as he had failed to live up to it in the past, so he must needs fail now. Nevertheless these repeated immersions in water that was so astonishingly cold did at least give his conscience the absolution it required. He could say at the inquest, and afterwards, that he had done his best; what a poor best that happened to be was nobody's concern but his own.

And so, here and there, up and down, he probed for the dear departed; and only when quite convinced that his

74

universe was empty of Davidina did he quit the scene of the disaster and run off to fetch help.

Poles, ropes, lanterns, and presently a drag-net gave to subsequent efforts a surface appearance of efficiency which his own had lacked; but below the surface, where lay all that mattered, they were attended with no more success. No body was found.

Going home to his bereaved family the gasping youth told a tale which was readily believed. His exhaustion, his lively distress, his drenched condition, and his chattering teeth gave evidence of the ordeal he had passed through, and verification to a story which nobody had any reason to doubt. He told how Davidina had lost her footing and tumbled in, and he, plunging after, had twice caught hold of her clothing; and how one garment had come off in his hand, and another had given way. Only when she sank from view, after diving for her repeatedly in vain, did he relinquish his saving efforts.

This was the story in its second telling; others down by the stream, in the intervals of their search work, had heard it all before; and there was so little to alter from the facts, so little to leave out, that at second hearing he had already become convinced of its truth; and only the sight of Davidina standing at the door, carrying the parcels he had forgotten, reminded him, with 'that sinking feeling' out of which patent medicines make their fortune, that another version of the story existed and would probably be told.

In the next few minutes he got the surprise of his life: Davidina did not tell it. She had, it is true, something of her own to tell which was a departure from fact; for she said the stream had carried her down a mile and over the

weir, at which point she had got upon her feet and waded
out; whereas having fallen from the bridge on the upstream
side she had become entangled in its central timbers, and
after keeping low for a while and watching her brother
safely out of sight along the further bank, had climbed out
again and gone back into the wood. And there, I regret
to say, she had wilfully stayed – warming herself with
sharp exercise the while – listening to Mr. Trimblerigg's
intermittent cries of distress, watching the flit of lanterns,
hearing the harsh shouts of the search-party, and calculating coolly how long they would take to give up quest for
the body that was not there.

And her motive for all this? Her motive was to give Mr.
Trimblerigg his chance: his chance to tell the truth, or to
do otherwise, just as he chose.

Now was this charitable of her? I do not know. I only
know that she genuinely thought it would do him good:
to give him the chance, just once, of his own accord, to tell
something against himself, bad for his moral credit, bad
for his future prospects, and bad for his self-esteem. And
yet, though that may have been her motive, I doubt
whether it was not practically overborne by her sharp
appreciative foresight of the actual shaping of the
event.

After waiting for well over an hour to give her brother
all the rope he needed to tie himself up in glory, she
crossed the bridge, collected the parcels, his as well as
hers, and went home. And so well had she timed herself
that it was just as the second telling finished that she
entered.

It took the family some moments to get over their surprise; but Mrs. Trimblerigg, an eminently practical

woman, did not let them wait for questions now. She ran
them up to their rooms, got them out of their wet clothes,
then brought them down again, bundled in hot blankets
to sit opposite each other by the fire; and now to be heard
once more, telling their tale more fully each in their own
way.

And since Mr. Trimblerigg pleaded exhaustion, his proud
mother told it herself; and Davidina listened gratefully,
fixing upon her brother Jonathan a kind and considerate
regard. Her mother told it all accurately, just as she had
heard it from Jonathan; and when it had all been re-
hearsed in her ears – our own Mr. Trimblerigg sitting
opposite the while and furtively regarding her, rather like
a Skye terrier that has just been washed and whipped –
she said not a word to question the accuracy of the story.
She accepted it; and when her mother said that she ought
to feel most grateful to brother Jonathan for all he had
done in trying to save her at the risk of his own life, she
said that she was. She said also that the last thing she
remembered was his voice calling, 'Davidina, where are
you?' And as, weary and weak of tone, she thus corrobor-
ated his story, she gave him a friendly look and a faint
smile; and then shut her eyes at him, as if to say, 'The
incident is now closed.'

And so upon Davidina's side, as far as words went, it
was. But with the mere shutting of her eyes she gave Mr.
Trimblerigg a sleepless night; and for many nights and
days after, she held him in a grip from which there was no
escape. And then some of her answers to the maternal
inquiries would flash into his memory with a horribly disturbing effect. 'But Davidina, however did you come to
bring the parcels along?' 'I went back for them: I thought

Jonathan might have forgotten them; and so he had.'
And when Mr. Trimblerigg defended such forgetfulness
as being only natural under the circumstances, Davidina
replied, 'He didn't forget the other parcel, he saved that.'
'Which parcel?'
'The one that fell in. He saw that, and thought it was me,
and swam after it; and it must have been a sort of satisfaction saving that, as he couldn't get me.'
Such clairvoyance was horrible; it was as if her eye
had flown with him like a firefly in the night watching
every movement not of his body only but of his mind
as well? And what made it so much more terrible was
that he could not understand her motive, or how it was
to end.
But day followed day, and no revelation was made; his
story stood uncorrected; neighbours came to call and congratulate and at each occasion the story was told again.
Sometimes Mr. Trimblerigg himself was made to tell it,
in spite of a modest reluctance which grew and grew; and
there always sat Davidina listening with kind eyes and a
friendly smile. Then the eyes would shut suddenly, and
the smile would remain.
When she had done this to him two or three times, Mr.
Trimblerigg was ready to scream; and when she also did
it to him the first time they were alone together, he wanted
either to die or to murder her. Then, finding he could do
neither, he gathered up his courage and was about to
speak. But it was no good. Davidina opened her eyes
again.
'I've god a horrid gold,' she said, flattening her conson-
ants in comic imitation of a stage Jew. 'Dat cubs of falling
indo de warder.'

78

CHAPTER SIX

She blew her nose meticulously (as certain modern writers would say), creating an atmosphere which made confession impossible. Mr. Trimblerigg had not a word left that he could utter.

Now, that Mr. Trimblerigg should have been puzzled by Davidina's acquiescence in the story he had told – that he should have been puzzled, that is to say, after perceiving what use she put it to – reveals the irreflective streak which was always dividing him from self-knowledge, and was presently to do him so much more mischief.

Holding her tongue had given Davidina a power over him which no exposure of his face-saving art of tale-telling could have equalled. The ignominy of that would have blown over; or he could stoutly have denied the push altogether, declaring it a figment of her imagination; and had she forced him to denial often enough he would have come to believe it true. But by saying nothing Davidina stewed him in his own juice without a bubble to show for it; and the tender mercy of her eyes made him sensitive where the accusation of her tongue would only have hardened him.

What Davidina loved was power; and power economically exercised is a far subtler luxury than power which requires repeated effort to sustain it. Davidina by doing nothing had acquired power not material but spiritual; and 'Thou, Davidina, seest me,' became more truly the motto of his life day by day.

But the reason why Mr. Trimblerigg failed to read her motive while wincing under the results, was partly because power of so static a kind had no attraction for him whatever, and partly because it contradicted the fundamental

79

notion of his whole scheme of life – that he was a man,
namely, of virtuous character, one with a destiny of re-
splendent goodness lying ahead of him. Across that conception of himself Davidina's contrary conception struck
like cataract of the eye. The two views could not co-exist.
Without his quite realizing it, Davidina's reading of his
character threatened to drive his own out.

In the privacy of his own chamber he had more than once
sat down to write his own epitaph – the epitaph which he
liked to think would appear on his entablature in that
day when Free Churchmen had got the run of West-
minster Abbey to burrow in. With the art of simplicity
after much trouble he had boiled it down to three words,
'Little – but good.' And if that were to represent finally
and truthfully his work on earth, what place was there
for Davidina's rival epitaph to stand, if, as he half-sus-
pected, it found its expression in the words, 'Good – for
nothing.'

If I had made him good (and surely I had done that, he
thought) was it to be 'for nothing' after all? Before he
could believe that, he must give up his faith. And when he
said 'faith,' he never understood that it meant, and meant
only, faith in himself.

So silently, invisible, with imperceptible pace, mind
against mind, Davidina tightened her grip.

One struggle to escape from the blast of her continued
silence he made; but it was no good. New callers had
come with their congratulations, and the story was to be
repeated once more. Summoned to a fresh drench of
ignominy under his sister's calm gaze, Mr. Trimblerigg
had a flash of inspiration. He laughed jovially. 'Oh, I just
pushed her into the water,' he said; 'so of course I had to

go after her. I tried to save her; but Davidina preferred to save herself. And that's all there was to it!'

The visitors laughed, thinking what a very charming and modest young man he was. And Davidina laughed too.

CHAPTER SEVEN

He Tries to be Honest

DAVIDINA GOT OVER HER COLD WITHOUT DIFFICULTY. But Mr. Trimblerigg, who from repeated immersion, had been in the water much longer and with opportunities for severe chills to take him between whiles, fell seriously ill.

It was with a sort of satisfaction that he took to his bed; for this at any rate was a genuine result of his life-saving efforts, and seemed in a way to affect their character, giving them the testimonial he craved.

Davidina accepted the duty which fate had laid on her, and nursed him with devoted detachment.

'It's wonderful how those two do love each other!' remarked Mrs. Trimblerigg, after viewing a sick-bed scene where Jonathan was as one hanging between life and death in Davidina's arms: 'And yet to look at them sometimes you wouldn't think it.'

That was on the first day of desperate symptoms, preliminary to the arrival of the doctor, when Davidina, for lack of higher guidance was nursing him with prescriptions of her own choosing. He had horrible pains; she pursued them with the old-fashioned remedies which, in remote country districts, still effect cures, and for which the undeserving doctor comes presently to receive the fee. Fore and aft, wherever a pain came catching his breath, she skinned him with untempered applications of hot raw mustard; and after five hours of it he still survived.

When the doctor came he could not but admire her handiwork. 'Well, you have punished him!' he said. He examined the patient and gave the illness its name — double pneumonia. Its importance was a satisfaction to

82

Mr. Trimblerigg and Davidina alike; they took it as a worthy occupation; – he to be ill of it, she to have the nursing of it. For the next fortnight brother and sister enjoyed each other thoroughly, more than they had ever done in their lives before. They even became fond of each other. But character remained; the fondness was critical.

The day that the doctor pronounced him out of danger, Mr. Trimblerigg had already felt so much better, that he wanted to get up. Life having become attractive again, he was impatient to go out and meet it once more on his own terms. And when he had seen from the medical eye that all was to be well with him, he was as anxious to have word of it as though it were a compliment on his good looks.

'What does he say of me?' he asked when his sister returned from seeing the doctor to the door.

Davidina, having measured him judicially with her eye, settled that he was well enough for an indulgence that would be mutual.

'He says you are out of danger,' she answered; 'so now you are in it again.'

'In what?'

'In your own way,' she replied, elliptically. 'It's done you no harm being ill. To be safe from yourself for a fortnight never happened to you before. Mother calls it a God's mercy you're still alive. Perhaps it is: I don't know.'

Mr. Trimblerigg lay trying to read her face and the meanings behind it. 'Have I been a great trouble?' he asked at last.

'People can't be as ill as you've been, without giving some trouble,' she answered.

Yet he had a consciousness that he had been good, as

83

goodness goes on a bed of sickness; and he hankered to have it said.

'Wasn't I a good patient?' he inquired in a tone of meek repentance. 'I'm so sorry.'

'You were as good as you knew how,' replied Davidina, 'and that's not saying a little; for you *know* more than most; if you'd only do it.' She paused, then added, 'You were very good when you were out of your senses.'

'What did I say?' inquired Mr. Trimblerigg anxiously; for the possibilities of unconscious goodness alarmed him.

'Your prayers.' (His anxiety increased.) 'You didn't say much. 'Twas either "God, I am not as other men are," or "God, be merciful to me a sinner", just those two things, one or other; and they both sounded real, as if you meant 'em.'

There was a long pause, while Mr. Trimblerigg calculated; he had got the right atmosphere for it at last; so gathering his strength he said:

'Davidina, it was I pushed you into the river.'

The avowal struck Davidina a cold blow: she had not reckoned that feebleness, or illness, or affection, or gratitude, or anything indeed but fear would ever have made Mr. Trimblerigg own truth against himself so long after the date. Then she looked deeper, and realized that it was fear: he was trying to get out of her clutches by telling the truth.

She countered him by telling a lie herself.

'I didn't know it,' she said; 'I never felt you touch me.'

'But I did!' he insisted.

'Well, if you did, you didn't do it on purpose.'

Into this trap he fell.

'Yes, I did!' he declared. 'I hated you: I pushed you in because I wanted you to drown.'

Reassured, she saw that once more he was telling lies. It comforted her to find that he had not got out of her depth; her old Jonathan, the Jonathan she knew, was safely hers again.

'Then why did you try to save me?' she inquired.

'I didn't try; not really. I only pretended to.'

'Who was that for?'

'Myself, I suppose. It would have been easier to think of afterwards, you see: that I – tried.'

Here she saw that he had given her a bit of the real Jonathan wrongly applied.

'Ah, yes,' she commented, 'you manage to pretend to yourself a good deal, don't you? I wish I could!'

Her voice was gentle, regretful, full of compassion and understanding. 'What would you like to pretend?' it encouraged him to ask.

Then she smote him.

'That I believed you,' she said.

So the victory was won.

He lay back, exhausted of his attempt. He had not escaped her after all; and his final word was uttered without any hope of reversing the issue now decided.

'Well, I've told you,' he said, trying to appear indifferent; 'and it's true, – every word.'

'Then we won't talk about it,' she replied; 'you can think it's true, if it amuses you. It would amuse me too, if I'd got the gift for it.'

She looked at him kindly, humorously; and then, speaking as one who tries to chaff foolish fancies out of a child, said:

'Some day, Jonathan, you'll look in the glass and be thinking you've got a halo; and it'll only be the moon behind you, or a haystack on fire, or something of that kind. If I'd got an imagination like yours, I should be afraid to believe anything!'

So she shut him down with his poor weak wish to be privately and confidentially honest. And as he lay back in the cage of her contemptuous affections, he realized how very nearly he had escaped. If he had only been content to tell merely the truth, Davidina might have believed him: but at the last moment his Devil – his decorative Devil – had tempted him to play the murderer; and to the lurid beauty of it he had succumbed.

He turned his head away on the pillow, for there were tears in his eyes.

Davidina said: 'It's time you took your medicine.' She poured it out as she spoke, and set it beside him, with the two lumps of sugar that were to follow.

'I don't want it,' he cried peevishly. 'Anyway, I don't want it just yet: you can leave it.'

'No, I can't; I'm going downstairs.'

'Well, you can leave it, I say.'

'And you'd empty it away and eat the sugar as soon as my back was turned. I know. You've done that before.'

It was true he had: but all humans of my acquaintance do similar things when left to themselves. It is their nature. But it was Davidina's devouring instinct for not leaving him to himself which made him desperate.

'Davidina,' he cried, 'why can't you be friends?'

'Friends?' she retorted, 'you are too anxious to be friends with yourself, to be a safe friend for anyone else, I'm thinking. The best friend for you is some one who knows how to make you honest to 'em from a distance.'

She gave him his medicine as she spoke, and saw him drink it.

'Well, there's one thing you're honest about at any rate,' she said.

'What's that?' he inquired, hopefully.

'You bite your nails, and you don't try to hide it.'

'What does that matter to anybody?' he demanded irritably.

'Nothing, except to yourself. I never knew anybody yet that bit his nails who was able to tell the truth. Not that that matters to you, I suppose you'll say.'

'I do tell the truth sometimes,' he declared in a tone of appealing *naïveté*. 'And when I do, you don't believe me.'

'When you do,' she said, 'you show a red light. That frightens me. It's like a train whistling and screaming to say there's going to be an accident.'

Whereat Mr. Trimblerigg put himself resolutely under the bed-clothes: and so she left him.

Yet, in the end, she did him good. It is a pathetic fact that from that day Mr. Trimblerigg left off biting his nails, hoping, perhaps, that as they grew an instinct for truth would be born in him. Eventually he even developed a habit of letting them grow quite long: securing, to that extent, a sense of escape from the supervision of Davidina.

I wish I could add that that little addition of grey growth made him become more truthful. But when in later years all his hair turned grey and he wore it long, almost like a woman's, even that did not alter the fundamentals of his character.

Where there's a Will, there's a Way

ON HIS RETURN FROM COLLEGE FOR THE SUMMER vacation, his course almost completed, Mr. Trimblerigg found Uncle Phineas with his feet gathered up for death, though not immediately. He was confined to the house and did not go out; presently did not even come downstairs. Caroline, of course, was still with him, somewhat colourless as a companion, but efficient as a housekeeper.

It would be difficult to say whether she was also a True Believer, in the doctrinal sense, because to her doctrine meant nothing. She was one of those comfortable characters who, in matters of faith, can believe anything, and never actively disbelieve anything they are told by those whom they respect and look up to. Otherwise, in worldly affairs, she was quite sensible.

When she opened the door to Mr. Trimblerigg she showed pleasure in his arrival. He called her 'cousin,' and kissed her, thereby committing himself to nothing but a more open acceptance of the kinship which had existed before intimacy began. Still it prepared the ground provisionally, and the blush with which she accepted the salutation made her look almost pretty: in her large cream-coloured way, with under-edges of pink, she was personable though she lacked personality; and she was very pleasant to touch, a point which with Mr. Trimblerigg mattered on the whole more than good looks, and very much more than intellect.

In the balm of her smile she said, 'Uncle has been expecting you.'

'So have you,' said Mr. Trimblerigg; 'and I've been

CHAPTER EIGHT

expecting myself.' Thus, footing it easily, he came into
the house of his expectations, and went up to his uncle's
room.

It was a momentous interview. The old man's beard had
whitened and was beginning to slope from the horizontal
to the perpendicular: voice and hand were tremulous; but
his eyes, whether he saw well or ill with them, retained
their keen look: and Jonathan still felt, in a lesser degree,
as he did with Davidina, that he was being examined as to
his character. For in spite of submissive hours in the past,
he suspected that as yet Uncle Phineas had never quite
trusted him; that there was something missing which all
his art and solicitude could not supply.

Indeed it was so; temperamentally Mr. Trimblerigg was
not cut to the pattern of True Belief; whereas, for Uncle
Phineas to be outside True Belief, was to be spiritually in
chaos; and the small ugly chapel which he had built for
his own ministry of the Word was to him a veritable city of
light. And now he knew that he was leaving it.

'I'm glad you've come, Jonathan,' he said. 'We haven't
got a preacher, only one that comes once a month; it's only
praying and reading most Sabbath days now; and there's
some that aren't faithful. Are you willing to take the work
now you're home again?'

Mr. Trimblerigg said that he would.

'I wonder,' said the old man, fixing him with his gaze,
'whether you'll be contented to stay here after I'm gone?'

'I shall do what the Lord tells me,' said Jonathan.

'Let's ask Him now,' said Uncle Phineas. 'Bring me the
Book.'

There was no reason why Mr. Trimblerigg should re-
fuse; but it was a curious experience to see that the Book

89

opened where a marker had been placed in it; to see the old man pass his hand over to the left, measure his finger up the page and lay it on an exact spot. Nor did he wonder then, when the text was read, that his future had been fixed for him in terms that he could not dispute.

'And Laban said unto him, I pray thee if I have found favour in thine eyes, *tarry*; for I have learned by experience that the Lord hath blessed me for thy sake. And he said, "Appoint me thy wages, and I will give it".'

After Heaven had thus spoken there was a pause; then Phineas said, 'The word "Tarry" is in italics, Jonathan. That seems to point, doesn't it? Have you any doubt left in you now, about what God means you to do?'

'No, Uncle,' replied Mr. Trimblerigg, 'I have none.' The text, in fact, had not altered by a hair's breadth his views of the career he was to run.

' "Appoint me thy wages and I will give it," ' went on the old man. 'That comes in too. But it isn't wages exactly, is it, Jonathan? Though you may call it so for want of a better word. You know that I've made two wills, don't you, Jonathan?'

Yes: Jonathan had heard it.

'I haven't forgotten you, Jonathan. I've remembered you in both; but I haven't left you so much in the one as in the other. You see, I'd got Davidina in my mind, then: and there was Caroline, too. . . . I should be leaving you more, Jonathan, if it wasn't for Caroline. But now, she's lived with me all these last years, I've got to provide for her – differently to what I meant.'

He spoke slowly, picking his words a little. Mr. Trimblerigg listened to them without disappointment or dismay. He had no objection to Caroline being provided for on a generous scale; and as his own share was apparently to be increased, Davidina was now evidently the one who would have to give way.

'And then,' said his uncle, 'there was the chapel to think about. Now that you've accepted the Lord's word I know what to do.'

With quavering hand he drew out a key, and directed his nephew to a drawer with certain contents.

Under instruction Mr. Trimblerigg brought him the two documents. He looked them through, and separating the one from the other had it returned to the drawer and locked back into safety. He then did something which convinced Mr. Trimblerigg that at last he trusted him. He put into his hands the remaining document.

'When you go downstairs, Jonathan, put that into the fire,' he said, 'and see that it burns. It's not wanted now.' And as he heard those words Mr. Trimblerigg felt that his future was assured (and incidentally Caroline's also). His anxieties were all over, but curiosity remained.

When Uncle Phineas dismissed him he went downstairs with spirits quietly elated; and seeing that his future wife was then busily occupying the kitchen, he went into the parlour to consider matters. First he opened and read the discarded will; its contents were not sensational, but they would, had they outlived the testator, have disappointed him. His uncle had left him an income of a hundred pounds, and his books. The chapel went to Trustees with a small stipend for the ministry of the Word according to the tenets of True Belief. The residue of his property, real and personal, was divided in equal portions between Caroline and Davidina; Caroline's share including the house he lived in. This meant that Caroline and Davidina would have each got an income of over two hundred a year, of rising value.

When Caroline went up aloft at the ringing of Uncle Phineas's handbell, Mr. Trimblerigg went into the kitchen and without reluctance put the document into the fire according to his instructions. And when Caroline came down again to go on with the cooking, he proposed to her and was accepted.

This was the beginning of quite the happiest three weeks in his life, for as soon as Mr. Trimblerigg made up his mind to marry Caroline, he also made up his mind to be in love with her. He did not find any more difficulty in this swift embrace of new affections than in the equally swift embrace of new convictions as soon as they suited him. Circumstances had provided him with sufficient reasons for making Caroline his wife; and as love made the proposal so much more palatable, he bestowed upon her that extra gift with the demonstrative ardour that was his nature; and in the extended opportunities afforded by courtship he continued to find her very pleasant to the touch: a little unemotional perhaps, but good-tempered, contented, and an excellent cook; and it was clear that in her quiet, half-motherly way she very much admired him.

Uncle Phineas received the news without comment; and three weeks later, with a final gathering-up of his patriarchal feet, died in the beginning of his eighty-seventh year just about tea-time.

Mr. Trimblerigg ran for the woman who was to lay him out (since in that matter old age requires extra haste when the legs have died bent), then walked on to give instructions to the undertaker. Returning presently to a house where the womenfolk were busy at their obsequious duties, he sought and found a key which he knew by sight, and got out the will. Under it lay a sealed letter addressed to Davidina. This puzzled and slightly startled him; but for the present he laid it by as an item of comparative unimportance. What startled him much more, however, were the provisions which he found in the surviving will. His own share of it was indeed larger. He found himself owner not only of the house, the books and the furniture, but of the chapel also, with an accompanying income of a hundred and fifty pounds, to be his so long as he remained the local minister of the True Believers. This stipend was in the hands of Trustees. All the rest of the estate, amounting to an annual value of five hundred pounds went to Davidina.

Mr. Trimblerigg lost his temper; for a moment it almost seemed that his uncle had made him destroy the wrong will. But there, for himself, though tied by conditions, was the larger bequest; he could not but admit that here a modest livelihood was provided for him: enough in that retired district where all lived simply to enable him to marry and have a family. On the other hand, it bound him to the place, and bound him still more stiffly to the tenets of True Belief. There was the further bewilderment that Davidina got all the rest, the bulk of the estate; and that Caroline got nothing.

And now, of course, the letter to Davidina became important. He went upstairs, got it from the drawer, and brought it down. The seal was a purely conventional precaution, easy to get through and to replace; while as for the adhesive flap there are ways also of dealing with that which every one knows. Adopting one of them he became cognizant of the contents. It appeared then that, after all, his Uncle Phineas had not trusted him; and that, in spite of their apparent estrangement of late years, he did trust Davidina absolutely. The letter informed Davidina that while her benefit under the will was without legal condition, it was the testator's wish and request that if fifteen years after his death her brother Jonathan was still an active minister of the True Believers she should surrender to him one-half of the estate now bequeathed to her; and that, as a necessary precaution, she should make a will securing him the same advantage under the same conditions. And following on this came a statement more startling than all: 'I have made no special provision for Caroline, as I intend that she shall marry Jonathan.' And with that the communication ended.

Mr. Trimblerigg looked up from it into a changed world. Just as he thought to be starting on his forward career, he had become a cypher in the hands of others. The word 'Tarry' stared him in the face; in italics, as his uncle had remarked. Here and now he had been left to Caroline, in order to provide her with a home; and in the future to the tender mercies of Davidina – who was not even legally bound, when the time came, to act on her instructions.

Fifteen years! The time was fatal to his prospects; it mattered nothing to his career that now, in his twenty-first year, he happened to be a member of the antiquated sect of True Believers; it would matter everything if he were bound to it for another fifteen years. He would then be nearing forty; how could he become the leader of the Free Evangelicals, foremost figure of the Free Church Union in its march toward liberal Theology, if in fifteen years' time he was still saddled with the tenets of True Belief to the extent of having to preach them? He saw the meaning of it. His uncle had not trusted him; and was as far from trusting him as ever, at the moment when he had placed in his hands the other will to have it destroyed. It stung him to the quick that a simple and rather stupid old man should thus have got the better of him — to the extent at least of controlling the offer or withdrawal of a prospective income of four hundred a year. A hundred and fifty of it depended on his remaining in the local ministry; that did not so much matter; but the rest depended on his remaining in the connection at the very height of his powers; and that he did not for a moment intend. No; even in the shock of disappointment and all the callowness of untried youth, he knew that he was worth more. And in a moment he had decided: henceforth his career was to be a tussle between him and old Uncle Trimblerigg; they would see which would come out first.

While thus he straightened out his problem below, Uncle Phineas was being straightened out upstairs. It was the easier job of the two and would soon be over; Jonathan had no time to lose. And so collectedly, with presence of mind, he restored the letter to its envelope, licked and sealed it, and returned letter and will to the drawer from which he had taken them, leaving them to be found by others.

Three days later he prayed and preached at the funeral with great success. People flocked to hear him, for it was already known in the surrounding district, which had sampled his early efforts, that he was going to become a great orator. Within a year he was due to enter the ministry: and the True Believers swelled with a sense of triumph that once more they were going to have among them a shining light.

In the domestic privacy of the Trimblerigg family, when the funeral was over, the will was ceremonially opened and read; and Jonathan received with Christian resignation the announcement that Davidina was her uncle's chief beneficiary.

A few days later he gave Davidina a chance to speak of the thing he knew, by inquiring:

'Uncle Phineas left a letter for you, didn't he?'

'Yes,' said Davidina, and was for saying no more. But Mr. Trimblerigg could not quite let it stop at that.

'Anything that concerns others besides yourself?'

'Yes,' said Davidina again. 'He told me that you were going to marry Caroline, and sent you his love.'

So apparently Davidina meant that he was not to know. For once he had beaten her; and even if it were to bring him nothing in the end there was satisfaction in that thought.

Some Women and a Moral

MR. TRIMBLERIGG'S CALL TO BE MINISTER TO THE TRUE Believers of Horeb was independent of the theological test of his College which qualified him for election to a pastorate among the Free Evangelicals. But practically it gave him a two-years' start; the Free Evangelicals did not as a rule adopt pastors unless they were either twenty-three, or married. Mr. Trimblerigg was only twenty-one, but there among the True Believers the vacancy was waiting for him, and he reckoned that two preliminary years devoted to establishing his fame as a preacher and emancipating himself from the narrower doctrines of True Belief would not be spent amiss.

In the short while which must elapse before his marriage with Caroline, she and Davidina changed places domestically; and brother and sister lived queerly together at the house adjoining the chapel; an arrangement which, more than anything else could have done, decided Mr. Trimblerigg that his engagement should be short.

Of course it was impossible from the first that Horeb should absorb all his energies. He started at once as a mid-week missioner, first among the neighbouring chapels of the connection, then going further afield; and so as to avoid for the present the problem of an exchange of pulpits with easier denominations contrary to the traditions of True Belief, speaking in hired halls where connection did not count; thus, without taking up the revolutionary standpoint, he began to sit loose to the exclusiveness into which the True Believers had reduced themselves, and to make himself known among the Free Churches.

G

He had passed his theological degree brilliantly; a brilliancy slightly reduced in his own estimation by the fact that Miss Isabel Sparling had tied with him for first place. Thus, except for the sex-barrier, her qualification for the ministry was mathematically the same as his own.

Now among Free Believers the idea of women in the ministry had been so unthought of that in their constitution there was no word against it; and Mr. Trimblerigg was, by his outspoken advocacy of their claim during his college career, a predestined champion of the cause.

He had not occupied his pulpit a month before Miss Isabel Sparling reminded him. She asked for three things: that he would circulate a Women's Ministry petition to the Annual Conference for the signatures of his congregation, that he would himself present the petition and make an accompanying motion in his ministerial capacity, and that meanwhile he would invite her as a lay-preacher to his own chapel.

Mr. Trimblerigg was of a divided mind: had the proposition at that time been welcome among the Free Evangelicals, he could not have wished for a better means of effecting a breach between himself and the True Believers, when occasion was ripe for it. But among the Free Evangelicals vacancies in the pastorate were not going begging as they were among the True Believers; and for that and other reasons the rank and file of Free Evangelicalism were either opposed or indifferent. The question had indeed already been debated in that great body of Free Churchmen, and they had decisively turned it down as inopportune. The opposition ranged from support of the Pauline doctrine of womanly silence in the assembly, to the argument that as they could not go out as missionaries to be eaten by savages they had not a complete qualification for ministerial office; and when some protested that they were quite willing to take their chance of being eaten like the rest, it was pointed out that savages did other things to women besides eating them; at which point it was considered that the discussion had become unsuitable for open debate; and the previous question was moved and carried.

After considering the matter for awhile, therefore, Mr. Trimblerigg decided to plead his youth and inexperience. It was the only time that he ever did so; as a rule he revelled in the sense of freedom attaching to both, finding inexperience quite as valuable as youth in the formation of those momentary opinions on which he ran his career. Tentatively, however, as a sop to self-approbation he put the matter to his own chapel-members, – did they wish to have a woman come and preach to them? The shade of Uncle Phineas presided over the gathering: they were startled – emphatically they did not.

Mr. Trimblerigg, fortified by this verdict, told Miss Sparling that being nothing if not democratic, and his own local democracy having decided against it, he could go no further at present in that particular direction; but that in his own time and in his own way he would work for the enlargement of popular opinion, and as soon as he saw an opening resume advocacy of the cause.

Thereupon ensued a long dispute between Mr. Trimblerigg and Miss Sparling as to what 'democracy' really meant. Was democracy, in matters spiritual, the will of a single congregation or community, or of the whole Church Militant? Mr. Trimblerigg said that democracy was merely what you could make it, a thing not of theory but of practice; and the whole Church Militant being highly divided on party lines, democracy was divided also.

Miss Sparling then created an argumentative diversion by asking, 'Why did you kiss me when you converted me to True Belief?' And thereafter the duel which went on between them was mainly upon those two questions — what democracy meant, and what the kiss had meant. Mr. Trimblerigg gave to both alike a spiritual and a brotherly interpretation. Whereupon Miss Sparling adumbrated a letter in which he had signed his name with five crosses after it: what did the five crosses mean? Mr. Trimblerigg said that they stood for an unfinished communication — unfinished for lack of time; and that educated people called them 'asterisks.' Miss Sparling refused to be so educated, and thenceforward was his enemy.

In the holiday season she took lodgings in the neighbourhood, and became a member of his congregation. Mr. Trimblerigg found that he could no longer preach and pray freely, while Isabel Sparling sat with her eye upon him, saying 'Amen' in a loud voice whenever he came to a full stop, pretending to think then that his prayer had finished. Thus by attacking his nerves she destroyed his spiritual efficiency. Constantly he received letters which he did not answer.

She followed him up on weekdays also, attended his mission services in the neighbouring villages and towns; and though he had ceased to speak to her, was to be seen following him at a few paces distance, as though somehow he belonged to her.

Mr. Trimblerigg walked fast, and sometimes, on turning a corner, ran to get quit of her. One day, in front of his gate, she was seen to make five crosses in the mud, indicative of an unfinished communication. She left it at that.

In desperation he was driven at last to consult Davidina, who had remained silently aware of what was going on, amused but saying nothing.

Davidina asked how many crossed letters she had had from him. Only one, he assured her. 'One may be enough,' was her comment, which he did not deny.

Davidina thought awhile, then said:

'Have you forbidden her the house?'

'She has never come.'

'If you forbade it, she would.'

'Then I won't.'

'You had much better. Tell her that you are in to-morrow between four and five, and that you will not see her.'

'And what if she comes?'

'You have only got to be out; I'll see to her myself. It's a pathological case, and the sooner you get married the better.'

For once he trusted her; and as Davidina arranged it, so the thing happened. Miss Sparling called; Davidina opened the door, and said, in reply to inquiry, that Mr. Trimblerigg was out. Miss Sparling, not believing her, walked in. Davidina requested her curtly but civilly to walk out again; and when she refused, closed the door and fell upon her.

In the struggle that ensued Miss Sparling was no match for Davidina. Within two minutes her bosom was rifled of its guilty contents, and so far as written documents were concerned Mr. Trimblerigg's reputation was safe again; that is to say Davidina had it in her keeping.

She explained her course of action quite coolly to the flabbergasted Isabel: 'You forced my door; I forced your buttons. Now we are equals; you'd better go.'

She opened the door again as she spoke. Eye to eye they looked at each other; then Miss Sparling walked out. And as Davidina watched her depart, she said to herself, 'I wonder whether she's going to be the making of him?'

Davidina had got it firmly into her head that it was better to provide Jonathan with enemies than with friends. She saw that popularity might be the ruin of him; it was sisterly partiality which made her think that unpopularity would be a corrective.

In the event Isabel had the making of him in a direction that Davidina could never have dreamed.

When Mr. Trimblerigg came home, creeping in by the back way after dark, Davidina presented him with the letter ending in five crosses, saying that Miss Sparling had left it for him.

'Have you read it,' he inquired uncomfortably.

'No; did you want me to?' said Davidina in a calculated tone of surprise.

He could not quite credit her with not having read it; but it was a great comfort to pretend she had not read it, and to have the pretence shared.

And if a human can understand that state of mind he will understand a good deal of the mind of Mr. Trimblerigg.

Mr. Trimblerigg as soon as he was alone, read the letter carefully through. He remembered the occasion of it, but had forgotten the actual phrasing; he was astonished at its moderation.

'I don't believe she could ever have used it!' he exclaimed

to himself. Then he put it into the fire and watched it burn; and as he did so, he remembered Davidina's advice: 'The sooner you get married' (meaning to Caroline) 'the better.'

It may be – I am not quite sure – that this was what really decided him to marry Caroline. His feelings toward Caroline had undergone, since his uncle's death, not a revulsion, but a diminution. He had begun to have his doubts whether he was the right husband for her; if she could find another and a better, he did not wish to be selfish. There were episodes in their courtship which had disappointed him; she was still pleasant to touch; but her mind was the sort which seemed only capable of responding with a 'just so' to whatever was said to it: equable, comfortable, and contented, but not stimulating.

Like a soft cushion, leaning on which you leave an impression, and the mark stays for awhile then slowly effaces itself, so she. Looking ahead he could see the sort of wife and mother that she would be; and if ever it should chance that one of her children were taken from her, or if he himself were to die young – she would be more like a mother cow separated from its milk than from its calf. Caroline was uneventful.

It was not an exciting prospect to look forward to. Nevertheless – and perhaps Miss Sparling had something to do with it – within a year of his uncle's death, Jonathan Trimblerigg married Caroline.

And Davidina, out of her newly inherited wealth, gave them £100 to start their housekeeping; returning herself to the parental roof, where she stayed till a couple of years later Mr. and Mrs. Trimblerigg senior shared an influenza and died in the same week, and in the same bed.

After that, for some while Mr. Trimblerigg was comfortably rid of her. She developed a craze for travelling. But regularly every year, when a new child was born to them, Davidina sent them a present of £20.

He Rides for a Fall

IT WOULD NOT HAVE BEEN WELL FOR MR. TRIMBLERIGG —
for his training as an adept in the art of getting on —
had his early ministerial career been entirely without
obstacles. Had circumstances not kept him on the jump,
his native agility might possibly have diminished; but
from the very beginning obstacles presented themselves,
and they were not all of one kind.

The first which confronted him was intellectual and
temperamental. It had been all very well in his early
novitiate to act as occasional lay-preacher to that sect of
rigid Believers with bottle-necked minds; a callow and
undogmatic theology was then permissible. But now,
being called to the ministry, he must get to the heart of
things, and let his light shine there. True Believers
expected it; and elders from afar, men placed in authority,
came to listen to this young and rising hope of a diminished community, in order to discover whether his oratory
had weight and substance, or was merely words.

It was Mr. Trimblerigg's fixed intention to get himself
driven out of that narrow communion so soon as he could
afford it; but meantime he had to maintain the verbal
verities of the faith, a difficult matter when his ministry
extended to three discourses a week, two on the Sabbath
and one every Wednesday.

For awhile he kept himself going on the Song of Songs,
the literal interpretation of which provided him with
poetic flights and passages of local colour congenial to his
youthful temperament. Poetry in the pulpit was a new
thing. His spiritual interpretations of love attracted the
courting couples of the neighbourhood; youth flocked to

hear him, with occasional results which made the watchful elders uneasy. It is true that on Sunday evenings the chapel was always crowded, but his congregation of youths and maidens, coming from a distance, showed more punctuality in arriving than in returning home; and now and then, as a consequence, marriages had to be hasty.

Before long Mr. Trimblerigg's Watch Committee called upon him to talk less of love, with its bundles of myrrh, its vineyards and gardens of spice, and to concentrate a little more on those starker and more characteristic verities of the faith – sin, death, judgment and damnation.

Under this doctrinal pressure Mr. Trimblerigg became futurist. He started a course on the literal interpretation of prophecy. It was a branch of theology which the modern school of Free Evangelicalism had neglectfully allowed to go out of fashion, fearing perhaps what definite repudiation might involve. Here Mr. Trimblerigg saw his way. Unfulfilled prophecy had this advantage: it could always be apprehended and never disproved. Also the sleeping atavisms of human nature favoured it; just as they favour palmistry and table-turning, and the avoidance of going under ladders or looking at the new moon through glass. When these currents of instinctive credulity are wisely drawn into the service of religion they may do great things. And so it was that Mr. Trimblerigg made a slight mistake when without meaning to do great things in his present connection, he let himself go.

Before he had realized the danger, his chapel became full to overflowing; crowds far larger than it would hold waited at the door; and through that, and through windows set wide, his word went forth into the world and stirred it more than he wished it to be stirred.

Reporters came to listen to him; Free Evangelicals of the older school wobbled and came over; and while his own congregations increased, down at the larger chapel below Grandfather Hubback's diminished, and relations became strained.

This was not what Mr. Trimblerigg had intended; meaning only to temporize he had exalted himself to a height from which it would be difficult, when the time came for it, to make an unconspicuous descent. He did not wish his ministry among the True Believers to remain memorable; but when upon the platform the word came to him with power, it was very difficult to refrain. It was also very difficult to remember afterwards what he had actually said: Mr. Trimblerigg had too much verbal inspiration of a momentary kind. If this sort of thing went on long, he might establish a record against himself fatal to his future career.

The Free Evangelicals were beginning to feel sore; the door which he wished kept open for him in a friendly spirit, might narrow, might even close against him in the day of his need.

And then two things happened which he turned briskly to account.

The first was an invitation from the Synod of True Believers to deliver the set discourse at the Annual Congress.

It was a great, an unexpected, and an embarrassing honour; for the set discourse, by unwritten tradition, was always given in defiance of modern theology and in defence of the literal interpretation of Scripture.

If he did this to the satisfaction of the True Believers, his secession to the Ministry of Free Evangelicalism in the immediate future would become almost impossible.

But Mr. Trimblerigg, though his other virtues might be fleeting or fluctuating, had a nimble courage which stayed fixed. After humbly and fervently informing me of his intention, under the guise of a request for guidance, he accepted the invitation and sat down to write the thesis which precipitated his career two years ahead of the course he had planned for it.

The second circumstance, embarrassing but helpful to the same end, was the reappearance of Isabel Sparling, heading a deputation of women who, feeling called to the ministry, now saw an opportunity which they were not going to let slip. As select preacher before the Assembly it was, they told him, his bounden duty to crown his allegiance to their cause in public advocacy of the ministration of women; and when he pleaded that the literal interpretation of Scripture must be his theme, they replied by requiring him to concentrate on the literal interpretation of certain texts – mainly in the Old Testament – conclusive of their claim.

In the discussion that followed, the deputation saw their opportunity slipping away from them. Mr. Trimblerigg was willing to support their cause, but only, as he said, 'in his own time and in his own way.' And that time was not now, and his way was not theirs. Tempers grew hot, words flew, the deputation went forth in dudgeon; Isabel Sparling gave him a parting look; it meant business, it also meant mischief. She was, he knew, a woman of high ability, and a determined character: and now, on public and on private ground, she was become his enemy.

In the six months which intervened before the day of Congress, the women's spiritual movement broke into flame and heat, and they began that phenomenal campaign of Church Militancy which has since made history. They began by entering a motion for Congress in support of their claim; but as women, though congregational electors, could not sit in the Assembly, and as they could get no member to give his name to their motion, it was ruled out of order and returned to them.

Then in the chapels of the True Believers the word of the Lord was heard by the mouths of women; what Congress sought to silence, at meeting they made known; they went forth in bands of three or four, or sometimes they went solitary, and entering into the congregations like lambs became as wolves.

When it seemed good to them that the preacher should end his prayer, they cried 'Amen', and in the midst of his discourse they spoke as the spirit gave them utterance. It was a demonstration that the gift of prophecy, like murder, must out, and that if a place in order be not found for it, it must come by disorder. So they presented their case, by example and not by argument, and the congregations of True Belief dealt with them, or tried to deal with them, in various ways painful or persuasive, but none prevailed. For this phenomenon, they claimed, was spiritual, and could only be cured spiritually in the granting of their demand; while the coercion practised on them, being merely material, must necessarily fail.

And so spiritually chaining themselves to their chairs, they were materially carried out, and spiritually interrupting the eloquence of others were materially suppressed under extinguishers which deprived them of breath; and for what they truly believed to be their unconquerable right True Belief could find no remedy.

From the moment when it had first sparkled into life, this sacred flame had, of course, found at Mount Horeb an altar for its fires, and in Mr. Trimblerigg a victim suited to its need. There Isabel Sparling came in person, for the first time openly, but afterwards in disguise, and there they wrestled together for an eloquence which tried to be simultaneous but failed. And though, with preparation and practice, he did better against interruption than she, yet even there she beat him; for if her remarks were disjointed and ejaculatory it did not much matter, whereas for him sound alone was not sufficient, but he must keep up the thread of his discourse, rise superior in eloquence as well as in sense to the reiterated 'Alleluias' of Miss Sparling's inspired utterance, and all the while put a Christian face upon the matter, which was the most difficult thing of all.

Three times was Miss Sparling cast forth from the midst of the congregation, before the doorkeepers became efficient in penetrating her disguise. The third time Mr. Trimblerigg, losing his temper, had used what sounded like incitement to violence, and Miss Sparling getting her leg broken, brought an action and obtained damages, fifty pounds.

This was regarded by the movement as a great spiritual victory, and a victory it was. The law of the land, finding that True Believers had no fixed ritual of public worship, and that male members of its congregations might preach or pray without comment when the spirit moved them, acquitted Miss Sparling either of brawling or of conduct conducive to a breach of the peace, and held responsible for the damage those who had so ruthlessly ejected her. It admitted, however, that they would be within their rights in keeping her out. This for the future they did, and when, as her next spiritual exercise, Miss Sparling returned and broke all the chapel windows as a way of joining in worship, they got her sent to prison for it. There, still led by the spirit, she hunger-struck and got out again; just too late unfortunately to hear Mr. Trimblerigg deliver his sensational discourse to the Annual Congress, a discourse to the force of which she had, without knowing it, contributed: for six months of the women's Church Militancy had been enough to convince Mr. Trimblerigg that a connection in which they had become active was one from which he himself must sever.

And so, on the opening day of Congress, setting the note for all that was to follow, Mr. Trimblerigg delivered his mercurial and magnetic address on 'The Weight of Testimony.' Therein he upheld without a quiver of doubt the verbal inspiration of Scripture; it was, he argued, the true and literal setting forth of things actually said and done by a chosen people finding their spiritual way and losing it; but in that to-and-fro history of loss and gain many things were recorded for our learning upon the sole testimony of men whose minds still stumbled in darkness, and who, therefore, had not the whole truth in them; but where their fallible testimony infallibly recorded by Scripture actually began, or where it ended, was not a matter of inspiration at all but of textual criticism, because in ancient Hebrew manuscripts quotation marks were left out. Thus Holy Scripture, once written, had become subject to vicissitudes at the hands of expurgators, emendators, and copyists, even as the sacred ark of the Covenant which, having at one time fallen into the hands of the Philistines, and at another been desecrated by the pollut-

ing touch of Uzzah, was finally carried away in triumph
to pagan Rome, and there lost.

Having thus shown how the most sacred receptacles of
the Divine purpose were not immune from the accidents
of time, he drew and extended his parallel, and from this,
his main thesis, proceeded to give instances, and to restore
quotation marks as an indication of where textual criticism
might be said to begin and inspiration to end.

Before long holy fear like a fluttered dove fleeing from
a hawk had entered that assembly, and beards had begun
to shake with apprehension as to what might come next.

Mr. Trimblerigg warmed to his work; his sensations
were those of a fireman who, in order to display his courage and efficiency in the fighting of flames, has set a light
to his own fire-station; and while it crackles under his feet,
he strikes an attitude, directs his hose and pours out a
flood of salvation.

When he started to give his instances, their devastating
effect was all that he could desire. He tackled Joshua's
command to the sun to stand still, restored the quotation
marks, pointed out how in that instance Holy Scripture
had expressly referred it back to its only authority, the
Book of Jassher: and how the Book of Jassher being outside the canon of Scripture was of no standing to impose
its poetic legends on the mind of a True Believer. Why
then, it might be asked, had reference been made to it at
all? He adumbrated a prophetic significance, a spiritual
value, to which by that parable the human race was afterwards to attain.

Joshua's command to the sun now found its true address
in the human heart, and the reason why Scripture had
recorded it at so early a date was in order that it might

find fulfilment and illustration in that greater Scripture uttered upwards of a thousand years later by St. Paul in his Epistle to the Ephesians, 'Let not the sun go down upon your wrath.' That was the true meaning of Joshua's command for those who read Scripture, not by picking at it in parts, but by reading it as it ought to be read as one great harmonious, consistent, homogeneous, and indivisible whole.

On that uplifting string of adjectives Mr. Trimblerigg stopped to breathe, and his hearers breathed with him loud and deep.

That answering sound, whatever it might mean, gave Mr. Trimblerigg the poetic push which the gasp of a listening audience always supplied, 'Yea, I say unto you, yea!' he cried, and paused. He was in deep waters, he knew; so, breaking into an eloquent passage about ships – ships at sea, ships that pass in the night, ships that have Jonahs on board, ships that cling to the anchor, and ships that have no anchor wherewith to cling, ships of the desert seeking for water and finding none, ships that making for the North Pole stick fast in ice, yet continue moving toward their destined goal, ships that go out like ravens and return no more, ships that come home like doves to roost carrying their sheaves with them – so experimenting on wings of poesy in that seaward direction to which, though he had never been there, his pulpit oratory so often carried him, he almost succeeded, or almost seemed to succeed, in carrying his audience with him; for indeed it is very difficult, when beautiful spiritual similes are being uttered, for an audience to remain cold and critical, and remind itself that figures of speech have nothing to do with sound doctrine.

It is also difficult when a speaker speaks with so much

beauty and fervour and imaginative mimicry, as on this occasion did Mr. Trimblerigg, not to see him as he sees himself; for the self-hypnotism of the orator is a catching thing – and nations have often been caught by it to their destruction, and churches to heresy almost before they knew.

But the True Believers, though momentarily moved, were not carried away; and when Mr. Trimblerigg returned to his instances his audience was still against him.

He took the characters of the Hebrew prophets and examined them; he showed that the sins and shortcomings of Eli's judgeship, for which Eli had been condemned, were reproduced under the judgeship of Samuel when he, in his turn, grew old, and that it was really only as Samuel's own word for it that the people stood condemned in asking for a King. Holy Scripture had truly recorded that incident; but was Samuel, the ineffective ruler whose sons took bribes and perverted judgment, was he a witness altogether above suspicion when his own deposition from power was the question to be decided on? And so round the testimony of Samuel he put quotation marks, and relieved Scripture of the burden of that unjust judgment the approval of which was Samuel's, and Samuel's alone.

And then he took Elisha and the cursing of the children, and the she-bears tearing of them, and there, too, he restored the quotation marks. He threw no doubt upon the incident, but its reading as a moral emblem was the reading of Elisha, and the tearing of the forty-two children had found its interpretation in the wish of the prophet misreading it as the will of God. Other instances followed: there with the testimony of Scripture before him, stood

CHAPTER TEN

Mr. Trimblerigg inserting quotation marks for the restoration of its morals, dividing the sheep from the goats, trying to show where inspiration ended and where textual criticism began.

Judged by outside standards it was not a learned discourse, even Mr. Trimblerigg would not have claimed that for it; but it was vivacious and eloquent, and not lacking in common sense; and as common sense was pre-eminently the quality for which in relation to the interpretation of Scripture the True Believers had no use, the result was a foregone conclusion.

When he had finished Mr. Trimblerigg sat down to a dead silence, and the presiding minister rose. Deeply, bitterly, unsparingly Mr. Trimblerigg's thesis was there and then condemned as utterly subversive of the revealed Word. More than that, Congress by a unanimous vote expunged it from the record of its proceedings; not by the most diligent search in the archives of True Belief will any reference to Mr. Trimblerigg's address on 'the Weight of Testimony' be found.

But the discourse had done its work, and Mr. Trimblerigg knew that he left the Congress theologically free for the new-shaping of his career.

It was true that the Chapel of Mount Horeb, with house attached, was still his own; but within a week the stipend pertaining thereto had been withdrawn, and the Trustees, believing themselves to be deprived of the chapel, had already begun the hire of temporary premises.

But Mr. Trimblerigg's instinct did not play him false; and when acknowledging his dismissal at the hands of the Trustees he informed them that the chapel was still open to them, free of charge and without condition. He was

sure, he said, that this was what his uncle would have
wished.

And having done all this, he felt that he had committed
a great act of faith; he felt also that he had done at last
something which could not fail to win the admiration of
Davidina.

Davidina was not herself a True Believer; but she had
done him the compliment to come from a distance to hear
his discourse; and much he wanted to know what she
thought of it. There was the added circumstance that she
had a direct interest – not theological but financial – in
the severance which had now taken place, and it was with
elated curiosity that he looked her in the eyes – with a look
more straight and unembarrassed than he could usually
muster – to see how she had taken it.

He found her waiting for him outside.

'Well, what d'you think of that?' he inquired.

'I think you'd have made a wonderful jockey,' she replied.
'You'd have made your fortune.'

'Jockey?' he said, puzzled. 'I didn't exactly pull it off
this time, at any rate.'

'No,' she replied. 'Did you mean to?'

'Yes; I did my best.'

'That I'm sure.'

'How d'you define a jockey?' he asked uneasily, irritated
by her fixed abstention from further comment.

'There's your own definition,' she said, 'you wrote it in a
school essay. I kept it because I thought it was good. I
won't spoil it; I'll send it you.'

And the next day the essay, which he had entirely forgotten, written in a round boyish hand, reached him by
post.

CHAPTER TEN

'A jockey,' he read, ' is one who had trained himself from early years in the dangerous and delicate art of falling from a horse.'

Accompanying it was a cheque for a hundred pounds. 'No wonder!' said Mr. Trimblerigg, 'she feels that she owes me something now. For by what he had just done he was giving her the right, twelve years hence, to continue as main beneficiary under the will of Uncle Phineas.

Nevertheless he was pleased that he had pleased her. It was almost the first time he had known it happen. Davidina's opinion of him counted much more than he liked. All his growing years he had tried to escape from her, and still he had failed.

Scene-shifting

MR. TRIMBLERIGG'S FALL FROM THE GRACE OF TRUE Belief – or from the good graces of the True Believers – had a famous reverberation in the Free Church Press; and at the age of twenty-four he became for the time being – next to the great Dr. Giffard himself – the most controversially talked-of person among the high lights of Nonconformity.

For just at that time the Free Churches had nothing on which to grit their teeth, and badly wanted a new bone. The New Theology of Dr. Ramble had come almost to nothing: its author had deserted it upon the door-step of the more ancient faith into which he had retired; and the fight about it had died down. But here was a fight, not more suddenly sprung than ended; and in a single round this young Jonathan of a David had been knocked out by the older Goliath. The common sympathies were with him, for the True Believers were not a popular sect; a time had come when it was generally felt that they were doing harm rather than good by an insistence on the literal truth of things which no one really believed. Nevertheless many old school Free Evangelicals considered that Mr. Trimblerigg's method of attack had been inconsiderate and rash; for if one started to put quotation marks round everything one did not wish to accept, where would the process end? The world still believed in punishment for the wicked; Samuel and Elisha stood high among the prophets; and if harvests were not liable to be cursed for a nation's sins, how then consistently could they – or alterations in the weather – be prayed for? As for the tearing of the she-bears, in primitive times primitive punishments were not regarded as they are now. Besides, as somebody pointed out in the correspondence which followed in *The Rock of Ages*, the she-bears may only have torn them slightly though sufficiently, killing none; merely teaching them to behave better in the future.

But though then, as always, Mr. Trimblerigg's plunges in exegesis provoked criticism, they had at least abundantly released him from the restricting inhibitions of True Belief, and the way to wider pulpits now lay open.

And then in the very nick of time, on a Saturday night of all days and hours in the week, Grandfather Hubback was taken ill, and Mr. Trimblerigg, who had been much in doubt where to go for his next Sunday's worship, came down at short notice and preached at Bethesda so beautifully, so movingly, and in so charitable and resigned a spirit, that there was no question of asking anyone else to come the following Sunday and take his place.

And so, informally, with the goodwill of a congregation where he was native and known, Mr. Trimblerigg became temporary preacher to the Free Evangelicals; and when, after a six weeks' illness, Pastor Hubback died, Mr. Trimblerigg was congregationally recommended to take his place; and after a certain amount of prayer, deliberation, and inquisition before a Committee, in answering which Mr. Trimblerigg found no difficulty at all, his ministerial status was confirmed and the appointment made.

In the month following, to make it as easy as might be for the faithful at Horeb to find and accommodate a new pastor, Mr. Trimblerigg moved his wife, family, and furniture to the larger abode of his late grandfather. But though the chapel was then left to them free of charge, and the house at a fair rental, the True Believers of the locality thenceforth dwindled to a small remnant; while the congregation at Bethesda increased and multiplied.

Mr. Trimblerigg, however, had made his exit so handsomely that though henceforth a suspended and disconnected minister (for the fiat of the Synod had gone forth against him to that effect) there was nevertheless between him and his old congregation a certain measure of goodwill; those who parted from him parted with regret; a few, younger members mostly, came out and followed him.

In that matter, indeed, more followed him than he could have wished; for no sooner had he been cut off from the communion of True Belief, than it became evident that in that narrow and reactionary following the woman's ministry propaganda had not a dog's chance of success. Possibly also, with him out of it, the sect ceased to attract the forward spirits of feminism. Whatever the cause, within a few weeks the agitation, so far as True Belief was concerned, died the death; but unfortunately came to life elsewhere, more vigorously and more abundantly than ever.

The long struggle of women, in the broad fold of Free Evangelicalism, to obtain sex-equality is not to be told here. Its main importance, so far as we are concerned, is the effect it had on the career of Mr. Trimblerigg. The recrudescence of Isabel Sparling and her followers in congregations drawn together by his growing reputation as a preacher became a sad impediment to the flow of his oratory. The manifestations were epidemic through all the loosely-knit communions of the Free Churches; but against himself they were directed with a personal animus of which only he and Isabel Sparling knew the full inwardness. For public purposes it was sufficient that, after first disclaiming all further obligation to their cause – since only in the bonds of True Belief had he stood fully committed thereto – he now sought to postpone the question of their admission until the corporate union of the Free Churches, and a few other reforms (Disestablishment amongst others), on which he had set his heart, had been accomplished. A piecemeal extension of the ministerial function to women would, he maintained, have a disturbing and a disuniting effect on communions which he sought to draw together in closer bonds of brotherhood. 'I am in favour of it,' he said (to the deputations which continued to wait on him), 'but I am not so much in favour of it, as of other and more fundamental things which must come first.'

Fundamental: the word kindled in the hearts of women who had felt that fundamental call of the spirit, a flame of resentment that crackled and spread. Who was he, who was anybody to dictate times and seasons, when the signs of that spiritual outpouring were here and now?

And so there was War in all the Free Churches which strove to fulfil themselves under the ministry of one sex alone; and Mr. Trimblerigg's prayers and preachings were in consequence broken into shorter paragraphs than was good for them.

But the violence with which those spiritual interruptions were carried out could not go on for ever; it was not in human, it was not in heavenly nature to utter messages born of the spirit with the drilled regularity and mechanism of a firing-squad. The things they said lacked conviction, did not come from their hearts or their heads, but only from their tongues and their tempers; and when in certain selected cases, Mr. Trimblerigg was inspired to pause so that they might speak as the spirit gave them utterance, the spirit left them badly in the lurch, they faltered and became dumb. For Isabel Sparling had enlisted in her cause many who were the poorest of poor speakers and had no wish whatever to become ministers; and when these heard themselves speak to a congregation which was artfully prevailed upon to listen they trembled and were afraid, and felt themselves fools.

And so, for a while, in his own particular congregation, it almost seemed that Mr. Trimblerigg was on the way to restore order and recover the undivided attention of his audiences.

But once again the pin-prick policy of Isabel Sparling got the better of him; and in the third year of her Church Militancy, forces of a new, a more placid, and a more undefeatable type were let loose against him.

They came, they behaved themselves, they said not a word, cloven tongues of inspiration no longer descended upon them; but in the most moving passage of prayer or sermon, they would feel imperatively moved to get up and go. And with much deprecatory fuss and whispered apology, always from the centre of a well-occupied row – they would go forth and presently return again, finding that they had left book, or handbag, or handkerchief behind them, or that they had taken away their neighbour's in mistake for their own. And it was all so politely and apologetically done that everybody, except the preacher, had to forgive them.

And so it came about that after Mr. Trimblerigg had been at Bethesda for a little more than two years, he accepted with alacrity a post at the Free Evangelical centre for the organization of foreign missions. And when he went out to preach it was at short notice here, there and everywhere, where the sedulous attentions of Miss Isabel Sparling and her followers had not time to overtake him.

That great work of organization, and the addressing of meetings for men only, gave his energies the outlet, the flourish, and the flamboyance which they imperatively demanded; and while he discovered in himself a head for business and a leaning toward speculative finance, in the great Free Evangelical connection his spiritual and oratorical reputation continued to grow.

And meanwhile, in his domestic circumstances, Mr. Trimblerigg was living an enlarged life and doing well. His wife had presented him with three children; and he in return, by moving them from a remote country district of primitive ways to one of the big centres of civilization, had presented her with a house containing a basement and a bathroom.

The basement enabled them to keep a servant; while the bathroom – a matter of more importance – enabled me to obtain a clearer view (which is not quite the same as a complete explanation), of Mr. Trimblerigg's character.

CHAPTER TWELVE

Theory and Practice

IT IS AS A RULE (THOUGH NOT ALWAYS) WHEN MEN ARE not under the observation of others, that they most surely reveal themselves. Word and face and gesture are not then the concealment which at other times they may become; and though when a man talks or gesticulates to himself he is often very far from telling the truth, he is generally near to revealing it.

And that, I suppose, is why writers of fiction have so generally taken the impossible liberty of following their characters into places of solitude and the privacy of their own thoughts; and from this godlike vantage-ground have pulled the strings of their puppets, imposing upon the reader a shoddy romanticism which pretends to be science.

But the gods can very seldom gaze into the secrecy of the things they have made, with so omniscient and cock-sure a spirit. Between mortal man and his maker there is a remove which sometimes baffles each alike. Free will, inside a fixed radius of determined environment, creates an obscurity. The outer integument, the limited view-point, the competing interests and motives, which go to make up one of those small self-centred individualities called man, are often obstructive to the larger and more serene intelligence which accompanies the spiritual stand-point; and I confess that in his privacy Mr. Trimblerigg used often to puzzle me.

It was seeing the puzzle at work – putting itself elaborately together, then pulling itself to pieces again – which gave me the clearer view; though it remained a puzzle still. But it was something to discover, suddenly and unexpectedly, that Mr. Trimblerigg had a passion for sincerity – towards himself at any rate – which took him to strange lengths; and though I recount what came under my observation, I do not pretend that I am able to explain it.

It was my privilege, more frequently at this particular point of his career than ever before, to see Mr. Trimblerigg take his bath; a function which, so far as his wife and the outside world knew, took place every morning of his life. It is more accurate to say that he went to the bathroom every morning, and that every morning, to anyone who cared to listen, the sounds of a bath being taken came through the door.

Mr. Trimblerigg had committed himself to the bath-habit with characteristic enthusiasm from the day when, with enlarged means, he found himself in a house containing a bathroom. But the house did not – in the first instance at any rate – contain a hot-water system; except on occasions of special preparation the baths remained cold.

But Mr. Trimblerigg's tenancy began in the summer quarter, when cold baths are almost as much a pleasure as a virtue. He was young, robust, vigorous, a preacher of the strenuous life; and facilities for the daily cold bath having come his way, he first boldly proclaimed his faith, and then got into it.

His faith carried him on, even when colder weather made it a trial; and often it was beautiful to see, after a timid bird-like hovering on the brink, how boldly he would plunge in, and with pantings and rapid spongings cross the rubicon of agony which leads to the healthy glow of a stimulated circulation.

On these occasions he would be very proud of himself, and standing before the glass gaze with approval on the ruddy blush which suffused his body and limbs under the hard rubbings of the towel. But a day came when he quailed and could not bring himself to get in at all; for the bath-habit was not in his blood as it is in the blood of those who have had a public-school training. The hill-side-chapel clan from which he sprang bathed only on the day of its baptism, or medicinally at the order of a doctor; and early habit, or the lack of it, counts with people as they grow older. So now there was controversy between Mr. Trimblerigg and his bath.

He tried it first with his hand, then with his foot: then he drew a breath and said 'Brrrr!' loudly and resolutely, and continued saying it as he drove the water up and down the bath with his sponge. He splashed it artfully across the wooden splash-board, and down on to the floor; he dipped his feet and made wet marks on the bath-mat, and all the while he spluttered and panted, and at intervals stirred the bath-water to and fro, and round and round with his sponge. Then he stood in front of the glass and rubbed himself hard with his towel until he felt quite warm, until his body glowed with a similar glow to that which followed an actual bathing. And, as he did so, he looked at himself roguishly in the glass; and shaking his head at himself – 'Naughty boy!' he said.

He was quite frank about it – to himself; and when he had done the same trick several times, as the mornings remained cold, he gave himself what he called 'a good talking to.'

'You are getting fat!' he said, 'you are getting self-indulgent; you want whipping!' And so saying he let out at himself two or three quite hard flicks with the towel – flicks that hurt.

CHAPTER TWELVE

It was a new invention for the establishment of pleasant relations between his comic and his moral sense; and when occasion required he repeated it. That little bit of self-discipline always restored his self-esteem, leaving his conscience without a wound; and he would come out of the bathroom feeling as good as gold, and sometimes would even remark to his wife how fresh a really cold bath on a frosty morning made one feel. And she would assent quite pleasantly, only begging him not to overdo it; whereupon he would explain how constant habit hardens a man even to the extremities of water from an iced cistern. And who, to look at her, would have any suspicion that she did not entirely believe him?

But on more than one occasion on very cold mornings, when Mr. Trimblerigg was safely downstairs, I have seen her go into the bathroom and inspect, with a woman's eye for details: appraise the amount of moisture left in the towel, and various other minute points for the confirmation of her hope that he was not overdoing it. And when she has quite satisfied herself, I have seen her smile and go on down to breakfast, a good contented soul, full of the comfortable assurances wives often have, that though husbands may be clever in their way, to see through them domestically is not difficult.

Later on, when Mr. Trimblerigg moved to a house efficiently supplied with a hot-water system, his baths were taken daily, but they were not always cold ones; and though he still pretended that they were, the modifications were so various and so habitual, that he left off saying 'naughty boy!' when he looked at himself in the glass. Also, when he really did begin to become chubby he left off telling himself that he was getting fat. Sometimes he would look at himself a little sadly, and in order to avoid the moral conclusion that you cannot have the fat things of life without the adipose tissue, preferred to reflect that he was 'getting middle-aged,' which was still ten years away from the truth.

But the sadness was only momentary; he had so good an opinion of himself that he was almost always cheerful, and easy to get on with. And if after he had turned thirty he did begin to become a little ball of a man, he kept the ball rolling with energy. The amount of work he could do, and do happily, was phenomenal; and under his stimulus the foreign mission work of the Free Evangelicals grew and flourished.

A Virtuous Adventure

NOBODY WHO HAS FOLLOWED THIS NARRATIVE WITH any intelligence can suppose that Mr. Trimblerigg was a man who did not have his temptations. What happened when he immersed Davidina in the stream without intending it, what happened when he did not immerse himself in the bath on a cold morning, has been faithfully told. But what he did to Davidina had hurt him far more than what he did to himself. It had hurt him because Davidina had found him out, and then had not allowed him to exlain.

He liked explaining. Explaining always made him feel right again with his own conscience. Even the look of understanding which he exchanged with himself in the glass, after some involuntary reversion to type, was sufficient as a rule to restore him to his own good opinion. To explain things, therefore, which generally meant to explain them away, was spiritual meat and drink to him.

But there were two people in the world to whom he very seldom explained anything: his wife, the quiet Caroline, who understood so little that it was not worth while; and his sister Davidina who understood so much that it was dangerous.

And between these two Guardian angels – who should have been his confidantes, but were not – he led a life of temptations. Not gross, or serious in kind, or extreme in degree, but temptations none the less, and all having their root in a very laudable trait of his character, his abounding love of adventure.

All his life Mr. Trimblerigg had been respectable: when he married he had no bachelor episodes to conceal from his wife, except perhaps that sixpenny sale of a kiss to Lizzie Seebohm, of which he had ceased to be proud, and his temporary infatuation for Isabel Sparling which had afterwards so embarrassed him. And this rectitude of conduct was not for lack of opportunity or inclination; for women attracted him and he attracted them. Puritan training and Puritan ancestry had no doubt something to do with it: the bath-habit which he had failed in his youth to acquire materially, he had acquired spiritually.

And so also with other things. He had never drunk wine or spirits; only once or twice a glass of beer, and that not for its potency or taste, but because it had froth on the top, and he liked dipping his lips into it. Surreptitiously, for the mere pleasure of concealment and doing it with boys older than himself, he had smoked a pipe a few times before becoming an adherent of True Belief, and he had not, upon escaping from the confinement of its doctrine, relinquished the abstention which had become a habit. Nor had he ever betted; though now, with a little money to turn round in, he had begun to speculate; but that was different. Finally he had never travelled.

In all these ways he, to whom change and adventure instinctively appealed, had been cut off from adventure; and adventure — even when it could not be called wrong — tempted him more than most people. To see himself in a tight place, and get out of it, meant self-realization; to find his way into unaccustomed circumstances, and fit them perfectly, was intellectual and moral training of a stimulating kind. During his days at College in the annual students' rag on the Fifth of November, a plot had been formed by the anti-feminists to make a Guy Fawkes of him dressed as a woman preacher. And he had escaped by stealing a policeman's helmet, truncheon, and overcoat, which were all much too large for him, and had then helped to batter the heads of the turbulent crowd which was out seeking for him and breaking the windows of the lodging-house where he was supposed to be.

That was a memory which he very much enjoyed: he had then drawn blood for the first time and heard a skull crack under his inexpert handling of the truncheon which a trained policeman only employs in the way of kindness. His man had gone to hospital. And that was at a time, too, when Mr. Trimblerigg considered himself a pacifist.

If the truth must be known he had more thoroughly enjoyed that brief hour of a violent laying-on of hands than the subsequent day of his ordination for which all the rest was a preparation. It had been more of an adventure.

And there you have the key to the temptations of Mr. Trimblerigg. Neither then, nor subsequently did he ever wish to do any man wrong; but he did wish to experiment. And whether it was the thickness of a fellow-student's skull, or the rise and fall of a market, or the gullibility of the common herd, or the pious employment of superstition for high and noble ends, or his own susceptibility to a woman's charm, or hers the other way about – he never had any other aim or object, or desire, except to experiment so that he might get to know and manipulate human nature better, including his own. Life itself was for him the great experiment.

And it so happened that at the very centre of his life was Caroline; and Caroline was dull.

Therefore their marital relations were imperfect.

It struck him one day that Caroline would be more interesting if he could make her jealous. Without giving her

131

serious cause, he tried, and failed. But, in the process of
his experiment, he engaged the affections of the instrument he employed much more than he intended.

It was a great nuisance. He had done everything to make
such a *dénouement* unlikely; had chosen her indeed rather
with a view to the stupidity of Caroline than to the attraction he found in her. She was rich, married, considerably
older than himself, had in fact a grown-up daughter and a
husband who was then in the process of earning a title for
her and himself, together with a handsome retiring pen-
sion, in the Indian Civil Service. She also had a motor-car
which she could drive independently of chauffeurs.

When he found that the affair had become serious he
began avoiding her; and being, as a pedestrian, the more
agile of the two he might have done it; but he could not
avoid the motor-car. And so one day, having gone to a
distant town to preach and to stay the night, he found the
lady and the motor-car awaiting him at the chapel door,
with an offer to motor him back to town all in the
day.

In that there seemed a hazardous sort of safety; tender
passages while on a high road and going at high speed,
were compatible with virtue; there was also a spice of
adventure in it; a half-engagement that they should meet
abroad under platonic but unencumbered conditions, must
now probably either be renewed or broken; to renew it
would, he thought, be the safest way of temporizing with
a situation which must end. Caroline had no capacity for
jealousy, and the affair was becoming ridiculous.

And so getting into the car, with four hours of daylight
left, and a hundred and fifty miles to go, Mr. Trimblerigg
accommodated himself to the situation that was soon to

end, and renewed with a warm asseveration of feelings that could not change.

They were still over fifty miles from their destination, and the darkness of night had settled, when the spice of adventure increased for Mr. Trimblerigg in a sudden shock. The car had irremediably and unaccountably broken down in a way which its owner announced would take hours to repair. They found themselves upon the outskirts of a village to which the requirements of motorists had added a small hotel; and before Mr. Trimblerigg could make up his own mind what to do, his companion had taken command of the situation and made retreat impossible, by entering in the visitors' book a Mr. and Mrs. Somebody: names not their own.

She had done this, while leaving him in charge of the car. They were booked, he found, to stay for the night; and the accommodation was as their names indicated.

Mr. Trimblerigg was not prepared to have a scene; but neither was he to be coerced from the ways of virtue. If he ever left them it would be in his own time and in his own way. And so presently, when they had dined together very pleasantly, and when Mr. Trimblerigg, in order to restore his sense of adventure, had experimented by taking wine, he simply stepped out casually into the darkness of the night and did not return.

His suit-case he left as a prey to his lady of the situation now ended; and walking to the nearest station, five miles away, waited there rather miserably for a midnight train which brought him back in the small hours to the virtuous side of his astonished Caroline.

He had a good deal to explain, including the absence of his suit-case; which forced him to say things which were

133

not all of them true. And when next day the suit-case arrived 'forwarded by request,' addressed on an hotel label to the name left in the visitors' book, there was a good deal more to explain; and for the first time Caroline became jealous. But it did not make her more interesting; it took the depressing form of a tearful resignation to the inevitable. She supposed that he had become tired of her, which was true; she added, less truthfully, that it was what she had always foreseen would happen, when as a matter of fact her mind had never been sufficiently awake to foresee anything so undomestic as suspicious circumstances pointing toward divorce.

Being simple, she spent the rest of the day trimming herself a new hat; at 6 p.m. she fortified herself in maternity by giving the three children a hot bath before bedtime; and then, as it was the servant's evening out, she descended to the kitchen and made pancakes for Mr. Trimblerigg's supper; and sat to watch him eat them with her hair unbecomingly tied up in a large pink bow.

These mild symptoms of jealousy expending itself in domestic steam, ought to have interested him but did not. He merely recognized and accepted the fact that Caroline's jealousy was as unimportant as had been her previous lack of it. Perhaps his mind was too preoccupied to give it all the attention it deserved.

He was amazed by the return of the suit-case under a name not of his own choosing; and yet somehow it raised the lady in his respect. For he had in him a touch of the sportsman; and on being struck so shrewd a blow, was quick to recognize that in going out into the night without warning he had left behind him a situation difficult for the lady to explain. He wondered how she had explained

134

it, and was a little fretted because he could not quite make things fit. All he saw clearly was that the open forwarding of the suit-case by rail to name and address, gave to it an air of *bona fide* which might have served to allay suspicion. But unless it was to avenge herself why had she given the right address? Was it, he wondered, an unusual combination of vindictiveness with plain horse common-sense; a straight one in the eye for him, and a bit of smart dodging for herself? If so, she was more interesting than he had thought: that was just the sort of thing that Isabel Sparling would have done. In that direction he was beginning to have definite regrets.

So, after the pancakes, he sat and thought, while his wife, a mellow picture of domesticity, bent under the lamp-light darning his socks.

And then the evening post came and a letter, in a hand-writing which he knew and had hoped never to see again. It was very brief.

'Whatever happened?' it ran. 'Did you get your suit-case?'

That beat him altogether; it interested, it bewildered him. His spirit of adventure was suddenly revived; because it would be difficult, he felt that he must go and explain – explain that he had suddenly seen somebody at the hotel whom he recognized, and who would recognize him, and that the only way of safety for both was instant flight. And so, not because he loved her any more, or wished for a renewal of the entanglement, but because he loved explaining himself out of difficult situations, he felt that on the morrow or the day after, he would go and see her again.

And though this particular episode here finds no further

chronicle, since thereafter it became in kind only one of many — suffice it to say that, on the morrow, he did.

Just before bed-time, folding up her work, his wife, who had been thinking her own thoughts quite quietly, looked across at him and said:

'If you died before me, Jonathan, should you like me to wear widow's weeds until I married again?'

Mr. Trimblerigg was startled almost out of his skin. Had it come from a woman of different character he would have found it a tremendous utterance. But in another moment he saw that this was only Caroline, Caroline composedly thinking aloud where other people did not.

'Now that,' replied Mr. Trimblerigg, 'is a very interesting question. But it is one which your second husband not I had better decide for you.'

Caroline saw that she was being laughed at. But she had already forgiven him. She kissed him, and went up to bed.

As the door closed behind her, Mr. Trimblerigg uttered a half-conscious ejaculation. 'O, God!' he cried, 'how dull, how dull you are!'

This personal remark, though it might seem otherwise, was really addressed to his wife.

Spade Work

THE FREE EVANGELICALS HAD LONG BEEN HONOURABLY
known for the extent and zeal of their labours in the
mission field. In Africa, in the larger islands of the
Pacific, and elsewhere, there were whole tracts from which
their spiritual competitors were cut out – districts of which
they had a practical monopoly. But in others, of recent
years, the monopoly had broken down.

Mr. Trimblerigg, with his shrewd eye for business, investigated the cause, and found it. He discovered that a
gospel-teaching which would not go down in the modern
world of civilization was the most successful, being the
most convincing, among the primitive races. And though
the missions of True Belief had everywhere dwindled for
lack of funds, they had nevertheless left their doctrines so
firmly rooted among certain tribes that those coming after
had found it advisable to take them over without much
change or enlargement of view. For the coloured races a
form of faith divorced from reason was for practical purposes the best. And so it became Mr. Trimblerigg's work
to persuade into the mission field such minds among the
Free Evangelicals as tended most nearly to the doctrines
of True Belief, and to head off as unsuitable those of a
more modernist tendency who were better suited at home.
And when, as sometimes happened, there was doctrinal
war among the missionaries themselves, Mr. Trimblerigg's influence was always subtly on the side of those
who preached, as the true word of revelation, those things
which the natives accepted most easily and liked best.

It was a point of view for which there is much to be said;
for the knowledge which comes to man mainly through

his five senses, and which has similarly to be passed on to others, cannot in the nature of things be absolute knowledge; and directly that is granted and given due weight, knowledge, even of things spiritual, has to adapt itself to forms which bear a sort of proportion to the minds waiting to receive it. And so under the stimulus of reports brought back from the mission field, Mr. Trimblerigg developed his doctrinal thesis that truth is but relative, thus anticipating in the spiritual world the discovery of Einstein in the material.

It was a thesis which when first put forward provoked a great deal of controversy; and many of the older school, for whose larger influence in the mission field it had been practically designed, denounced it in unmeasured terms as incompatible with Revelation and dangerous to the integrity of the human conscience.

But it was such a convenient doctrine – especially for the establishment of a *modus vivendi* among missionaries – that it made its way; and within ten years of Mr. Trimblerigg's first lubricating touch to the machinery put in his charge, the Free Evangelicals had redoubled their efficiency in the old world and the new, by setting forth the evidences of religion on two entirely different and incompatible lines, and producing as a result forms of faith as diverse in complexion as were the black and white faces of the respective communities to which essential truth was thus made relative.

As a further result Mr. Trimblerigg brought about, more by accident than by design, an informal alliance in missionary effort between True Believers and Free Evangelicals. For out there in the mission fields True Belief was now having won for it the battle which at home it had

lost; and by a strange irony the man most responsible for
that turn in its fortunes was he who, once its rising hope,
had been so uncompromisingly cast forth for a too-relative
adherence to revealed Truth.

One day word was brought to Mr. Trimblerigg that certain elders of True Belief had been of a mind to search the
Scriptures concerning him: and the word had come, not
inappositely – though open to different shades of interpretation: 'Cast thy bread upon the waters, and after many
days it shall return to thee.' And it was reported that the
said elders had been impressed and had made a note of it.

Mr. Trimblerigg was pleased by the news, for it meant
that a door still stood open; and though he had no intention of passing through it again, he liked it to be open.
For he was now busy opening a door to them; and theirs
being open in return, they might eventually pass through
it to him. The idea of relegating the mission field definitely to True Belief under an agreed coalition of the
Churches began to attract him, for it was becoming clear
to him that among the mentally deficient True Belief was
the quickest and most effective way to conversion, if only
it could be made non-sectarian – a means rather than an
end. He saw, with speculative instinct that looked like
faith, how a place might be found for all on a plan of his
own making. Thus the great fusion of the Free Churches
toward which he was working came a step nearer to
practical politics.

His work being the organization of missions, it was often
his duty to entertain missionaries. And as the best time
of all, for establishing confidential relations, was to meet
them in friendly intimacy immediately upon their arrival,
it was beginning to be his practice to invite as guest to his

house any prominent missionary who had come home on leave. Thus in the course of a few years the very cream of the Free Evangelical mission world, and a few others from connections that were friendly, passed through his hands.

It was from one of these latter that Mr. Trimblerigg received news of the swift civilization that was taking place in parts scarcely heard of as yet, owing to the beneficent efforts of certain missionary centres not only to sow the seed of the faith but to develop the wealth and resources of the fields in which they laboured. This paticular missioner was an optimist about his own districts. 'In fifty years' time,' he said, 'it will be for its size, the richest country outside Europe and the States.' And as its size was nearly half that of France such a forecast suggested big possibilities.

He went on to tell with what prudent and fatherly care those in control of the missions had headed off the rapacious traders and concession hunters, who follow in the missionary's track, by obtaining from the native chiefs exclusive rights strategically based upon the routes of trade, such for instance as the building of landing-stages at the junction of rivers, and the setting up of white settlements on the high table-lands of the interior.

As a consequence the economic future of the country was controlled, not indeed by the missionary society itself, but by a humane-minded organization of business interests working with and through it. And under this happy cooperation the Native Industries Company in the Ray River territory to the north of Puto Congo (not then the familiar name it has become since) had opened up commercial relations at the cost of only a few score thousand pounds, which in the near future might be worth millions. They were already paying an interest on shares which compared favourably with larger ventures of longer date; and as the total number of shares was comparatively small, they offered to early investors a great future.

And so Mr. Trimblerigg, who had a taste for speculative transfer, sold out and reinvested a few hundred pounds in Native Industries Limited; and receiving his dividends thereafter on the scale promised, thought very little further about it, except as something sound which carried with it the larger hope of value that might increase.

The sense in which he thought very little about it, was as to the actual source of its profits – oil, rubber, copra, or ivory – the methods of its working, and the men who worked it, or what it really did for the native beyond making him more accessible to the influence of missions and of trade. As to that last, a very slight preliminary inquiry had satisfied him that it was so; and there he left it. It never occurred to Mr. Trimblerigg, who was eloquently opposed to corporal punishment in his own country for crimes of violence and such like, to inquire whether corporal punishment played any part in making his dividends from Native Industries Limited nearer ten than five per cent per annum. And why indeed should it occur to him? The shareholder system, on which modern trade is run, does not prompt such mental occurrence; and where so many millions are satisfied that their responsibilities end in the acceptance of the reports of their directors, can any particular blame attach to one, however eminent in the organization of the mission field, if he also was satisfied, and become in consequence forgetful?

Mr. Trimblerigg had then – as always – a perfectly clear

conscience. He was very busy, he was doing good work; his doctrine of relative truth was giving theology a more modern and a much more sensible mind about all the things it could not really prove but loved to fight about; the coalition of the Free Churches was advancing under his manipulation by leaps and bounds; behind that loomed Disestablishment. Given a greater corporate union of Nonconformity, the argument for it would be irresistible; and when it came he would be the up-to-date Luther before whose assault that final stronghold of religious privilege toppled to ruin. For Mr. Trimblerigg had been busy not only in the organization of missions but upon the political side also; and would no doubt by this time have gone into Parliament had not somebody already been there before him who was doing what he would have done in exactly the same way – with the same brilliance, the same elasticity, the same eloquence, the same hand-to-mouth conviction, and the same enthusiastic and catchword-loving following. Parliament did not need two wizards to cast upon it the same spell. That was the reason why Mr. Trimblerigg kept his wizardry for the Churches.

And so, through strenuous years Mr. Trimblerigg laboured to make Free Evangelicalism greater, and more powerful, and more feared than it had ever yet been; and before he had touched middle age he began to be spoken of as candidate for the high office of President at the Annual Conference – a post for which previously no head without grey hair on it had ever qualified.

It only wanted some great cause, some big agitation led by himself, to carry him through and make him, before he reached the age of forty, the most prominent figure in the Nonconformist world. And then, while he was looking for

CHAPTER FOURTEEN

it, came, just in the nick of time, the story, the horrible
story of the Puto-Congo atrocities.

He was no missionary and no trader, but a mere outsider
who brought it to Europe; and when, for reasons, Government threw a belittling doubt upon it, questioning the
motives and veracity of its reporter, then Mr. Trimblerigg
saw his chance, and blew a blast to the Free Evangelical
mission world. He took up the cause, made it his own,
and gave it all the publicity it required.

The Sound of a Trumpet

WHEN THE CAMPAIGN STARTED THE PUTO-CONGO Consolidation Company was paying its shareholders from 20 to 30 per cent, independent of bonuses which dropped to them like manna every alternate year; and its shares stood in the market at 200 per cent above par. It had held its own against a six months' exposure of its methods, not only without a drop in the quotations, but with a slight rise when official cold water had been thrown on the report of the egregious Mr. Morment, whose unfair and superficial investigation had caused all the trouble.

But when Mr. Trimblerigg took the matter in hand, hiring halls in all the big towns for monster meetings, and thumping the Free Evangelical war-drum, within a month the shares came tumbling, and the Government had begun to hedge by promising a commission of inquiry – not, as had almost been previously suggested, into the character of Mr. Morment, but into the conduct of the Company.

Even though the world is said to be wicked, it often pays and pays well to be on the side of the angels. For trade and commerce, and politics are largely run on a sort of agreed pretence that man, though now a little lower than the angels, is not much lower, or only in his bad moments, or only because he doesn't always have time to look into things. The side on which the angels are, may for a time be violently disputed by guilty interests: but give it a clear view-halloo and a sight of its quarry on the run, and you have the great-hearted public up and after it, quite oblivious to its own record in matters closely similar.

CHAPTER FIFTEEN

So now: the strewings of the feathers of angels' wings across the landscape made Mr. Trimblerigg's lightning campaign look like a paper-chase from the heavenly or bird's-eye view; and tens and hundreds of thousands of virtuous shareholders, in companies of whose ways and doings they did not in the least know or very much care, attended his meetings to denounce the shareholders of a Chartered Company which was paying 20 and 30 per cent upon methods that were now being exposed.

I have said before, and I say again, that Mr. Trimblerigg was a man of absolute sincerity to the convictions of the moment; so also were his audiences, all people of sincerity; but it was a sincerity which, rising to the surface like cream, when it has been skimmed off leaves a poor thin material behind it. But it was national material after all; and how, as somebody once asked, can one indict a great nation? Its greatness is the refuting answer.

And so it was, when those cheering crowds hung upon Mr. Trimblerigg's eloquence, and when, being so much carried away by it, he hung upon it himself – there was not one, speaker or listener, who, while sincerely denouncing the cruelties which had wrung 20 and 30 per cent profits from the blood and bones of indentured black labour, ever thought of denouncing the system which enabled any who had capital to invest, to make money out of ventures and industries as to the workings of which they knew nothing. It was not the system which was being denounced, but individuals who had been oiling the wheels of the system by methods of civilization pushed to logical extremes. And so, when you strike an average, Mr. Trimblerigg was just as innocent and just as sincere as the bulk of his fellow-countrymen.

The only difference was that nobody else enjoyed his innocence and sincerity as much as he did, or thought so highly of it. For now, being so gloriously upon the side of the angels, it was with the voice of an angel – and a powerful one – that Mr. Trimblerigg spoke. And the angels and the herd-instinct having got hold of him together, he did wonders: not only did he surprise me, he surprised himself.

One day he had before him and behind him, around him and above him, an audience of ten thousand breathless listeners – breathless not for any difficulty, his fine voice being easily heard, but for the mere joy of him. He was making visible to all, the forests and swamps and malarious rivers to which he had never penetrated save with the eye of vision and pity and compassion; and also the things that were being done there for shareholders in a country calling itself Christian. He gave chapter and verse: before him had come a speaker, fresh from the district itself, with terrible lantern-slides, some showing life, many more showing death. As a prelude to his peroration he demanded the last of the slides, one that had been specially reserved for the occasion. It appeared and a great gasp went through the audience; they sat so silent for his concluding words, so motionless that actually not a pin dropped. And after he had ended, for some seconds the silence lasted, so deep was the emotion of his hearers. When he sat down he felt that he had made the speech of his life.

His auditors apparently thought so too, having recovered they stood up for five minutes to applaud, while Mr. Trimblerigg, feeling a little faint but very happy, sat and drank water.

146

CHAPTER FIFTEEN

When silence was restored for the announcement of the next speaker – a rather reluctant Archbishop had been captured for the occasion – a cold staccato voice came from the back of the hall:

'Is not the gentleman who has just spoken himself a shareholder in the Puto-Congo Consolidation Company?'

A buzz of horrified consternation went sibilating from stalls to gallery: the whole movement tottered to its base. Mr. Trimblerigg was on his feet.

'It's a lie,' he said; and to show that was the end of it, sat down again.

The audience took a free breath and applauded.

Once more came the voice:

'Does the speaker deny that he draws any profit from investment in the forced labour of these unhappy natives?' And again Mr. Trimblerigg was on his feet.

'Not one pound, not one penny, not one farthing. I would die rather.'

The applause at this was terrific. All heads turned towards the interruption: lost in the dense crowd gathered at the back of the hall it remained merely a voice.

There was a pause, the voice said: 'I am quite satisfied. I was misinformed.'

A sharp burst of laughter rang through the hall; and everybody was happy again. Mr. Trimblerigg received another ovation; and when he rose to reply to the vote of thanks the noise was deafening.

But though he replied beautifully and in moving terms, he was not at ease. During the speech of the Archbishop he had sat thinking:

' What shares remotely resembling the Puto-Congo Con-

solidated do I possess? Whatever can the man have got
hold of?'

Suddenly the words, 'Native Industries Ltd.' flashed into
his mind. Those shares paid him about fifty pounds a
year, on an investment of two hundred; and every year the
directors sent him a reassuring report of the well-being
and prosperity of the natives in whose interests it was run.
But what had these to do with the Puto-Congo Consolidation Company? He was not good at geography; beyond
the fact that they both hailed from the same continent he
was aware of no possible connection.

All the same, as soon as the meeting was over he sped
home in trepidation, and after a short search through a fat
bundle of small but varied investments he found the share
certificate he was in search of. The sight of it froze him,
as it had been the eye of Davidina fixed in judgment:
terror and desolation opened under him as a gulf into
which he descended alive. For though in the original certificate the name of the Puto-Congo Consolidation Company was nowhere mentioned, the certificate bore endorse-
ment of a later date (he remembered faintly sending it, at
request, for that purpose) from which it appeared that
Native Industries had become affiliated – consolidated
was perhaps the awful and correct word – with certain
other companies operating in the same district, the Ray
River Rubber Company being one of them: and 'Ray
River Rubber' with its beautiful rolling sound had now
acquired a horrible familiarity to his ears; only that very
night he had himself rolled it upon his oratorical tongue,
enjoying the rich flavour of it. And though the name of
the Puto-Congo Consolidated did not even now appear,
his certificate bore nevertheless that notorious official

stamp which he and the Free Churches had so fiercely held
up to scorn – a large adhesive label of embossed paper,
blood red, bearing as its emblem a white man and a black
holding hands, and over them the punning motto 'Nihil
alienum puto' – I hold nothing foreign.

How devoutly he wished that for him the motto could
have been true. But that he did hold this damnable
and damning share in that commercial atrocity which
he had been denouncing, there was no longer room for
doubt. And how, in Heaven's name, or the name of
anything equally incredible, how was he to explain it
away?

That was the question which, for the next hour or two,
he continued putting to me with great fervour and insis-
tency. I listened, but I said nothing; for though I was
much interested, I did not intend to intervene. That is
not my method. And so, while I paid due attention to
what he actually said, I let the nimbler speed of his brain
for one moment escape me; and was taken suddenly by
surprise when I saw him jump up from his knees and start
into definite action.

During the next forty-eight hours the meteoric speed of
his career, his swift adjustment of means to ends, his
varied and almost instantaneous decisions, and above all
the driving force of the moral arguments which he
addressed to those larger shareholders of Native Industries
Limited whom in so brief a time he succeeded in running
to earth, all this gave me a conception of his abilities to
which, I confess, that till then I had hardly done justice.
Nor do I think the average reader could follow through
all its ramifications that inspired *sauve qui peut*, which,
in such short space of time, carried moral devastation to

so many Free Evangelical back-parlours – fortresses for all the virtues.

Suffice it that Mr. Trimblerigg, having obtained a complete list of the shareholders in Native Industries Limited, discovered for truth what his sanguine mind had envisaged as a blessed possibility – that nearly half of the Company's shares were actually in the hands of Free Church ministers and of other prominent and privileged members of their congregations, and that all unknown to itself the Free Evangelical Body – that great instrument for the establishment of God's Kingdom on earth – had got one of its feet well planted in that very stronghold of the Devil against which it was directing its assault – an awkward, or an advantageous position according to the use made of it.

Mr. Trimblerigg, whose apprehension and anguish had been so great that in the first ten hours after his discovery he could eat no breakfast, had during the next ten, with travel, telegram, and telephone, done such an enormous amount of work and to such good purpose, that before the day was out he had begun almost to enjoy himself.

In that brief space of time he had captured not only the council of the Free Church Congress, and three of its ex-Presidents, but the President-elect and five of its most shining lights in the financial world as well – men who had always maintained publicly that they held their wealth as a sacred trust from the Powers above for the service of humanity.

Now he showed them their chance. While the shares of the affiliated companies in Puto-Congo Consolidated lay battered on the market, opportunity for good Samaritans

CHAPTER FIFTEEN

presented itself on a large scale. For the preaching missionary, who also travelled for Native Industries Limited,
had done his agency thoroughly and well, and Mr. Trimblerigg's saving hopes were abundantly realized. Here
they all were, almost without knowing it – some not knowing it at all; others knowing it but lying low, trusting that
affiliation carried with it no responsibility for the administrative acts of Puto-Congo Consolidated, and finding
much virtue in the difference of a name – here they all
were in the same box, and the lid of it suddenly opened
like graves for the day of judgment.

Yes, they were all in it; but, so Mr. Trimblerigg assured
them, with this important difference. They were there of
set purpose and intent like himself: had gone into it,
for strategical reasons, with the sword of the spirit, to pre-
pare the way of the Lord and bring deliverance to the
oppressed. They heard from Mr. Trimblerigg how he
had invested his little all for that purpose alone, watching
and waiting, with never a penny of profit, biding his time
for the great day of deliverance. (He had, in fact, that
very day, sold out all his other investments in order to
secure a yet larger holding for the confirmation of his
case.)

They also, he had not a doubt, had invested for a like
purpose – or if not, were eager and willing to do so
now that the time had come for that purpose to be
declared.

For here was the case; the Free Evangelical Church
could now at a push in a falling market obtain a shareholders' majority in one of the most important and prosperous companies which had come together under the
ægis of the Puto-Congo Consolidated: had, therefore,

power to call and control a special meeting of the shareholders for the reform – root, branch, lock, stock and barrel
– of the whole abominable system to which it had become
linked.

Free Church Presidents, Evangelical financiers, shining
lights in the Temperance movement, and others with
reputations above suspicion, listened, sat up, and were
amazed; only too thankful in that dark hour to have good
motives so generously imputed to them and their way of
salvation made plain. Very few attempted to remain irresponsible, incredulous, or indifferent; when they did, Mr.
Trimblerigg launched his attack, and their opposition
wilted and crumbled. Nor did he mince the inspired word
which came to him: his brisk little figure sparkled with
flashes of divine fire, even as the wireless apparatus
sparkles with the message which descends to it from the
outer air; and there to hand was the circular appeal which
within twenty-four hours would have received the signatures of over a hundred Free Church ministers and elders
calling for an emergency meeting of the shareholders. At
that meeting the Puto-Congo atrocities would be denounced, and the present Directors of the Company called
on to resign and make room for others. Native Industries
Limited, by reason of its secured monopolies, held the key
to the position. Though small, it could impose its terms;
close its depots and landing-stages to proved abuse of contract by the affiliated companies, and if it became a question of law, dare the rest to come on; for now it would have
the entire country behind it, even, if need be, the power of
Parliament. Let them blow their blast loud and long
enough, and the whole huge financial fabric of Puto-Congo
Consolidated which had sought to absorb them into

identity with its own guilty prosperity, would have to cleanse itself or go.

And as these reverend elders listened, and bent their heads for the whitewash provided by Mr. Trimblerigg, there was the offered vision before them of the great Free Church body, too long couchant in moneyed ease, rising upon its hind legs at last, and uttering no meek lowing of kine, but the combined roar and scream of the Lion and the Eagle – and over them in feathers of silver and gold, the covering wings of the Dove; and there was the Visionary himself wanting to know, here and now, whether their voice would swell the chorus or only be raised in futile opposition. That question received but one answer.

So, like fire through stubble, did Mr. Trimblerigg burn his way into the consciences and fears of the Native Industries shareholders; and by the time the sun had set upon the second day of his labours he knew that he had won.

The next day a letter from the 'Voice' – or from its informant – appeared in the press challenging once more Mr. Trimblerigg's publicly uttered denial of having lot or share in the nefarious activities of Puto-Congo Consolidated. The letter made no assertion, but presented a series of neat interrogations – yes or no; and ended with the smooth reposeful sneer of one certain of his facts.

Mr. Trimblerigg's reply gave that dirty platter the clean lick it required inside and out. In the Puto-Congo Consolidated he held no shares at all: in the affiliated 'Native Industries Limited' he did hold some, and since the meeting in question had succeeded in getting hold of a few more.

His purpose, which together with others, he had been

obliged hitherto to conceal, lest the Puto-Congo Executive should get wind of it and take steps to prevent, he could now declare. He did so resoundingly.

The same paper which contained his letter, contained notice of the special meeting convened by its Free Church shareholders to purge the Native Industries Limited of complicity in the Puto-Congo atrocities, and to terminate all contracts forthwith. For himself Mr. Trimblerigg had only to add that never, in the years of waiting for the power which had now come to him, had he applied to his own use one penny of the dividends he had received from Native Industries; all had been saved up for a further investment when the moment should appear opportune. And with that — facts speaking louder than words — his defence was complete.

A month later he held the special meeting of the Native Industries shareholders in the hollow of his hand, and in a speech which the press reported verbatim lashed the administration of the Chartered Company of Puto-Congo Consolidated with a tongue like the whip of an inspired slave-driver. Powerless in the face of numbers the opposition fell away in panic; the conscience of the Free Churches asserted itself, all the Directors resigned, and Mr. Trimblerigg and nine others, with clean records like his own, were elected to their place. Two members of the new Board proposed Mr. Trimblerigg to be chairman; and he was elected without a dissentient voice.

Native Industries Limited was to be run henceforth on Christian lines, and set an example to the world by earning for itself on those lines larger profits than ever before. Mr. Trimblerigg was a consistently sanguine soul; believing the shareholding system to be a device well-pleas-

ing to God, he believed it could be done. And so that
night he went home to his house justified, in beams of
glory all of his own making, very tired, but more satisfied
with himself than he could ever remember to have been
before.

Reward of Virtue

WHILE MR. TRIMBLERIGG STILL WENT IN CLOUDS OF glory, high and uplifted on popular applause, Davidina, back from one of her adventurous expeditions and already preparing for the next, came to see him. She viewed him up and down admiringly.

'You don't look much the worse for it,' she said.

'I don't know that I am,' he replied genially, even while his dodging mind was at guess as to what exactly she meant by worse. 'But it's taken me off my work a good deal; and I was wanting holiday.'

'Take it,' said Davidina, 'I'll pay.'

'Oh, it isn't a question of paying,' he returned. 'Besides, if it were, I'm the better off of the two of us, now.' His eyes twinkled. 'You see, I made lucky investments.'

Davidina almost loved him; that hit at himself was so good-humoured and playful and apposite.

'Yes,' she agreed, 'but it was a narrow squeeze.'

'It was,' he replied, 'but I like being squeezed. It suits me. Then I always do my best.'

'Jonathan,' said his sister, 'I'm beginning to admire you. If I didn't know you so well, you'd take me in too – almost.'

'My dear Davidina, that is the last thing I have ever wished to do,' he said. 'Hopeless adventures do not appeal to me.'

She laughed, and let the argument drop to say: 'By the way, what are you now? What do you call yourself?'

'I still call myself Jonathan Trimblerigg,' was his reply. 'I don't propose taking a title, even if it were offered me.'

'It's fifteen years since Uncle Phineas died,' said Davidina, 'and I've a reason for asking.'

So? Here was Davidina proposing to broach the subject
on which till now no word had ever been uttered between
them. It did not exactly surprise him; he had always
believed that Davidina had a conscience; but often he had
wondered if, convinced in her own mind upon the point
at issue, she would trouble to tell him of it – unless spite-
fully to enjoy his disappointment.

But there was no longer any question of disappointment
now. In the fold of True Belief, Mr. Trimblerigg knew
that he could not have done anything like what he had
now accomplished, or have attained to such a standing or
such prospects. Nevertheless – had the bait been larger –
for there the door stood open waiting for him – who
knows? The great fusion of the Free Churches, in a form
to include True Belief, might have come earlier, and
he might have remained Free Evangelical in practice
and yet qualified in the letter and in the spirit for
that deferred benefit which he was now denying himself.

'I asked,' said Davidina, 'because I see that next Sunday
you are going down to preach to your old congregation at
Mount Horeb.'

'Yes,' said Jonathan, 'they've asked me. It's the first
time such a thing has happened, and my text is not going
to be the repentant Prodigal, either. I haven't changed.
We shall just go on where we left off.'

'That's why I'm asking – what you call yourself. Do you
still reckon yourself a True Believer?'

'I reckon that what I believe is true; but I do not regard
myself as a True Believer in the technical sense. I don't

think I ever was. A Relative Believer, Davidina, is what
I am.'

'It's a pity,' said Davidina, 'in a way. Uncle Phineas left
me a letter of instruction – not legal; but still I take it as
binding. If you had remained a True Believer till now, I
was to go shares with you.'

Mr. Trimblerigg had long since, in his own mind, got
the better of Uncle Phineas and his £200 a year. But now
he saw his chance of getting the better of Davidina. So he
said quietly: 'I know that, he told me.'

Davidina stared. 'What did he tell you?'

'He showed me the letter,' said Jonathan.

'And you never said anything!' cried Davidina, astonished

'Well, I did say something in a way. I mentioned the
letter to you once; but as you chose to say nothing about
it, I left it at that.'

'And you trusted me?' inquired Davidina.

'Absolutely. But very soon after that, you see, it didn't
matter. I got turned out.'

Mr. Trimblerigg was now feeling very happy, for he
saw that Davidina was right out of her bearings. But
without appearing to notice this unusual phenomenon he
went quietly on:

'After all it's a good thing as it happens. If you had to
divide with me now you wouldn't have enough for your
expeditions.'

'Plenty,' she assured him. 'Ah, to be sure, I haven't told
you. And yet that's why it was important that I should
know; for I didn't suppose his old two hundred would
matter to you much now. But the other day I got news:
opening a new quarry they struck a seam of something

else quite unexpected; it isn't exactly plumbago, or Cumberland lead as they call it; but it's rather like it; and as a consequence the property is up to something like twenty times its value.'

Mr. Trimblerigg took it very quietly; he made no sign; even now he was not sure that he wished things differently. He had a great desire, for his own spiritual comfort, to get the better of Davidina, just once.

'Well, I congratulate you,' he said; 'where will the next expedition be? The Sahara, Persia, Arabia? It looks as if you were going to be a famous woman traveller; you've always had the pluck and the brain; and now you've got the means for it.'

'Do you mind, Jonathan?' she asked him.

'Mind? I'm delighted.'

'This is the first time,' she confessed, 'that you've ever taken me by surprise. You knew, and you didn't say anything. You knew, and you let them turn you out. You knew, and you trusted me.'

'I've always trusted you.'

'Well, I haven't always trusted you. In fact, I've always suspected you.'

'I know it, my dear Davidina, but as it amuses you and had left off hurting me – why not?'

'And now,' she went on, as if he had not interrupted her, 'I don't know whether to suspect you or not.'

'You'd much better,' he said.

'The truth is I'm puzzled!'

'The truth often is very puzzling,' assented Jonathan, 'it's so relative.' Then he got up and stretched himself like a cat enjoying the sun.

'And I still think,' said Davidina decidedly, 'that you are

capable of being a villain, and a blood-thirsty villain too, if it suited you.'

Mr. Trimblerigg continued to stretch and to smile at her.

'Oh, Davidina,' he said, 'you are a comfortable person to talk to!'

And at that he let her go. For once, just for once in his life he had got the better of her. Davidina was puzzled at him. It was a great event.

And a week later he received from Davidina a voluntary transfer duly executed of one-half of the property, which at its prospectively enhanced value would make him comfortably off for life. It meant, it must mean, that at last he had won her approval. 'Thou Davidina seest me!' had no longer its old discomfort for him. In her eye too, as in everybody's, there was a blind spot, and he had managed to hit it.

Too Good to be True

THE DULLING OF DAVIDINA'S EYE HAD A FATAL EFFECT upon the career of Mr. Trimblerigg. It removed the last obstacle from his way to thinking himself good. His own conscience had been malleable; but hers, serving in its place, had kept an integrity of its own which always left him with a doubt. Now the doubt vanished, and on that mercurial and magnetic temperament it had a surprising effect.

I wonder whether readers have realized the extraordinary spiritual comfort which Mr. Trimblerigg had derived from the friendly disarmament of Davidina's suspicions. He had just come through a phase of success and public applause, with its accompanying sense of power, unprecedented in his career. But behind it all was the uneasy sense that he had been remiss in the protection of his own interests – that it had been a tight squeeze, and that only by the kind favour of Heaven had he got through not merely creditably, but with so much to spare.

The Native Industries shares might soon be – as he had joked to Davidina – a good investment; but he had blundered in holding them, or, at least, in not getting rid of them before starting on his campaign; and it always hurt Mr. Trimblerigg very much to feel that – even in his own eyes alone – he had made a fool of himself. It was obvious therefore that to make a fool of the redoubtable Davidina, who had for so many years given him an uneasy conscience whenever she wished, had redressed the balance. And so, according to his own practical standard, Mr. Trimblerigg stood purged and purified of self-reproof, with his conscience beautifully easy once more. He had fought upon the side of the angels, and the battle was won hands down; in the process, by embarking all his savings in a venture which temporarily had crashed, he had seriously reduced his income; but even that, thanks to the prospect presented to him by Davidina did not now concern him, it even pleased him, for it was a proof of his disinterested devotion to the cause he had championed. And so, looking at himself from all sides, the spiritual, the public, and the domestic, he was abundantly satisfied with what he saw. Having made good, he felt good; and elated by that feeling, he decided that the family – that part of it which was not away at school – should have a holiday.

In order to begin the holiday as soon as possible – for himself as well as the others – he sent off Caroline and the little ones, remaining himself for a few days to clear up a few ends of work still in arrears at his central office, and in spite of those arrears, when he had seen Caroline into the train, his sense of holiday had already begun. For in spite of all the goodness that was in him, he continued to find her dull, with a dullness that did not diminish. And yet, he told himself, he was fond of her, and had never denied her anything that was her due. So, in that matter also, his conscience had left him nothing with which to reproach himself.

That day, when his office work was over, he took recreation in a characteristic way. Having bought some quite good cigars, he mounted to the top of a bus, and started to explore the metropolis, or, more accurately, to let destiny explore it for him. His method was to accompany the bus to its terminus, and there change into another, leaving chance to decide in what fresh direction it should carry him, east or west, north or south. In this way, through a variegation of lighted streets – from some wearing the shadiest subterfuge of life to others of a flamboyant brilliance, and back again, for a couple of hours and more he thoroughly enjoyed himself – seeing unconsciously in the kaleidoscopic life seething around him a reflex image of his own, and in it felt justified. It was all so quick, unexpected, and yet congruous, so criss-cross and various, and vitally abounding, and yet, in its main current uniform, flowing on with one general purpose common to all – meaning business, whatever the business might be. And here, sitting enthroned above it on the front seat of a swift-going motor-bus, he, a man who on the right side of middle age, had become almost famous, went happy and unrecognized, his hat drawn low over his eyes, his coat collar turned up to meet it, absorbing that large life of the crowd with which so deeply and instinctively he felt himself to be one.

And meanwhile destiny did its work. To the seat beside him, vacated at the last stopping-place, came a fresh occupant – a woman quick and alert of movement, well-dressed, not elderly. Before he had been able unobtrusively to get a look at her face, the conductor was collecting her fare. He heard a familiar voice naming a suburban destination; a moment later, quick and decided, annoyed rather than dismayed, the voice said, 'I've lost my purse!'

'Allow me!' said Mr. Trimblerigg. 'Good evening.' He tendered the money as he spoke.

One look at him, and Miss Isabel Sparling rose to go. 'You shall do nothing of the sort,' she said, 'I'll get down.'

And then – destiny. In the road below a coster's barrow, cutting across the track of the swift-moving traffic, collided, shed a wheel, and sat jammed under the head of

the oncoming motor-bus. The impact which lifted all
the seated occupants from their seats, caused Miss Isabel
Sparling to disappear from view. Breaking her fall by a
well-sustained clutch upon the rail, she struck the hood,
and slid sideways into the upset apple-cart.

Mr. Trimblerigg, with admirable agility, heels first,
scrambled after her. The first to get to her, he found her
conveniently unconscious, and taking possession of his
implacable foe in her now defenceless condition, he hailed
a taxi and carried her away to hospital.

There, having learned that she was not dangerously hurt,
and would probably have recovered sufficiently to give
account of herself in an hour's time, he left money to pay
for conveyances or telegrams, and took himself off, a
nameless benefactor, whose identity Miss Isabel Sparling
might either nose out or ignore according to taste, but
could not do otherwise than suspect.

And so, if there was one spot in his kaleidoscopic world
where Mr. Trimblerigg, in retrospect, had not hitherto
felt quite happy, he was able to feel happy now. His
embrace of Isabel Sparling's inanimate form, the first time
for more than fifteen years – had given him the sudden
inspiration that now, in his own time and in his own way,
he should take up and fulfil the rash promise of his early
youth, and be voice and champion of the ministerial call
to women.

For now at last he had the standing and a following
whereof he was the accepted leader, which would make
the achievement no longer theirs but his, and give credit
where the credit was due. Through him, almost through
him alone, the chains of the Puto-Congo natives were
already being struck off; following upon that, through

him, the chains of sex-disability should go likewise. There was no time like the present. He would take a brief holiday, and then he would begin.

He dined at an old-fashioned restaurant in the city, which had its traditions; the head waiter, with recognition in his eye, but not a word said, installed him in the seat of honour, the seat once habitually occupied by one of the great eighteenth-century emancipators of the human brain. The attention pleased him, still more the respectful silence with which it was done – the acceptance of his right to be there incognito without remark.

He ate well of a wonderful pie containing oysters, and he drank white wine, followed by Stilton cheese, port, and a cigar. To all these good things life had gently led him away from the early training of his childhood. He accepted them now without scruple and felt the better for them.

When he got home, the elderly domestic, now in sole charge of the house since the family's departure, had gone up to bed. About half an hour later, Mr. Trimblerigg, comfortably sleepy, went up to his own.

From habit, because he usually needed it, he took a bedside book and began briefly to read; five minutes generally sufficed; it did so now.

The book he had chosen was of poems by an author whom he felt that he ought to admire more than he did; there was a splendour of beauty in them which yet managed somehow to escape him. This slight intellectual separation of mind from mind was good as a sedative: it helped his own to wander. His first selection from the poems was a very famous one, but too spiritual and elusive for his present mood: a transcendental game of hide-and-seek, he could not quite follow. He passed on to the next; large drops of sleep were already entering his brain, and he knew that presently it would be making nonsense; but the opening lines attracted him, gave him a picture of which he himself became a part. In the middle of every line there was a star — why, he did not know; but it gave an effect. He liked it, and making an effort to keep awake for a few moments longer, he read on:

'Athwart the sod which is treading for God* the poet paced with his splendid eyes;

'Isabel Starling he stately passes —'

No, that wasn't right; Sparling, not Starling. No, no, what was he thinking about? Not Sparling, or Starling, or anything resembling it. 'Paradise verdure he stately passes.' That was better. The following line had long words in it which he didn't understand. The next verse started pleasantly —

'The angels at play on its fields of Summer* (their wild wings rustled his guide's cigars).' No, not cigars, something else, word he didn't know: cigars would do.

'Looked up from dessert at the passing comer* as they pelted each other with handfuls of stars.'

Ah! That was why the stars were there, they'd got loose on to the printed page: stars did, if you happened to get a knock or a fall.

'And Isabel Sparling with startled feet rose,* hand on sword, by their tethered cars.'

Wrong, wrong! not 'Isabel Sparling' — 'warden spirits': whatever made him say Isabel Sparling? she wasn't a warden spirit or anything like one. But 'tethered cars' was right: 'motor-bus' would have been better.

After that his reading ceased to be consecutive or to

convey any sense – only colour and a sort of atmosphere.
'Plumes night-tinctured, englobed and cinctured,' then
a star, followed by 'saints': 'crystalline pale,' and another
star: 'Heaven' – ah, yes, Heaven, the place the stars came
from: then 'the immutable crocean dawn' – crocean meant
yellow – 'enthusing' – no, not enthusing 'effusing.' 'Crocean dawn effusing' meant 'yellow dawn coming.' If that
was what he meant, why couldn't the fellow say so? Why
did poets always choose the difficult words? Ahead lay
more light and colour, mixed with other things he didn't
fully understand – or want to; he was getting too sleepy
for it. 'Bickering Conference': no, not conference: 'gon-
falons': better go back and read again, he was only making
nonsense; but 'Crocean dawn effusing' was nonsense too.
'Ribbed fire,' 'flame-plumed fan' – 'globing clusters,' and
stars everywhere with no sense to them. But the poet had
splendid eyes – must have had, to see all that!

His lids closed, then opened again: he had almost gone
to sleep with the light still on. 'Crocean dawn': half consciously he switched it off – not the dawn, the light; and
with the crocean dawn still in his head slept till morning.

Nouveau Riche

A CROCEAN DAWN WAS OUTSIDE AND AROUND HIM
when he awoke — yellow, of the metropolitan variety;
it was, that is to say, a fog. But in spite of the dullness of
the outer world, Mr. Trimblerigg awoke happy, with the
happiness of a man whose prayer has been answered.

For many days he had been praying fervently that his
character might be placed above suspicion: and now that
Davidina's suspicion of him had gone, and his own with
it, he had just everything for the present that he could
pray for. And on the top of it, he had forgiven an enemy
— in such a way that, if he did not miscalculate, his
enemy would presently have to forgive him.

There, in that purified spiritual atmosphere, another
great work was awaiting him. All omens were auspicious;
he knew now for certain that he was going to achieve fame,
and that very soon, among the Free Churches, he would
be able to have almost whatever position he liked, and do
almost anything he chose. And so, as he got up in that
crocean dawn, he felt all about him, but especially in his
brain, an effusing sense of well-being and happiness. And
as he looked at himself in the glass before shaving, he
smiled: and it seemed to him then that his countenance
was wonderfully bright.

Presently, as he shaved, he began to have a suspicion
that the illumination was different and strange: that there
was a curious absence of shadow about his chubby cheeks
and under his chin, which made shaving easy; and this,
too, on a dark morning.

This fact only dawned on him gradually; for close above
his head hung the electric pendant, with its bulb of power-

168

ful light directed downwards by the white porcelain shade. But when, thoughtful of the high price of electricity, he turned it out and once more faced his glass to give a final polish to his hair, there could no longer be any doubt that he was in the presence of something which waited to be explained – something too mysterious, too incredible to be described as a phenomenon.

'Crocean dawn': the embodied phrase looked him in the face. But how had it located itself? Was it physical, or spiritual, or was it only mental? 'Miracle' he did not think of calling it; his Free Church upbringing had given him an instinctive repugnance to such Romish things as modern miracles; though he admitted the possibility (but that was different) of miraculous answer to prayer. But miracles of a personal and a phenomenal kind he regarded with a certain suspicion – had indeed published in *The Rock of Ages* an article against them, wherein, with unrelenting logic, he had traced them to spiritual agencies – if spiritual they might be called – not of good but of evil. And now – this!

But if it was not a miracle in the accepted sense, if it was only something seen with the eye of the spirit, nevertheless there it was, carrying implications, and imposing if not exactly a burden – a problem, a weight of responsibility, which he did not quite know how he was to solve.

He could not help feeling that, for the present at least, he would like to keep it to himself, until he was a little more sure. But then a sudden sense of elation carried him away; for of what he had hoped might be true, this surely was proof; he really was – good! Even if it was only a recognition – an encouragement sent confidentially, for his eye alone, it meant – it must mean – that Heaven approved of him. The beauty of holiness was upon him in visible form – a certificate of chara&ter unimpeachable in its completeness; and yet, for an uncomfortable instant, the thought had flashed – how was he going to live up to it? Could he be as holy in practice as this advertised him to be? No, for the present at least, he would rather that it should not be seen. This was early dawn: he was hardly up to it. He must acclimatize himself.

So here, in the privacy of his own chamber, he examined the portent at leisure, and from all points of view. Trying to see himself, as others might presently be seeing him, he continued his study of the glass. Around a face broader than it was long, a wide forehead, puckered eyes, short nose, a neat bunch of a mouth, and hair worn rather long, turning up at the ends like the hair of the knave of hearts, a faint lemon-coloured radiance emerged, effused, flowed for a few inches, and then suddenly stopped short.

It was that abrupt ending which gave it so uncanny a chara&ter. Earthly radiance diminishes as it travels from its source; but this behaved differently – was indeed, if anything, brighter where it ended than where it started. Thus, from a front view, it had that plate-like appearance with which stained-glass windows and pictures of mediæ-val saints had made him familiar.

Going to his wife's dressing-table he took up the hand-mirror, so as to get a better side-view. The plate-like appearance persisted: quarter, three-quarter, and back view were always the same. The emanation was not flat, then, but round; a glory of three dimensions encircled him, and he moved in a globe of light which, like a head of dandelion seed, was brightest toward the edge, yet so faint and unsubstantial, it seemed as though a breath might blow it away.

Once more he brushed his hair for experiment. The lemon-coloured flame did not deflect or waver from its outward symmetry; nor did his head experience any electric thrills, as though virtue were passing either into him or out of him. With a slight sense of disappointment he laid his brushes down, and put on his coat. This, he found on consulting the glass, had made no change, except that upon the black cloth fell a slight radiance; but when for further experiment he once more switched on the light, it almost disappeared; and against the window, looking back at himself in the hand-mirror, for a moment he persuaded himself that it had gone. But if an involuntary wish had fathered that thought, he had only to move away from the light for its form and colour to reappear as strongly as ever; and as it responded with unvarying consistency to all the experiments he played on it, so did his sense of its reality become a conviction. It was not merely an idea, it was a fact.

And then the feeble tinkle of a bell below told him of breakfast. He went out on to the landing and peeped over the banisters.

Hearing dilatory sounds among the breakfast things, 'Mrs. James,' he called, 'you needn't wait.' And a minute later, on hearing her descend to the basement, he came downstairs at a run.

At table, in case Mrs. James should find excuse to return, he took his wife's place instead of his own, sitting with his back to the window; and found, in that position, though the morning was still dark, that he could see into his egg quite easily. Thus, even while away from his

mirror, the sense of something real, not imaginary, remained with him.

But it gave him no joy; for though in himself he felt at
unity with this day-spring from on high that had visited
him, he was doubtful how it would appear to the outside
world – whether the world was ripe for it – whether, indeed, it was intended for the outside world at all. It was
already in his mind that if he entered his Mission Centre
office by the ordinary way, he would have to run the
gauntlet of a roomful of clerks; and that his unexplained
accompaniment might provoke comment, possibly even
mirth. And Mr. Trimblerigg, even with reason on his
side, was not one who liked to be laughed at.

Unable to make up his mind what he felt about it himself, now, as he considered the matter from the worldly
point of view, he began to regard it with less and less
favour. He could not but feel that for such a manifestation as this the world needed preparation; a publicity campaign should have gone first and some more obvious
occasion should have been found for its first appearance –
this, in all humility – than one so merely personal to himself, a testimonial to the integrity of his character.

And then – to give the first test to his doubts – came the
interrogative Mrs. James, merely wishing to know what
meals he would be in for, and whether, if callers came to
inquire for him, he would name any time when he should
be at home.

Mr. Trimblerigg, keeping his head in the light of the
window, gave her the required instructions, and saw at
once from the uneventful expression of her face that she
had noticed nothing.

This threw him suddenly back upon doubt; and no

sooner had she returned to her kitchen than he ran up-stairs again, and looked once more in the glass.

The visitation was still upon him; but now that there was more daylight he saw it much less; nor had it so definite an edge where the radiance left off. Had he been a woman a broad-brimmed hat with plenty of veil about it would have made what was there quite unnoticeable; or had he been a missionary in India wearing a turban in all the glare of the Eastern sun. But fate had decreed other-wise; the environment he had to face was not of so obscuring a kind.

Then all at once the thought occurred to him – what would it be like at night? He drew down blinds, closed curtains, and went back to the glass.

The vivid result made him realize, with a shock, the actual state at which his mind had now arrived with regard to facing his fellow-men.

'I shan't be able to go out at night,' he said to himself. 'I should frighten people.'

But as a matter of fact he was getting frightened himself. He knew definitely now that he wished it had not hap-pened: and so, being of that mind, more and more did he entreat to be told how it could have happened. Was it from his brain, or his body, or his soul, that these rays emanated; and were they a symptom – physical, mental, or spiritual – of sickness or health; and if of sickness, were they to be temporary or permanent?

So he debated; yet when it came to addressing himself directly to the possible source of all this trouble, he was hesitant what to do. He did not wish to seem ungrateful, or to confess to moral cowardice, or even to plead the most plausible excuse – that he was unworthy; and so after hesitating for awhile he kept his thoughts unobtrusively to himself on the earthly plane. What never struck him for a moment was that he had done this himself — that, just as when you put water in a kettle upon the fire, it boils till presently it boils over, so if you put self-belief and self-worship into an ebullient and imaginative brain, the belief will out, like murder, in one form or another; and as pictorial imagery was Mr. Trimblerigg's strong point — to the point, one may say, of intoxication — this halo was but the bouquet or visible fragrance of the life within. And just as his own and his wife's mirror between them reflected it with accuracy and completeness, with equal accuracy and completeness it reflected him.

It ought, therefore, to have done him good; but the experience was too wild and sudden and strange; for this was the very first time in all his life when he had wished to keep himself to himself, under circumstances which apparently made it impossible. Nor did he yet realize that this was but the preliminary stage — the eruption stage — the stage of concentrated effort outwardly expressed, in which it sought to establish itself in his mind and consciousness as a fixed part of a pervasive and expansive personality, destined to go much further in the world than he had ever yet dreamed. Being a temperamental halo — pale at first, rather uncertain of itself and of its relations to the society into which it was born, it was not yet all that it would wish to be; it had not yet made itself at home. But even in the first few hours of its existence it fluctuated, waxing and waning in response to the spirit within; and when the time came for him to go out into the street and face the world, when for a few uncomfortable moments he stood hesitating by the hat-stand, it almost died out.

CHAPTER EIGHTEEN

But this would have been to deny himself entirely; and this he could not do. He put on his overcoat; then with a wavering mind asked himself what hat he should wear with it – with IT, that is to say. It seemed almost to savour of irreverence that he should wear a hat at all. But unwilling to make himself more noticeable than necessary, he finally selected one. Then, before putting the hat on, he went upstairs, to have a last look at himself. It was then – he saw, or hoped – almost undetectable; but when he put on his hat – a black one – it once more leapt into local prominence, disappointing his hope that what covered his head might have covered that also. On the contrary, his hat failing to contain it, it seemed rather to contain his hat.

As he went forth, the undemonstrative Mrs. James looked out at him from her window. She had not detected, she did not detect now, the thing he had striven to conceal: but his fluttered manner and his talking to her with his back to the light had made her suspicious: 'It's my belief he's been having a night out,' she remarked to herself as she watched him go. And though she owned it was no concern of hers, she allowed the suspicion to entertain her all the rest of the day; and when in the afternoon a rather agitated lady called, with a bruised face, wishing urgently to see him or to know where he was to be found, but refusing to disclose her name, she did her best for his morals by giving the address which in another twenty-four hours would be his; where, she explained pointedly, he had gone with his wife and family to have a little rest and be away from people.

And while Mrs. James was thus providing adventure for him, according to the light that was in her, he by reason of the light that was not in him but on him, was having adventures of his own.

Upon opening the street door he was pleased to find that it was beginning to rain. He went back, fetched his umbrella, opened it, and emerged holding the umbrella rather low in order to protect – his hat. Then he stepped out briskly, trying to think and to move naturally; but the terrible literalness of the streets troubled him. In such surroundings he felt more than ever the incongruity which under modern conditions, separates matter from spirit. To walk in the light of the gospel had hitherto seemed to him easy; but now to walk in his own light was difficult.

He was getting along, however, and so far had not attracted attention.

On the other side of the street went a whistling boy, casting down newspapers through area railings. As he passed he felt that the boy had become aware of him, for the whistling had stopped.

A moment later from behind, from across the street, came the cry, 'Hullo, old lamp-shade!'

Was that from the boy? Was it intended for him? And was it as a lighted scarecrow that the world was going to regard him? He did not turn to find out; he made no sign that he had heard; but passing a shop front he sidled, and tilting his umbrella took a look at himself. Yes, under the shade of the umbrella, it was painfully distinct. He lifted the umbrella away; it almost disappeared.

That decided him. It was only humility, he told himself; he did not wish to be seen of men; he furled his umbrella, and stood with his best hat exposed to the rain.

Cabs and taxis passed him; he could, of course, have taken one; but those dark interiors would make more show of him than an umbrella; a bus with its glass sides, or better still its top open to the sky, was what he now waited for. And then down came more rain, making a bus-top ridiculous. He screwed his courage up to the sticking point; after all, it must be done; he must test his public and find out if life – life on earth, life inside as well as outside a bus, life in a modern city – was possible.

Round the corner came the right numbered motor-bus. As it drew up he had a cowardly sense of relief; there was no one on the top, and the inside seemed full. The conductor dispelled his hope. 'Room for one,' he said; and Mr. Trimblerigg got in. It was unfortunate; he had to go to the far end, where there was less light.

An old lady, as he settled beside her, said to her companion, 'I do believe the sun's coming out!' 'It can't: it's raining too hard,' was the reply.

Before long he was aware that those opposite were studying him with curious gaze. Elderly gentlemen lowered their papers, wiped and refixed their glasses, but did not resume reading. Their eyes bulged a little as they tried to believe them. Mr. Trimblerigg grew irritated; he wished they would make up their minds and have done with it. Presently a woman, sitting opposite, with a bandaged infant in her arms, leaned forward and remarked confidentially:

'So you've been 'aving it too, have yer?'

'I beg your pardon?' said Mr. Trimblerigg. 'Having what?'

'Haven't they been X-raying you?' she explained inquiringly. 'They done it to this one 'ere six times; but it don't show like that on 'im. Does it 'urt much?'

'Not at all,' said Mr. Trimblerigg, smiling: and then,

taking a plunge at his public, for others were listening. 'This is merely a first experiment, I didn't think anyone would notice it.'

He was aware that, as he spoke, the eyes of all his fellow-passengers had gravitated towards him; that he was exciting more undivided interest now than when he first got in.

Just then the conductor came along to collect his fare, and Mr. Trimblerigg, who knew the amount of it, tendered a three-penny bit, without comment.

'Angel, sir?' inquired the man encouragingly, naming a destination, intent on his job. Somebody at the far end tittered, and a smile went down the row of faces opposite.

That remark, and its reception, revealed to Mr. Trimblerigg more than anything which had yet happened, the unfortunate position in which any approach to the truth placed him. The spirit of the age was not attuned to receive it seriously, far less with reverence. Dispensations of Providence such as this no longer entered into the calculations of men's minds; nor was seeing believing, except on lines purely material. Surrounded by that atmosphere of scepticism which he felt in his bones, Mr. Trimblerigg had himself succumbed, and spoken, not as a man of faith having things of mystery to declare, but as an experimentalist, peddling in science – so adapting himself to a public which had no use for things spiritual: truly an inglorious demonstration of his famous thesis that truth is only relative.

The old lady and her companion got out, looking back at him as they went with slightly scared eyes and puzzled smiles. One of the newspaper readers moved up and sat next to him. The bus had halted under the gloom of a broad railway arch, and he became aware that a gentle light, emanating from himself, fell upon the faces on either side of him. The newspaper reader, making acknowledgment with a pleased smile, tilted his newspaper so as to obtain the benefit. 'Very convenient,' he murmured; 'quite a new idea. Where can one get it?'

And so challenged Mr. Trimblerigg still had not the courage to explain. 'I haven't the maker's name,' he said. 'It isn't mine. I'm only trying it.'

And hearing himself so speak, he sat aghast; it was horrible thus to be denying the light that was in him. Yet what else could he say, so as to be believed?

'How do you put it on?' pursued his interrogator. 'What is it, luminous paint?'

'No, nothing of that sort,' he replied. 'It's a secret. I mustn't explain.'

And then, though he had not reached his destination, unable to bear it any more, he called for a stop and got out.

Having alighted on the pavement, feeling painfully the concentration of at least twenty-four pairs of eyes upon his back, he put up his umbrella to cut off the view, though it had really ceased to rain, and made haste away.

Somebody had got out after him. He heard steps insistently close following him; then a voice speaking the American accent.

'Say! pardon me, sir. Do you mind telling whether you are advertising that as a patent? Can be got anywhere?'

'No, it can't exactly be got,' said Mr. Trimblerigg, whose own more insistent question was whether it could be got rid of. 'It isn't mine. I'm just trying it.'

'It's very remarkable, very striking,' said his interlocutor. 'There's a future in that contraption, sure; or I'm much mistaken. You've patented it, I suppose, before bringing it out? If you're needing capital to develop it, I'm your man.'

'No, no,' said Mr. Trimblerigg hastily. 'I don't want to develop it. It's developing itself; and – and,' he hesitated – 'it isn't for sale!'

Then, trying for once to have courage, and stand a faithful witness for truth: 'It's not what you think it is,' he said. 'It's not material; it's spiritual – a visitation; but the revelation of its meaning has not yet come to me.'

And so saying he took a perilous run into the traffic, and dodging death on nimble feet, got safely away to the other side.

He left behind him a stunned patriot.

'America, you're beaten!' said the voice with the accent.

The Conversion of Caroline

MR. TRIMBLERIGG JOINED HIS FAMILY IN A SMALL retired bungalow, standing between estuary and sea, on the outskirts of a large health-resort looking south. It was the very place for him to be – if not exactly alone – unobserved. The shore was shadeless; across an arm of the estuary a rickety foot-bridge led to copse and field, and across the railroad to a wide expanse of heath. After that came the littered margin of the town, with its cheap and scrubby architecture run up as a trap for holiday-makers.

He had arrived by daylight, and occupying a window-seat on the sunny side of the carriage had managed to get through without further adventures. At the office also he had done fairly well, entering by the door marked 'private,' and working with the electric light well over him.

His children, who always loved him when they saw him, but forgot him easily again in absence, ran boisterously to greet him, and each in turn entered the charmed circle without making remark. So did Caroline. They kissed him, noticing nothing.

This cheered him, but he knew it could only be for a time, and as soon as they got to 'The Mollusc,' which was the bungalow's name, he said to his wife, 'I want to speak to you,' and drawing her into a room apart, waited – to see.

She was slow to realize that anything was amiss; and this ought to have cheered him still more. But now that it was his wife alone – a public of which he was not afraid – he was irritated. It was an instance of the extreme slowness of her mental uptake.

181

'Well?' he said at last, challengingly, 'don't you notice anything?' He moved from the window as he spoke. Then she did.

'Good gracious!' she exclaimed. 'Jonathan, what have you been doing to yourself? Have you been going about in town looking like that?'

This tone, from Caroline of all people, he could not stand; she at least should be taught to look at the thing properly – with respect.

'I have been doing nothing to myself – nothing!' he replied. 'As it is the will of Heaven, you might try to speak respectfully about it – or else hold your tongue!'

She looked at him in pained bewilderment. 'Do you mean you can't help it?' she said at last.

'That is exactly what I *do* mean,' he said. His pent-up bitterness broke out. 'I've had two days of it – about as much as I can stand. Yes! you round your eyes, but you don't realize what it has made me go through. It's been spiritual desolation. I was like an owl in the wilderness, with all the other silly owls hooting at me, taking it for a show, a trick-turn, a patent night-light that burns all through the day to amuse itself; and now *you*! No; it's not X-ray; it's not Tatcho for the hair; it's not luminous paint; nor is it a mechanical adjustment to prevent people tumbling against one in the dark or help them to read newspapers in omnibuses. All those things have been said to me in the last twenty-four hours; and if only one of them were true, I believe to God I should be a happier man than I am! The plagues of Egypt may have seemed all right to Moses, but Pharaoh didn't like them! Why Heaven has seen fit – I don't know.' He paused. 'But there it is, so I must learn to bear it.'

182

Caroline said: 'When you've had your supper, you'll feel better.'

'I shall not feel better; I shall never feel better until I know – either what sense to make of it, or how to get rid of it. It's just as if – as if Heaven didn't know that the world's mind has changed about things. I shall become a laughing-stock. What good will that do?'

And then Caroline, who had been brought up on biblical knowledge, was very annoying. 'Didn't Jeremiah shave one side of his head?' she inquired, 'or roll in the dirt and eat books, and things of that sort? Or was it Isaiah!'

'I don't know,' said Mr. Trimblerigg shortly. 'It wasn't me, anyway. If one did that sort of thing to-day, one's use in the world would be over.'

Mr. Trimblerigg's view was the social: Caroline's was only the practical: trying to be resourceful, she said. 'You might try brushing it.'

'I might try cutting my head off,' he retorted. 'I wish you'd stop talking foolishly.'

Then Caroline, being a dutiful wife, and seeing how much he was put out, did her best to soothe him. 'I don't think people will notice it,' she said; 'not much if you don't want them to.'

'Then you'd better leave off thinking!' he said. 'Though I haven't wanted them to, they *have* noticed: they've done nothing but notice! If you like, I'll go and put my head into the kitchen now, and you'll hear that charwoman of yours faint at the mere sight of me.'

'No, she won't,' said Mrs. Trimblerigg, ' she's gone. She lays the table for supper and then goes home, and doesn't wash up till she comes again in the morning. And it's Jane's evening out; so there'll be nobody.'

These domestic details infuriated him; Caroline was so stupid. And she continued to be.

'Don't you think you ought to see a Doctor?' she inquired.

'I'll see the Doctor damned first,' replied Mr. Trimblerigg. Her suggestion of ice was no better received; it seemed as if she could only annoy him. And then one of the children outside shouted, 'Mummy, when are we going to have supper?'

'Go and give them their supper!' he said; and his tone was very bitter; bitter against her, and against the children, and against the whole world wanting its supper, while on his head fate had laid this burden of a blessing, too grievous for the flesh to bear. Yes, the flesh; that was the trouble. He saw the spiritual side of it – the symbolic splendour beckoning clear from heights which he could realize but which the world could not. He saw that, but he saw the other side also! There was no public for it; and if no public, where was the good – what could he do with it? Live it down? – or so arrange matters that it should never show? That meant cutting his life in half, and concealing the best of it.

There he was, a furtive fugitive in the bosom of his own family; the children wanting their supper, and he avoiding it; yet surely – if this thing was from Heaven – children, his own children at least, ought to be trained to grow accustomed to it, and take a right view of it. Then why not begin?

Caroline had gone into the kitchen to get the supper ready. He called her back. 'I'll come,' he said, ' they'll have to see it sometime. Tell them – for to-night at any rate – not to make remarks.'

CHAPTER NINETEEN

So Mrs. Trimblerigg went off to impose discipline on the family. To the maid she said, 'you can go out now.' To the children when the maid had gone: 'your father has got something the matter with his head. You are not to make remarks.'

Presently she went and told him that supper was ready. A lamp was upon the table; but it wore a shade; Mr. Trimblerigg did not, it would have been no use. He entered the room aware, in that half-light, that he had become conspicuous; nor could he be unconscious of the three pairs of eyes turning upon him an expectant gaze which became riveted.

Benjie, the youngest, gave an instinctive squeak of excitement; then, hushed by his mother but forgetting to close his mouth, he dribbled.

Mr. Trimblerigg, according to custom, stood to ask a blessing. 'For these, and all Thy other mercies,' he said, and stopped short: 'a mercy' was what he could not feel it to be. Conversation was slow to begin. All the children reached out with healthy appetites for the bread and butter. Amy, conscientious child, still all eyes, seeking an unforbidden topic of conversation, surmounted the impediment by saying, 'Ma, why didn't we have pancakes to-day?'

'Hush, my dear!' said Caroline, who had a feeling that the remark was too apposite; and indeed the barbed point had already gone home. So that – thought Mr. Trimblerigg – was how it appeared to a child's eyes!

He helped them all quickly from the dish before him; after that they looked at him less continuously, but not less admiringly. This eased the situation till Martin, the elder of the two boys, inquired concerning the food upon his plate. 'Mummy, why don't poached eggs have their yellow outside? Why don't they, Mummy?'

Caroline told him not to talk, but to go on eating.

Amy remedied matters in her own way, saying wisely, 'They do come outside when they're hatched; they turn into chickens then, don't they, Mummy?'

Martin said, 'No, they don't!' and looked corroboratively at his father. Benjie said: 'Yes, they do: eggs do.'

Caroline said: 'I told you not to talk.'

But children must talk, especially if there are three of them; and Martin being now silent, Benjie took up the running.

Laying his head on one side, and stroking it with his spoon, 'Mummy,' he said, 'if I was to catch fire, wouldn't I get burned up? Wouldn't I, Mummy?'

Then Mr. Trimblerigg could stand it no longer; he took up his plate, and left the room. As soon as he had closed the door he heard Benjie give a howl, and knew that Caroline, applying useless remedies, had slapped him.

Presently, having sent the children to bed, she came in to comfort him. 'They'll get used to it presently,' she assured him, 'if it doesn't go off. But I wish you'd see somebody.' This time she avoided the word 'doctor,' because it irritated him.

'I suppose they talked of me as soon as I'd gone?' he said, ignoring the suggestion.

'A little, naturally,' she replied.

'What did they say?'

'D'you think I'd better tell you,' queried Caroline, wishful to spare him.

'Yes, I may as well hear the worst.'

'Well, Martin said, 'Is Father a holy man, Mother?' Caroline had made her selection apparently: she uttered it without conviction; and to hear it so repeated gave Mr. Trimblerigg no joy. Truth from the mouths of babes and sucklings – even revealed truth sceptically reported – failed to comfort him.

'I think I'll go out for a turn by myself,' he said. Then stopped; for outside it was dark. He went into the bedroom instead; and Caroline took advantage of his absence, though too late for it to get through that night, to go and send off a telegram. It was addressed to Davidina, and it merely repeated what she had said to the children: 'Jonathan has something the matter with his head. Come at once.'

But though that was her view of it, Caroline had no notion how much really was the matter with his head – having only seen the malady in its fainter and less convincing manifestations; she had not encountered it in the dark.

When she went up to bed she found him already in it, with a lamp on the table beside him, reading; and at first, as she looked at him, she thought he was already cured; the globe of light had become quite unapparent.

Wise in her way, instead of exclaiming on the fact, she said nothing. 'Better wait,' she thought, ' and give it time,' – hoping that by the morning he would have quite got over it. And so with composed leisure, she went first to bed, and then presently to sleep, leaving him still at his reading. And only when Mr. Trimblerigg was quite sure she was safely asleep, did he put out the light and resign himself to the rest he so much needed.

The reason was that Caroline's composed materialism had got upon his nerves; her detached reception of Mar-

tin's godly suggestion had dealt him the shrewdest blow
of all. So little apparently was her mind open to conviction of a spiritual kind, that she had passed it over as
not worth a thought.

But in this Mr. Trimblerigg did Caroline an injustice;
she was merely dense to nuances; half-tones had not impressed her, and a thing which she could only half-see she
could only half-believe in. It was far otherwise when,
waking up in the small hours, she beheld Mr. Trimblerigg's head, unconscious but luminous, lying in a charger
of golden light – light so strong that she might have read
by it. So overwhelming was the effect of it then, that she
got out of bed, fell upon her knees beside him, and in
meek simplicity, though a little late in the day, gave him
the worship which was his due; for now truly he looked
beautiful.

Her mind experienced a revulsion; he had been concealing himself from her. All these years she had been married to a holy man and had not known it; had even had her
doubts of him. Now they were gone; that he should be
able to look like that while unconscious and asleep, convinced her utterly. Contrite, she wept. How could she
guess that in his sleep he was only carrying on with so
much more success that to which conscious life presented
difficulties? Mr. Trimblerigg was having a pleasant
dream.

" *The Desire of the Moth for the Star* "

HE WOKE FROM HIS DREAM TO CONDITIONS FAVOUR-
able to peace of mind; a rippling sea, a sunny shore,
and a day that promised to be cloudless. They break-
fasted in a verandah looking seawards, the children seemed
to miss something but said nothing; and Caroline's manner showed an improved change. Reserve and deference mingled with tenderness when she spoke to him.
When she suggested plans for the day she was shy and
a little nervous: for now her conscience was troubled:
she had Davidina on her mind, and was expecting
the reply-telegram. She had sent off the message
without consulting him, under what she now felt to be
a misapprehension. If Davidina wired that she was
coming she would have to break it to him; and fearing
that the news would not please him, she put off the evil
moment as long as possible. Her immediate anxiety
was to get him out of the house before the arrival of the
telegram.

This she managed to do: and all day nursed her guilty
secret that Davidina would arrive by a late train to know
what was the matter. And as a consequence, as much as
possible she avoided him.

Meanwhile Mr. Trimblerigg was thinking. Immediate
conditions were conducive to a quiet examination of the
problem; but though temporarily at ease, he was not getting more reconciled to the prospect. He had been long
accustomed to hear and speak of people being overtaken in
sin; but it had never entered his mind that, by a similar
involuntary capitulation to a stronger power, they could
also be overtaken in goodness – still less in goodness of so

conspicuous a character, attaching itself like a disease, independent of the will.

'The white flower of a blameless life' was a poetic phrase which, like that other about sin, had passed into the currency of the language: and mentally he had always been able to wear it, and feel the better for the consciousness that it was there. But it was a different matter when becoming visible and almost concrete, it turned into an evening primrose, catching him by the hair of his head, and refusing to let go.

Martin's question, 'Is Father a holy man?' was a child's way of putting it; but substantially it was so much his own point of view about the visitation now afflicting him, that he began to wonder whether he might not get rid of it by ceasing to be holy. If he went into the kitchen and kissed the charwoman, if he made himself drunk, if he went down to the marine parade and extracted cigarettes from the automatic slot-machine by inserting metal discs instead of pennies, or if – to make the matter worse – he were to add sacrilege to dishonesty, go into the church and rob the poor box – if he did those or other similar things, would this outward expression of his sanctity take itself off – go away and leave him?

But while entertaining the fancy that it might do so, he more than doubted it; for he felt that in his own heart he would not be doing any of those things; that it would not really be him; internally his good qualities and motives would remain unaffected. On such lines it would be useless, therefore, to experiment.

But mentally was there nothing which, if sedulously entertained, might bring him back to a more mundane and normal condition? Here, as he sat on the shore, with his children building sand-castles near by, and his wife making domestic sounds in the bungalow behind him, could he not definitely will away the manifestation by a slight deflection from his high ideals towards what is called temptation?

He began to think of Isabel Sparling; and to think of her pleasurably; she was still attractive to him; and that he had once again held her in his arms counted for something, gave to youthful memories a livelier flavour – a bouquet which hitherto they had lacked. He and Isabel Sparling had become enemies – or rather she had become his, and had all the more remained so because he had successfully evaded and got the better of her. But he had always liked her, her pluck, her perseverance, her capacity, and the spark of zealous fire for a cause which had burned in her for years, and which nothing could quench. Provocative, annoying, unscrupulous and vindictive though she might be, she was never dull. He knew that with her he would have had a more uneasy time than with Caroline – yet now he wished – or told himself he wished – that he had taken the risk, adopted her crusade as his own, and married her. It would have been harder, more uphill work – but looking back complacently on his successful career, due entirely to his own powers and intuitions – he believed he could have done it. And had he adopted that course, life, otherwise so interesting, would not have had at its centre that dull, that very dull spot which was Caroline.

So Mr. Trimblerigg sat and thought, indulging himself with the imagined sweetness of forbidden fruit. But as he was not in the very least ashamed or put out of countenance by the entertainment of these wayward fancies they had of course no effect upon him. His internal unity of purpose not consciously weakened, he continued to feel complacent and good, in the sense that he had always been – good to himself. It was not as if anybody had found him out; then it would have been different. The only person who ever found him out was Davidina; and as to her, since their last encounter, his mind was at peace.

The evening post brought letters forwarded from town; and Caroline, having to confess what she had done, made them the occasion for breaking into the solitude in which all day she had left him. An added reason was that one of the bunch was in the handwriting of Davidina. It was futile any longer to postpone the news that Davidina was on her way to see him.

Caroline handed him the letters, and as after sorting them through he seemed in no hurry to open them – Davidina's she noticed, he put aside from the rest – she opened, on her own account, the matter wherewith she was charged.

The Presence had begun to manifest itself again, though not as powerfully yet, as at the moment which had brought her to her knees and to conversion. She was moved, feeling very humble towards him; and her eyes grew full of tears.

'I am sorry, Jonathan, I have misjudged you,' she said.

The announcement, though it surprised, rather pleased him; for he saw plainly by her look that misjudgment was over.

'How have you misjudged me, my dear?' he asked.

'I – I didn't think you were always quite straight,' she said.

'Straight': the word had a certain sting. It stirred faintly the slumbers of that small sleeping dog – his conscience, which he was so accustomed to let lie. Then his sure instinct for defence brought him gaily to the attack.

'Oh, yes, I know, my dear child, sometimes you've been jealous.'

'No, no, never really,' she said, 'only I know I'm stupid – so, of course, sometimes – '

At that she left it and returned to her point – the point she had been wondrously cogitating all day in her slow mind. 'No, I mean straight in quite little things. You see, Jonathan, I know now Martin was right. I haven't understood you – not properly. And when I say 'not straight,' I mean in such little, little things, that never seemed to matter till now.'

This was a new experience altogether. Caroline was thoroughly surprising him. 'How didn't you think I was straight?' he asked.

'Well, for one thing,' she replied, 'I know now that you *do* take your cold bath. I thought you didn't.'

Had Heaven thundered and shaken off the roof, leaving nothing above but bare sky, Mr. Trimblerigg could not have been more startled than at those words. To poor honest Caroline, the acceptance of the spiritual interpretation of what had happened to him meant, meant necessarily that he had always not merely been good in his own sense of the term, but done the straight thing – taken his baths, and in all quite small things told the truth, the whole truth, and nothing but the truth.

And then, on the top of that, while the shock of it still reverberated through his soul, Caroline let go the thing she had come to tell him.

'Davidina is coming,' she said. 'Forgive me, Jonathan, I

didn't understand then. And when you refused to see a doctor I telegraphed for her.'

'What did you tell her?'

'Only that you'd got something the matter with your head. She's coming by the late train. It's nearly due.'

He sat so still that she grew frightened. She reached out a hand and touched him.

'Go away,' he said, 'let me alone!'

And weeping she got up and left him.

For a long while he sat on, motionless, unable to move. Doubt leapt in on him, engulfed him: blackness – such as he had never known before – was upon his soul. Not Davidina – no, not Davidina herself, whom he had now to expect by the late train – had ever dealt him so devastating a blow. 'Now I know you take your cold bath: I thought you didn't.'

O pellucid Eve: O rib of Adam, how naked hast thou made the man for whom thou wast formed! And this without in the least intending it, or knowing what she had done.

It was true that, even now, she had not found him out; but she had revealed to him with fatal clearness the fact that the shirking of a cold bath and the wearing of a yellow halo were incompatible. And this was the worst thing she had against him, this trivial doubt; but it was enough. Down came his castle. A horrid blush went over him – down even into his clothes; it went farther, had he only known.

'Thou, Lord, seest me!' he said to himself, got up, and went swiftly out into the starlit dusk carrying a red light.

And then the thought of Davidina, coming on the top of this, struck him cold. He remembered that he had upon

CHAPTER TWENTY

him a letter from her which he had not yet read; opening
it, he drew out the contents. There was no need to go in-
doors to get a light; that which he had was sufficient. The
letter was very brief and to the point. 'Found you out! but
no matter: you did the honest thing with your eyes open
– for once.' Enclosed was an old envelope, cut open across
the top, still bearing its seal, addressed to Davidina in
Uncle Phineas's handwriting. Minutely examining the
seal, he found – what Davidina also had found – traces of
his own handiwork, a scar showing where it had been
removed and put on again.

'Idiot!' he said to himself – why hadn't he covered up the
breakage with a larger seal? Or why, again, after all those
years had he troubled to tell a lie about it? But the reason
for that he knew; it was so that he might stand well –
better than he had ever stood before – in Davidina's eyes.
Just that once, so simply, so easily, by so slight a departure
from the truth – he had got the better of her; and now her
clutch was upon him again. She was coming through the
dark night; he must meet her face to face, and hear her
asking in hard matter-of-fact tone: 'Well, what's the
matter now?'

Through the house he heard a knock at the front door;
the thought that it might possibly be Davidina, come
earlier than she was expected, drove him down the garden
in flight and out by the back way. He was suffering badly.
The double buffet – Caroline's, followed by Davidina's,
had left him dazed; he had no spirit left. If there had ever
been doubt of him in his wife's easy-going and utterly
domesticated mind, how could he meet the all-seeing eye
of Davidina, in the expectation that his shining certificate
of virtue would, even for a moment, divert her from com-

mon sense? All the haloes in the world would not convince Davidina that he really took his bath of a cold morning: it would convince her of nothing of which he would
like her to be convinced, but only of other things that he
would rather she did not know.

And yet the thought stuck to him, 'I am good, sometimes.' To that anchor he clung like a drowning man who
happens also to be a little drunk. If he could only have let
the anchor go it would have given him a better chance.
But no – a sense of his sometimes exceeding goodness
still clung to him. Out into the night he went, and his
blush went with him – extending farther than he knew.

All the mercury of his composition had gone down into
his boots; and though he still believed in himself he was
very, very miserable. The fact that he attracted moths,
added to his depression. It was merely one more indication of the futility of the moral emblem which had fastened in on him. Coming to a stile leading into fields, he
made it his *prie-Dieu*, and kneeling on the foot-rest bowed
his head and prayed: 'O Lord, take away my life; thou
hast laid on me a burden too heavy for me to bear!' So,
characteristically – I had often heard him do it before –
still shifting the blame from himself to others.

One did for him what one could – stirred memories he
had striven to make dormant, suggested to him interpretations of his action in the past which at other times he
would have denied vehemently. All I could do I did to
make him shake off for good that halo of self-worship with
which he had surrounded himself. But, as always when he
took to his knees, he left me with a peculiar sense of helplessness. His tendency to defend himself in prayer not
only from the imputations the world made against him,

but from the imputations of his own conscience, was just as much in evidence as ever; and familiarity with the Scriptures continued to make sincerity of speech difficult. Quotations from the Old Testament kept coming into his head to be hurled at mine, as though, from such a source, they must needs be true statements of fact.

'I have been very zealous for the Lord God,' he cried; and then having chosen his prophet, started upon variations. 'The priests of Baal I have slain; I have broken down their altars; and I, only I, am left, desolate.' He was not arguing, he was telling me.

With his persistencies and his prevarications he made me really angry at last; for he would not leave off. As Jonah once had a great fish prepared for him, so I prepared and drove a cow up to the stile where he was kneeling. It touched him with its nose. In the darkness he mistook it for a passer-by, waiting to get over. Apologizing he got up and stood aside; and when he discovered his mistake it made him feel very foolish.

He ceased praying, and rambling quickly across the field, found himself presently at a level-crossing. Away on the other side he heard mixed music, shouting, laughter, and the crack of toy firearms, where the heath had temporarily become a fair-ground. From farther away in the distance came the mumble of an approaching train.

As he trod the metals, he wondered – his sense of direction being defective – which was the up and which the down line. He stood still on the track. Suddenly into his quick divided mind the thought flashed – suppose there were an accident ! He had heard of people standing to watch trains becoming fascinated by them, hypnotized, unable to move. Hypnotism would, he supposed, provide a comparatively happy death: it would also make the recipient irresponsible for his actions. Well, an express train might do it; but of local or luggage trains he was doubtful; they had not sufficient thunder or speed.

And so, between two rails, and still of two minds as usual, he halted and waited. The idea began to fascinate. him, as always where so much hung upon chance. Was he standing on the right track? Would it be an express, or would it be a local. And then the thought – if it were an express, and with track coinciding, would he after death display to a remorseful world that sign of divine approbation which as a living man now so encumbered him?

It was a wonderful and an inspiring thought; and as it came forthwith it blazed into a certainty; he became exalted and uplifted in spirit. Yes, posterity would see him in his true light, as he had always felt himself to be in those blessed moments when it was borne in on him that his whole life was a mission, and he himself the great modern evangelist making goodness a thing simple to the understanding. What a beautiful end! he thought. Even Davidina would be sorry then for her past misreadings of his character.

The train leapt into view. It did not leave him long in doubt; it was an express and a fast one at that. He watched it, and became fascinated. Power of control left him: his mind soared in a vague hopeful ecstasy toward the stars. He saw Sirius winking at him – Sirius, which had always been his special star, his affinity. He winked back at it: tears rushed to his eyes, he became blind.

Absolutely irresponsible for his actions now, he stood unable to move, his whole body possessed by the mighty rushing sound which filled his ears; the world around, the heaven above, the earth beneath grew full of the thunder of it. Upon those monstrous vibrations his soul mounted to bliss; he had become superior to his own body at last, did not mind, was not afraid. Heaven had been gracious to him after all.

Suddenly the engine, opening its throttle, gave a ghastly scream. With a blast of its nostrils, a rattling of chains, a grinding of brakes, and a screeching of wheels, which sent shuddering discords to the night, it came to a precipitate standstill, less than a dozen yards from where Mr. Trimblerigg stood with sapling feet waiting to be uprooted for another and a better world.

Those horrible noises, and the abrupt abatement of its speed snatched Mr. Trimblerigg from his trance. With loosened knees and presence of mind mercifully restored, now only apprehensive of detection and capture, he sped swiftly away; high-hedged night received him into its obliterating embrace; the track was clear.

A stoker, descending hastily from the arrested train, searched the line ahead. His voice swung back angrily out of the darkness:

'Red light? I don't see no red light. It's some damned fool's been having a blooming game with us – that was all.'

And so, with a rich accompaniment of expletives from stoker and driver, the express proceeded upon its way.

Mr. Trimblerigg, in a much more shaken state, did the same.

CHAPTER TWENTY-ONE

A Run for Life

THE SHOCK OF HIS ESCAPE HAD LEFT MR. TRIMBLERIGG dazed and tremulous. He went feebly, not yet quite reawakened to the world which, in that moment of exaltation, he had thought to be leaving behind him. But instinct, and the loud jolly sounds of his fellow-creatures drew him toward the glaring lights and bustle of the fairground. An illuminated crowd was a refuge from his condition; amid the flare of those naphtha lamps his radiance would be unapparent.

But while he thus moved toward the light, he forgot that his back was to darkness, and as he skirted the outer circle of the booths, standing shoulder to shoulder with their farther sides dressed to the staring crowd in gaudy habiliments of painted canvas, he was startled to hear a voice exclaim, 'What's that bloody sunset doing there?' and to perceive that it was directed at him.

The showman, jumping down from the back-door of his van, ran hastily towards him, thrust a bewildered face at him, and stopped amazed. 'Well, of all blinking wonders,' he cried, 'you take the cake!'

Mr. Trimblerigg, trying by superior calmness to control the awkward situation, wished him a good evening, and was for passing on.

The man caught him by the arm. 'Here! which of the blooming shows d'you belong to? I hadn't heard tell of you.'

Mr. Trimblerigg replied that he did not belong to any show. The man was dumbfounded.

'You don't mean to say you're going about here giving

yourself away for nothing?' he managed to say at last. 'You ain't advertising anything, are you?'

'No; I've just been taking a turn,' said Mr. Trimblerigg. 'Now I'm going home.'

'You aren't!' cried the show-man, with an eagerness that was almost like agony. 'Here, come along into my show, and you shall have half the takings. Honest, I mean it! And you shall have a money-box of your own to pass round too, if that ain't enough,' he added, seeing that his first offer had failed in attraction.

'You don't understand,' said Mr. Trimblerigg, assuming a mild dignity which he did not feel: 'This is entirely my own affair. I'm not a show.'

Stupefied, bewildered, outraged, the man stood and looked at him for a moment, to see whether he really meant it. Then, his admiration turning to hate: 'You aren't?' he shouted, 'Then what the blooming hell are you? If you aren't a show, what did you come 'ere for? Got a game of your own on, have you? We'll soon see to that. Hi!'

He shouted with all the strength of his lungs, and continued to shout, waving his arms to attract the attention of the crowd. 'Here's an escaped lunatic!' he cried.

Mr. Trimblerigg started to run. He heard the shouts of others gathering behind him, dodged round a canvas obstruction, doubled back, made a bolt through a hedge, and thus securing a good start made off across the open in the direction of home.

But in less than a minute he knew that the crowd was after him; jovial, but excited, – for the mere fact that there is something to chase kindles the blood – it hurled after him heavy-footed, a little slow in the uptake, but warming to its task at the sight of its quarry half a field away, a blister of red bouncing through the starlit night, and under it showing dimly a man's form.

As the crowd neared him, its uncouth epithets assailed his ears. 'Holy Moses!' was the cry of one; 'Go up, Elijah!' of another. Then as they got near him and marked how desperately he ran, 'Hullo, old fire-escape!' gave the more modern touch which the situation required.

Mr. Trimblerigg could not run nearly so fast as the crowd; but at the level-crossing fate was kind to him. An arriving luggage-train – not without some risk – allowed him to pass in front of it, and then with its slow length held up his pursuers. But the more active ones, running down the line turned the tail-light of the guard's van, broke fence, cut a slant and were on him again.

Once more fate favoured him. At the home stile the cow which had interrupted his prayer had couched itself for the night. Perceiving the recumbent obstruction too late, he planted his foot on it; with a spasmodic heave she hurled him across quicker than he could have vaulted, and plunging about broke momentarily the head of the oncoming crowd.

It was amazing with what spirit Mr. Trimblerigg – not being in running condition – had kept the pace; but he was a very spent man when he reached the narrow foot-bridge, and sped breathless to the crossing, his pursuers only a few yards behind. The tide was low: black glimmerings of mud stretched to right and left of him: he trod warily clutching at the hand-rail as he ran to stay the dizzying of his brain. Before he reached the end, a violent vibration told that his pursuers were now almost upon him; the bridge resounded to the weight and tread of a larger number than it was built for. Under Mr. Trimble-rigg's feet a plank started; the weight pressing it behind jerked it upwards. Somewhere with a sharp report a stay snapped, then another and another; and with a sense of general collapse going on behind him, from which he him-self was immune, Mr. Trimblerigg felt himself precipi-tated through the air in a long gliding curve, up, out, for-ward, and down. A shallow mud-bank received him into its merciful embrace. He stumbled out of it unhurt, but in so dark a disguise, that all the mothers in the world would not have known him.

Leaving his enemies behind in far worse plight, he stag-gered up to the door which had already opened to those sounds of break-neck disaster borne upon the quiet air.

He saw Davidina standing dark against the light, and even in the desperation of his present condition he felt the shock of it, and shrank back from meeting her – not because of the mud which now encased him, but because of that other adornment, which he could explain so far less easily. But the relief he had longed for had already been brought about: the mere sight of her had made him a changed man; and though her greeting word, as she ran down the path to meet him was, 'Jonathan, whatever *is* the matter?' she made no further remark indicative of sur-prise. All about him the night was beautifully dark; there was no reflected light upon her face as she bent forward to kiss him. The shock of meeting her had done it. Mr. Trimblerigg had no longer anything to conceal.

They cleaned him of the mud which smothered him. 'You don't *smell* of drink,' said Davidina, 'but you look like it. What's this Caroline has been telling me about your head? What's wrong with it?'

And, at the word, what he had already begun suspiciously to hope, he became sure of. Heaven was no longer making him conspicuous.

'What did she tell you?' he inquired defensively. 'There's nothing the matter with my head that I know of.'

'Said you'd been striking sparks – having a vision that your head was a hayrick that had caught fire; and now she won't tell me anything: says you've sworn her to secrecy.'

'She must have dreamed it!' said Mr. Trimblerigg.

He saw Caroline go white.

'Dreamed it?' exclaimed Davidina. 'If she dreams things like that she wants a doctor.'

She did. On hearing that she must not believe the evidence of her senses, Caroline fainted.

*

Full many a rose, the poet tells us, is born to blush unseen, and waste its sweetness to the desert air. Mr. Trimblerigg's rose had experienced a somewhat different fate; it may have wasted its sweetness, but it had not blushed altogether unseen; and though it died blushing for itself, it had not lived in vain. The conversion of Caroline to its spiritual significance had proved unimportant; the realization by Mr. Trimblerigg of its extreme inconvenience had made a temporary but not a permanent impression upon him, as further record will show. Davidina had not seen it at all, it had snuffed itself out at the sight of her. But somebody else had seen it, and had realized not merely its spiritual significance, but its potential value, which Mr. Trimblerigg had missed, or too hastily despaired of. And the person in question had seen it not once but twice, on two separate occasions.

When Mrs. James told Isabel Sparling that Mr. Trimble-rigg was not at home and had already left town, Miss Sparling had either the sense or the instinct not to believe her. And being a determined character, she had hung about at a respectful distance, keeping her eye on the door, rather expecting him to come out of it than to go into it. Muffled in veil and cloak — the former to conceal her bandaged face — she had walked up and down the farther pavement, with her senses alert for the coming or going of that familiar figure, until in the early gathering dusk, the apparition passed her, going with haste along the verge of the pavement in the line of the lamp-lights.

Isabel Sparling had this advantage over others who had seen, or doubted that they could have seen, that same mystical appearance in the earlier hours of the day. She was herself a spiritualist and a visionary; she believed in things which the world in general did not, and was on the look-out for them. She had recently, among her other beliefs, become a Second Adventist, and was looking for the end of the world; this event was to be preceded by a great war, by earthquake, by things happening to the sun and moon; by the opening of the seven seals upon a certain box which had recently come into her custody, and by the reappearance of saints from their graves, preparatory to the reappearance of others who were not saints. And for all these things she was already hungrily expectant, when she met a halo walking down the street. It came upon her suddenly round a corner, and had passed before she fully realized that it encircled the head of the man whose false friendship had changed her feelings to enmity. Her intention, in seeking him out and lying in wait for him, had been to return in person the money he had left for her; and though she had meant to thank him for his good services, she had not meant entirely to forgive him, but rather to explore his spiritual condition, and warn him, as she had begun warning the world at large, of the wrath that was to come.

But seeing him there, with head clothed in light, her feelings toward him changed. She was seized with an instant conviction that she had misread his character, or that she had not made allowances for the difficulties of one destined to fulfil a high mission in the spiritual crisis which the world was now approaching. The sight of him thus augustly changed, speeding furtively along, avoiding human recognition, filled her with awe and humility; she could not go and return money to a head in a halo; she could not, with the emotion of that discovery fresh upon her, follow him, ring the bell and ask for him — perhaps only to be denied. But twenty-four hours later, after much spiritual wrestling with herself and him (for her thoughts thereafter were never quit of him) she did find courage to go and knock at the door of the Mollusc wherein he had secreted himself from the world — the knock which he had heard and thought might be Davidina; and when the dull Caroline, without recognition or inquiry, had told her, in the double sense, that he was not at home, she let herself be turned away without protest; and standing forlorn, contemplative of that quiet scene of shore, river and star-brimmed sky, saw away in the mid-distance a globed cluster of moving light crossing the small foot-bridge, and making for the fields beyond. Then to her also came the sense of a mission, and prevailing in weakness she stole after him.

Following at a devout, that is to say at more than a

respectful distance, she saw him dimly by his light rather than by his form, cross the field and halt at the stile to pray.

Drawing nearer, she durst not then intrude on him; and when he had got upon his feet and passed on, she, following close after, found an impediment of an insuperable kind awaiting her.

Isabel Sparling was mortally afraid of cows; and there one stood in her way; and after standing for awhile and gazing at her with a munching movement of the mouth which she felt sure meant mischief, it lay down upon the footpath to wait for its prey to come over.

And thus it was that, without a full clue to its meaning, she became spectator to the unexplained scene of horror which followed after. She watched his light resting at the level-crossing to await the passing of a train, then saw it dwindle and merge in the broad band of fire amid which the junketing fair sat and bubbled; and wondered whether he had gone there to preach repentance like Jonah to the inhabitants of Nineveh. Her next sight of him was fleeing before a crowd that seemed thirsting for his blood, awhile holding his own, but presently losing ground, then by the intervention of Providence gaining more than he had lost. As he came headlong toward her, she nerved herself for his deliverance, was prepared to stand between him and the hungry crowd, declare his sanctity, die if need be instead of him; and so she would have done had not the cow got suddenly upon its feet – hindlegs first in that horrible way which cows have when they intend to toss people.

That finished her, she saw the rest of the chase from a distance, heard the crash of the broken bridge, cries, curses; and presently met a crowd of maimed larrikins, muddy, drenched and miserable, carrying each other home. But even had she then dared to go further, and inquire for more news that the angry comments of the crowd gave of his escape, the broken bridge prevented her; and the next day, stealing by furtive ways to watch unobserved, she saw Mr. Trimblerigg clothed and in his right mind, tended by female relatives, accompanied by his children, and his glory all gone from him.

And that, for the time being, was the conclusion of the matter; but not the real conclusion, for then came war; and Isabel Sparling, girding up her spiritual loins, preached that the world was to end, – that her people and her native country were to be punished for their sins, but other countries much more. Gradually, swayed by the patriotic crowds which gathered to hear her and cheer on others to do their fighting, she became harder upon the other countries, and let her own and its allies off; and before the war had been on a twelvemonth they had all become angels of light, chosen vessels, ministering spirits and flames of fire. For that is what war does; while in a physical sense it paints most things red, in a moral sense it paints them black or white; and the black is the enemy, and the white is ourselves; and the neutral, if neutral there be, is a dirty tint which badly needs washing.

As for Mr. Trimblerigg, having found that there was no public for it, he relinquished goodness of the first water, and fell back upon relative goodness and relative truth, in which, as a matter of fact, he had a more instinctive belief.

CHAPTER TWENTY-TWO

Intimations of Immortality

WHEN NATIONS WHICH PREACH CHRISTIANITY GO TO war, their truth has necessarily to become relative ; they cannot tell the truth about themselves; they cannot tell the truth about their enemies; still less can they tell the truth about Christianity. For doing that last, a Free Church minister in a certain land of hope and glory lying West, – he had merely issued the Sermon on the Mount as a circular – was tarred and feathered as a demonstration of Christian-mindedness by his belligerent fellow-countrymen. And nearly everybody said that it served him right.

So when Relative Truth became a spiritual as well as a military necessity, Mr. Trimblerigg, the inventor of the doctrine in its most modern form, came gloriously into his own. In other words he became the fashion.

The War gave him the time and the opportunity of his life. He had begun by adopting – first pacifism, then benevolent neutrality; but he saw quickly that there was not a public for either. And as he listened to the heart-beats of his countrymen roused for battle, a quick application of his doctrine of Relative Truth restored his mind to sanity. After that he never wavered; and though he often spoke with two voices, one day telling the workers, whom he was sent to preach to, that they were heroes, and another that they were slackers, and victims of drink; one day demonstrating that the National Executive's action had always come just too late, another that it had always come miraculously up to time; one day protesting the mildness and equity of his country's intentions toward those who were unnecessarily prolonging the war, another – when

prospects began to look brighter – threatening things of a
much more drastic character, in terms drawn from the
prize-ring; though thus from day to day and week to week,
he spoke in varied tones, fitting himself to the occasion,
always a forefront figure, occasionally pushing others out
of his way ; nevertheless his motive and aim remained
constant (nor when nations go to war is anything
more necessary for their salvation) – the ardent assertion,
namely, of the absolute righteousness of his country's
cause, and of the blameless antecedents leading up to it.

And though Mr. Trimblerigg's truth was often ex-
tremely relative, it was nearly always successful; and if
any man by tireless energy, resilient spirits, continuous
ubiquity in pulpit and on platform, alertness, invention,
suggestiveness, adaptability, rapid change of front in the
ever-shifting tactics of propaganda, – now conciliatory and
defensive, meek but firm ; now whole-heartedly aggres-
sive and vision-clear of coming victory – if by such qualities, richly and rapidly blended outside the direct line of
fire, any man could ever be said to have won a war, in a
larger and wider sense than the little drummer boy who
lays down his life for his drum, – that compliment might
have been paid, when all was done, to the unbloodstained
Mr. Trimblerigg, – and was.

In the person of Mr. Trimblerigg the Free Evangelical
Church had lifted up its head and neighed like a war-
horse, saying among the trumpets, ha! ha! to the thunder
of the captains and the shouting: and in the person of Mr.
Trimblerigg thanks were publicly tendered to it, when all
the fighting was over. And though Mr. Trimblerigg
received neither title, nor outward adornment, nor emolu-
ment, he became, from that day on, a figure of inter-

national significance, – the first perhaps since great old combative Martin Luther, to attain so high and controversial a prominence in divided Christendom on his spiritual merits alone.

It may sound cynical to say that the greatness of nations has very largely been built up on the lies they have told of each other. And yet it is a true statement; for you have only to compare their histories, and especially the histories of their wars (upon which young patriots are trained to become heroes), in order to realize that the day of naked and unashamed truth has not yet arrived: that so long as nations stand to be worshipped, and flags to be fought for, truth can only be relative. From which it follows that while nations are at war too much truth is bad for them; and not only for them but for religion also. And that is where and why Mr. Trimblerigg found his place, and fitted it so exactly. I leave it at that. He became a national hero; and truly it was not from lack of courage or conviction that he had seen no fighting. He was short, and fat, and over forty; and his oratorical gifts were more valuable where the sound of gunfire did not drown them; otherwise he would have preached his gospel of the relative beatitudes as willingly from the cannon's mouth as from anywhere.

A day came, gunfire having ended, when he, and an Archbishop, and a Prime Minister all stood on a platform together, and spoke to an exalted gathering too glittering in its rank and distinction to be called an assembled multitude, though its mere numbers ran into thousands. The Archbishop sat in the middle; and the two ministers, the political and the spiritual, sat on either side of him; and if they were not as like each other as two

peas, and did not, by both speaking at once, rattle together like peas upon a drum, they were nevertheless birds
very much of a feather; and when it came to the speaking,
they fitted each other wonderfully. The Archbishop came
first and spoke well; the Prime Minister followed and
spoke better; Mr. Trimblerigg came last and spoke best
of all. The audience told him so; there was no doubt of
it. Field-Marshals and Rear-Admirals applauded him,
Duchesses waved their handkerchiefs at him; a Dowager-
Countess, of Low Church antecedents, became next day
a member of the Free Evangelicals; the mere strength of
his personality had converted her.

Mr. Trimblerigg might well think after this that a visible
halo, though not necessary, had it reappeared just then,
would not have come amiss. From his point of view the
meeting could not have been more successful; he went
down from the platform more famous than when he went
up on it. And it was not his speech alone that did it: it
was in the air.

The great Napoleon was said to have a star: Mr. Trimblerigg had an atmosphere; and though it was not really
the larger of the two, to his contemporaries on earth it
seemed larger.

It was just about this time, when Mr. Trimblerigg was
obviously becoming a candidate for national honours after
his death, that he attended the public funeral of a great
Free Church statesman whose war-winning activities had
been closely associated with his own. And as of the two,
Mr. Trimblerigg had played the larger part, the prophetic
inference was obvious; and though in that high-vaulted
aisle, amid uniforms and decorations and wands of office,
his demure little figure looked humble and unimportant,

he was a marked man for the observation of all who had come to observe.

It was an occasion on which Free Churchmen had reason to feel proud. Impelled by the feeling of the nation – still in its early days of gratitude before victory had begun to taste bitter – the Episcopal Church had opened her doors to receive, into that place of highest honour, the dust of one who had lived outside her communion and politically had fought against her. But it was dust only (ashes, that is to say); and while to Mr. Trimblerigg's perception the whole ceremony, the music, the ritual, the vestments, the crape-scarved uniforms, and the dark crowd of celebrities which formed a background, were deeply impressive in their beauty and symbolism, the little casket of cremated ashes at the centre of it all was not.

In that forced economizing of space, the sense of the individual personality had been lost, or brought to insignificance. It gave him an uncomfortable feeling; he did not like it; he wondered why. So long as his thoughts went linked with the indwelling genius of that temple of famous memories he felt thrilled and edified; but whenever his eye returned to the small casket, he experienced a repeated shock and felt discomfited. The condition here imposed, to make national obsequies possible, seemed to him not merely a humiliating one; it spelt annihilation; what remained had ceased to be personal. The temple became a museum; in it with much ceremony an exhibit was being deposited in its case.

And so, pondering deeply on these things, he returned home; and added to his will (signing and dating it with a much earlier date) an instruction for his executors, 'My body is not to be cremated.'

213

Genius is economy. It could not have been more modestly done.

Somewhere or another, very near to where he had stood that afternoon, a grave was waiting for him. Those few strokes of the pen had decided that its dimensions should be not eighteen inches by ten; but five feet four by two.

But the time was not yet: the instruction added to his will need not begin to take effect for a good many years. Meanwhile his corner of immortality waited for him, measured by himself to suit his own taste.

It came back to him then as a pleasant simile of fancy, that he had had an uncle who was an undertaker. It ran in the family. Here was Mr. Trimblerigg – his own!

CHAPTER TWENTY-THREE

Peace-Work

To become the spiritual voice of a nation is a rare experience, and in the history of the race it has come to the individual but seldom. But when it happens, he is a greater power than military leader, or politician, or popular preacher, unless in one man all three functions find themselves combined; then, without much justification in fact, a people may mistake the combination for the more rare and genuine article.

It could not exactly be said of Mr. Trimblerigg at this time that he was a military leader; but the idea had been industriously disseminated, by his admirers and by himself during the war, that had he been he would have been a brilliant one. Nor was he exactly a politician; but he had been very busy and energetic in putting the politicians right, so that, as they went out of favour in public estimation, he came in. For the rest, a popular preacher he was, and a very wonderful one; though it is a curious fact that his sermons and speeches do not read well in print. Mr. Trimblerigg's orations were gymnastic exercises and histrionic performances combined; and these things lose their effect when reduced to print. Nevertheless he had now become a Voice, and the sound of him travelled wherever his native tongue was spoken, war-conditions having given it an atmosphere that it could fill.

His military instinct he had mainly shown by running about in moments of crisis and pinning his faith to commanders who up till then had escaped defeat. When he found he had made a mistake, he dropped them so quickly that nobody remembered he had ever believed in them; and having thus discovered three or four and lost them

215

again, he finally hit upon the right one. Having done that, he did not allow it to be forgotten, so that the reputation which survived the final and triumphant catastrophe remained partly his.

His political instinct produced more definite and more solid results; he persuaded the politicians to do a lot of things which at other times they would not have dared. Some of these things were not very scrupulous, and others were not very successful; but they were all military necessities, and as only the relative truth was told about them, they took their place in the general scheme of things; and if they did not exactly do good, they were good for the morale of the nation for the time being.

And while he thus persuaded the politicians to do things hitherto impossible for the benefit of the whole nation, he persuaded the Free Evangelicals also; and in his own time and his own way he secured for Isabel Sparling and others the desire of their souls which had been so long denied them. But in that matter, though the thing was done well and quickly when it was done, he missed something of his intended effect from the fact that the whole world was then so busy about war that nothing else seemed much to matter. The sudden admission of women to the ministry appeared then a mere side-issue, an emergency measure devised to meet the shortage of men theologically qualified for the vacant pastorates of congregations abruptly depleted of their young male element. Thus Mr. Trimblerigg's very real achievement in the pulpiteering of women was regarded, even among the Free Evangelicals, far more as a war-product than as his own.

Also for Isabel Sparling herself, whom he wished to impress, it had ceased much to matter. She had become a

Second Adventist; and among the Second Adventists it was admitted that women could prophesy as well as men. Miss Sparling had gone prophesying to America; and had caused a great sensation in New York by prophesying that Brooklyn Bridge had become unsafe, and would fall if America did not enter the war. She gave a date: and America saved Brooklyn Bridge to posterity only just in time. After that the success of Miss Sparling's American mission was assured; and whenever the States seemed momentarily to slacken in their purpose or diminish in their zeal for the rescue of a civilization they did not understand, Miss Sparling selected some cherished institution or monument, and began threatening its life; and when, after due warning a bomb was discovered inside the statue of Liberty just preparing to go off, she got headlines for Second Adventism which had never been equalled since Barnum's landing of Jumbo (representative of a still older civilization than that which was now imperilled) some forty years before.

All this is told here merely to indicate what a match to himself Mr. Trimblerigg had missed by not marrying Isabel Sparling in the days of his youth. Had they only put their heads together earlier, kingdoms might have come of which the world has now missed its chance – not knowing what it has missed; for there can be no doubt that its spiritual adhesions are not now what they were ten years ago; the pulpit has sagged a little on its foundations and congregations have become critical, sceptical even, though they still attend. The doctrine of Relative Truth has undone more than it intended; and though Mr. Trimblerigg was not a disappointed man at the moment when war declared itself over, disappointment was waiting him.

Not at first, as I say. At first, no doubt, as he pulled the wires, he thought he was plucking from harpstrings of gold, harmonies which could be heard in Heaven. But his atmosphere affected him; and just when victory brought him spiritual opportunities such as had never been his before, he had a sharp attack of the Old Testament, and his self-righteousness became as the self-righteousness of Moses and the prophets all rolled into one.

It was then, perceiving that a huge and expectant public was waiting for him to give the word, that he sent forth the fiery cross bearing upon it as the battle-cry of peace the double motto 'Skin the Scapegoat,' – 'Hew Agag.'

Both sounded well, and both caught on, and for a brief while served the occasion: but neither made a success of it. The skinning of the scapegoat lasted for years; but in the process, it became so denuded by mange that when the skin was finally obtained it proved worthless. As for Agag he did not come to be hewn at all, walking delicately; on the contrary he ran and hid himself in a safe place, where, though the hewers pretended that they meant to get at him, they knew they could not. And as a consequence Agag remains unhewn to this day.

And, as a matter of fact, almost from the first, Mr. Trimblerigg, having given his public what it wanted, knew that it would be so.

He also knew that in high places it was willed that it should not be otherwise. And here may be recorded the bit of unwritten history which brought that home to him.

Everybody to whom mediumistic spiritualism makes any appeal has, in these last days, heard of Sir Roland Skoyle, the great protagonist of that artful science, by which in equal proportion the sceptics are confounded, and the credulous are comforted. And that being, up-to-date, its chief apparent use in the world, it is no wonder that a certain diplomatist turned to it when he launched his great peace-making offensive, after the War was over. For diplomacy having to make its account equally with those who are sceptical of its benefits, and those who are credulous, it seemed to his alert and adaptable intelligence that a little spiritualism behind the scenes might give him the aid and insight that he required.

The direct incentive came from Sir Roland Skoyle himself. He had secured a wonderful new medium, whose magnetic finger had a specialized faculty for resting upon certain people of importance – people who had been of importance, that is to say – in high circles of diplomacy; and amongst them some who had been largely instrumental in bringing the world into the condition in which it now found itself. Among these – the war-makers and peace-makers of the immediate past – it was natural, war being over, that the latter should be in special request, where the problem of diplomacy was to construct a peace satisfactory to that vast body of public opinion which had ceased to be blood-thirsty on a large scale, but whose instinct for retributive justice to be dealt out to the wicked by a court of their accusers had become correspondingly active.

Sir Roland Skoyle, anxious to impress the Prime Minister with the value of his discovery, had the happy thought of employing Mr. Trimblerigg as his go-between. And Mr. Trimblerigg having heard a certain name, august and revered, breathed into his ear, together with the gist of a recent communication that had come direct, was not averse from attending a séance in such select and exalted company. He had an open mind and plenty of curiosity, and the idea of sharing with the Prime Minister a secret so compromising that no one else must know of it, strongly attracted him.

And so the sitting was arranged. And there in a darkened room the four of them sat, – Sir Roland, the medium, Mr. Trimblerigg, and the Prime Minister.

The medium was small and dark, and middle-aged; she had bright eyes under a straight fringe and she spoke with a twang. There was no doubt which side of the water she had come from. Until the previous year, except for a few days after her birth, her home had been the United States. The actual place of her birth was important; it helped to account for her powers; Sir Roland having recently discovered that the best mediums were people of mixed origin, born on the high seas. This particular medium, having been born in the mid-Atlantic, was Irish-American.

The theory of sea-born commerce with the world of spirits I leave to Sir Roland Skoyle and his fellow experts. My own reason for referring back to birth and parentage is merely that when the medium had entered into her trance she no longer spoke that rich broth of a language formed from two which was natural to her; but acquired an accent and a mode of delivery entirely different; the accent having in it a faint touch of the Teutonic, the delivery formal, well-bred, and courtly; even when the speech was colloquial there was about it a touch of dignity. And while she so spoke, in a manly voice, the little woman sat with an air like one enthroned.

The Prime Minister sat jauntily, thumbs in waistcoat, and listened as one interested and amused, but not as yet convinced. To Mr. Trimblerigg he said chirpily, ' If the other side got wind of this, and used it properly, they could drive me out of office.'

'That makes it all the more of an adventure,' replied Mr. Trimblerigg. 'I should be in trouble too. The Free Evangelical Church has pronounced against – well, this sort of thing altogether: "Comes of evil".'

Sir Roland said, 'In a year's time we shall have the whole world converted.' But Sir Roland was always saying that. Still, table-turning and its accompaniments had certainly received a great impetus since the War; for which reason Mr. Trimblerigg took a friendly view of it.

The medium's first remark in her changed manner was sufficiently startling and to the point:

'Where is my crown? . . .Put it on.'

Sir Roland resourcefully picked up a small paper-weight, on which a brass lion sat regardant, and deposited it precariously on the medium's hair.

'Who've you got here? Not Eliza, I hope?' said the Voice.

Sir Roland, in a tone of marked deference, gave the names of the company. Two of them were graciously recognized. 'Mr. Trimblerigg? We have not had the pleasure of meeting him before. How do you do, Mr. Trimblerigg?'

Mr. Trimblerigg, at a gesture from Sir Roland, bowed over the hand the medium had graciously extended.

'Do I kiss it?' he inquired, doubtful of the etiquette.

Sir Roland discreetly shook his head. The ceremony was over.

There was a pause. Then: 'Faites vos jeux, Messieurs!' said the Voice.

This was unexpected to all; and to one cryptic.

'What does that mean?' inquired Mr. Trimblerigg, in whose Free Church training French had not been included.

The Prime Minister rose lightly to the occasion. 'It means, or it practically means, 'Make your Peace, Gentlemen.' Then, to the unseen Presence: 'The game is over sir, – well over. Now we have only to collect the winnings.'

This statement of the facts was apparently not accepted: the game was to go on. 'Couleur gagne!' went the Voice; and then again, 'Faites vos jeux, Messieurs.'

'Our present game,' respectfully insisted the Prime Minister, 'is to make peace. To you, therefore, Sir, we come, as an authority – in this matter of peace-making a very special authority. We as victors are responsible; and we have to find a solution. The peace will not be negotiated, it will be dictated. The question is on what terms; under what sanctions; with what penalties? Under a Democracy such as ours –'

'Don't talk nonsense,' came the Voice, 'Democracy does not exist. Invite public opinion; say you agree; then ignore it, and do as you think best. Sanctions? You will not get good work from a man while the rope is round his neck; he wastes time and brain thinking how soon he will die. Penalties? Yes: if you think you can get hold of the really responsible ones.'

'We think we can,' purred the Prime Minister.

'Dig up the dead, eh? That was the mediaeval notion. You tar and feather their corpses, and you hang them in chains: most indecent, and no good to anybody. One of them is here now, – "The Man in the Iron Mask" as we call him, – a much improved character, his world-politics a failure, they no longer interest him; he plays on the French horn, – badly, but it amuses him; when he strikes a false note he calls it the Double Entente. He means that for a joke. He says they may dig him up and hang him in chains of iron, or brass, or glass-lustre, or daisies, or anything else if it amuses them. But you are not proposing to hang anybody, are you?'

Mr. Trimblerigg, voicing his notion in the scriptural phraseology which had prompted it, explained that skinning for the one, and hewing, not hanging, for the other was the process proposed.

'Who is your man?' the Voice inquired sharply.

Agag was indicated.

Came a dead pause; then, very emphatically, 'I won't have him here!' said the Voice.

Here? His auditors looked at each other in consternation.

What on earth, or above earth, or under earth, did 'here' mean?

The Prime Minister and Mr. Trimblerigg had both by now become convinced that they were in the actual Presence that had been promised them. But they could not admit to the world, or even to themselves, that there was a possibility of Agag going to the place where the Presence was supposed to be; or of the Presence being in the place where Agag was supposed to be going. They sat like cornered conspirators.

'I won't have it!' said the Voice, almost violently. 'We are not on speaking terms. He and I do not get on together. Send him to Eliza: she'll manage him!'

This was more awful still. The Presence and 'Eliza', it seemed, were not in that happy reunion which for Christian families is the expected thing. Yet as to where Eliza had gone no reasonable doubt was possible.

'On ne va plus!' cried the Voice, and the séance fell into sudden confusion. 'I won't have it! I won't have it!' shrieked the medium coming to, and casting off her crown at the feet of Mr. Trimblerigg. And the words, beginning in a deep German guttural, ended in Irish-American.

And that, if the world really wants to know, is why no real attempt was made to hew or hang Agag, or do anything to him except on paper in diplomatic notes which meant nothing, and at a General Election which meant very little more – only that the Prime Minister and Mr. Trimblerigg were saving their faces and winning temporary, quite temporary, popularity, which eventually did them as little good as it did harm to Agag.

The skinning of the scapegoat was not so expeditiously disposed of. In that case the goat suffered considerably; but the skin was never really worth the pains it took to remove from his dried and broken bones.

When will modern civilization really understand that its predilection for the Old Testament, once a habit, has now become a disease; and that if it is not very careful the world will die of it.

'Faites vos jeux, Messieurs!' Play your game! Sometimes you may win, and sometimes you may lose; but a day comes when you win too big a stake for payment to be possible. Then the bank breaks, and where are you?

CHAPTER TWENTY-FOUR

Circumstances alter Cases

HAD THE RESCUE OF THE NATIVE TRIBES OF PUTO-CONGO
from the squeezing embrace of modern industrialism
and its absentee shareholders been a fairy-tale, they would
have remained a happy people without a history, and here
at least no more would have been heard of them. But this
being the real story, things went otherwise.

It is true that Native Industries Limited not only became
itself a reformed character, but managed, by its control of
the river routes and depots, to impose repentance on the
great Puto-Congo Combine also. There, too, a rout was
made of the old Board of Directors, and the missionary
zeal of Free Evangelicalism, with an admixture of True
Belief, held the balance of power. In the first year shares
went down at a run from a thirty to a ten per cent divi-
dend, and the mortality of indentured labour was reduced
in about the same proportion.

Of course the shareholders grumbled – not at the reduced death-rate in itself, but at the awkward parallel
which its proportional fall suggested between toll of life
and that other toll of a more marketable kind which mainly
concerned them. It was not pleasant to feel that a reduced
ten per cent profit was always going to be the condition
of a reduced ten per cent death-rate: that fifteen per cent
of the one would cause fifteen per cent of the other, and
that, by implication, a life-saving of five per cent might be
effected if the chastened shareholders would stay lan-
guidly content with a five per cent profit. Mr. Trimblerigg himself felt this to be a reflection upon the reformation he had effected. He had practically promised the
shareholders that decent treatment of the natives would

225   P

eventually bring larger profits. He was annoyed that it
had not done so, and was already taking steps to secure
more co-ordination and efficiency in the combined companies when the war supervened and gave to the relations
of the brother races, white and black, a different complexion.

To put it quite plainly, under war conditions so far-
reaching as to affect the whole world, humanitarian principles had to take second place. For the white race, or
tribe, or group of tribes in which Mr. Trimblerigg found
himself embraced by birth and moral training was now
saving the world not only for private enterprise and democracy, but for the black and the brown and the yellow
races as well, all round the globe and back again from San
Francisco to Valparaiso. And so the enlistment of the
black races in the cause of freedom – even with a little
compulsion – became an absolute necessity, a spiritual as
well as a military one, and unfortunately the blacks – and
more especially the blacks of Puto-Congo – did not see it
in that light of an evangelizing civilization as the whites
did. They did not know what freedom really was: how
could they, having no politics? Their idea of freedom was
to run about naked, to live rent-free in huts of their own
building on land that belonged to nobody, to put in two
hours' work a week instead of ten hours a day, and when
an enemy was so craven as to let himself be captured alive
to plant him head downwards in the earth from which he
ought never to have come. That was their view of freedom, and I could name sections of civilized communities
holding very similar views though with a difference.

Slavery, on the other hand, was having to wear anything
except beads, and nose-rings, and imitation silk-hats made

of oilskin, having to work regularly to order for a fixed wage, and to pay a hut-tax for the upkeep of a machine-like system of government, for which they had no wish and in which they saw no sense. And that being so, it really did not matter whether the power which imposed these regulations was benevolent in its intentions or merely rapacious, whether it secured them by blood, or blockade, or by bribing the tribal chiefs (which was the Free Evangelical method) to get the thing done in native ways of their own. They did not like it.

Puto-Congo, having sampled it for twenty years, had definitely decided that civilization was bad for it; and when, under the evangelizing zeal of Mr. Trimblerigg and his co-religionists, civilization modified its methods, they beat their drums for joy and believing that civilization was at last letting them go, ran off into the woods to play. And though, here and there, their chiefs hauled them back again and made them do brief spells of work at certain seasons of the year, they regarded it rather as a cleaning-up process, preparatory to leave-taking, than as a carrying on of the old system under a new form; and so they continued to play in the woods and revert to happy savagery, and especially to that complete nudity of both sexes which the missionaries so strongly disapproved.

It was that holiday feeling, coming after the bad time they had been through under the old system – a holiday feeling which even the chiefs, stimulated by bribes, could not control – which did the mischief; for it came inopportunely just at the time when, five thousand miles away, civilization had become imperilled by causes with which the Puto-Congo natives had nothing whatever to do. If civilization was so imperilled all the better for them.

It was all very unfortunate: for while the fact that civilization was at war did not make civilization more valuable to the natives of Puto-Congo, it did make the natives and their trade-produce very much more valuable to civilization. Quite half-a-dozen things which they had unwillingly produced under forced labour in the past – rubber was one – had now become military necessities. It was no longer a mere question of profits for shareholders – civilization itself was at stake. Production had suddenly to be brought back to the thirty per cent standard; and that holiday feeling, so natural but so untimely in its incidence, was badly in the way. And so powers were given (which are not usually given to commercial concerns – though sometimes taken) and under government authority – a good deal at the instigation of Mr. Trimblerigg – the Puto-Congo Combine became exalted and enlarged into the Imperial Chartered Ray River Territory Company, which was in fact a provisional government with powers of enlistment civil and military, of life and death, and the making and administration of whatever laws might be deemed necessary in an emergency.

Endowed with these high powers, the Directors at home, with every intention to use them circumspectly and in moderation, instructed their commissioners accordingly. But when the commissioners got to work they found, in the face of 'that holiday feeling,' that moderation did not deliver the goods. And since the goods had to be delivered, lest the world should be lost to democracy, they took advantage of the censorship which had been established against the promulgation of news unfavourable to the moral character of their own side, and took the necessary and effective means to deliver them. And when the profits once more began to rise, these did not go to the share-holders but to the Government as a form of war-tribute, and that, of course, made it morally all right – for the ten per cent shareholders at any rate – since they knew noth-ing about it.

And thus, for three or four years, Puto-Congo natives did their bit, losing their own lives at an ever-increasing death-rate, and saving democracy which they did not understand, for that other side of the world which they did not know. They got no war-medals for it and no promo-tion; nor were any reports of those particular casualties printed in the papers. Enough that the holiday feeling went off, and the goods were delivered. Over the rest, war-conditions and war-legislation drew a veil, and noth-ing was said.

And that is why, while war went on, Mr. Trimblerigg and the rest of the world did not hear of it; or if they heard anything, did not believe what they heard; for that too is one of the conditions that war imposes. Truth, then, becomes more relative than ever; which is one of the reasons why Mr. Trimblerigg was then in his element. But when the war was sufficiently over for intercommuni-cation to re-establish itself, and when the skinning of the scapegoat had become a stale game, and when the hewing of Agag had emphatically not come off, then Mr. Trimble-rigg, and others, began to hear of it. It was the others that mattered. Mr. Trimblerigg – his war-mind still upon him, and still suffering from his severe attack of Old Testament – did not believe it; but the others did, and the others were mainly the most active and humanitarian section of the Free Evangelicals. Having already ex-pressed their disapproval of skinning the scapegoat and hewing Agag, even to the extent of pronouncing against it at their first annual conference after the war, they now fastened on the recrudescence of ugly rumours from Puto-Congo and the adjacent territories, and began to hold Mr. Trimblerigg responsible.

They had at least this much reason upon their side, that Mr. Trimblerigg was still chairman of the Directors of Native Industries Limited, and, by right of office, sat upon the administrative council of the Chartered Company. And when, as the leakage of news became larger, it seemed that everything he had formerly denounced as an organized atrocity was being, or had but recently been done on a much larger scale by his own commissioners, the cry became uncomfortably loud, and the war mind, which can manipulate facts to suit its case while they are suppressed by law, began to find itself in difficulties.

Mr. Trimblerigg, faced by certified facts which he continued to deny or question, began jumping from the New to the Old Testament and back again with an agility which confused his traducers but did not convince them; and the allegiance of the Free Evangelicals became sharply divided. The reunion of the Free Churches for which Mr. Trimblerigg had so long been working, already adversely affected by the divergencies of the war, was now strained to breaking.

On the top of this came the news that the natives of Puto-Congo had risen in revolt and had begun massacring the missionaries, and Free Evangelical opinion became more sharply divided than ever – whether to withdraw the missions and cease to have any further connection with the Chartered Company, or to send out reinforcements, less spiritual and more military, adopt the policy of the firm hand, and restore not liberty but order.

Mr. Trimblerigg then announced that he would do both. To the Administrative Council he adumbrated a scheme for the gradual development of the Chartered Company, with its dictatorial powers, into the Puto-Congo Free State Limited, with a supervised self-government of its own, mainly native but owing allegiance to the Company on which its commercial prosperity and development would still have to depend.

Matters were at a crisis, and were rapidly getting worse. Mr. Trimblerigg had made too great a reputation over Puto-Congo affairs to risk the loss of it on a mere policy of drift. Something clearly had to be done, large, spectacular, idealistic in aim, to cover up from view a record of failure which never ought to have seen the light. Not only must it be done; it must be done at once, and he was the man to do it.

The Administrative Council was wise in its generation. Without quite believing in Mr. Trimblerigg's proposals it gave him a free hand; for as one of them said: 'This is a matter over which he cannot afford to fail. If he does, he is done for. Give him rope enough, he may hang others, but he won't hang himself; of that you may be quite sure.'

Without being quite sure, they made the experiment, and Mr. Trimblerigg, with full powers, went out as High Commissioner of the Chartered Company to sow the seed, plant the roots, or lay the foundations of the Puto-Congo Free State Limited. His mission was twofold – to save the Puto-Congo natives from themselves, and the shares of the Chartered Company from further depreciation. Incidentally he had also to save himself.

CHAPTER TWENTY-FIVE

Kill and Cure

I CAN UNDERSTAND PEOPLE LIKING MR. TRIMBLERIGG, I can understand them disliking him; I can understand them finding him incalculable and many of his actions puzzling (I used to do so myself); but I do not understand why they should ever have been puzzled as to his main motive, since his main motive was always himself.

Like everything else in life, character is a product, the inevitable outcome of its constituent parts. When I invented him, I gave Mr. Trimblerigg brains and a good head for business; I also gave him imagination and an emotional temperament. Why, then, should it be wondered at if he made a calculating use of his imaginative powers, or indulged his emotions with a good eye to business?

Could you find me any occasion on which the fervours of his oratory got in the way of his worldly advancement, or did anything but add size to his following, I would admit that his character puzzled me. But more and more I found this to be the rule – that the fervour of his prayers, public or private, meant the same thing; and whenever the encounter was a private one, and the fervour more than ordinary, then I knew that Mr. Trimblerigg was in a tight place, and that he had come to me not to admit that it was the place in which he deserved to be and to stay, but to ask me to get him out of it.

Crocodiles cry: it is their nature. But they do other things as well: they eat – not only people, but practically everything else in the world that lives and breathes and is at all eatable. I gave them a good digestion for that purpose. They are scavengers; and when they scavenge, they do not always wait till the about-to-become-nuisances die. They make, however, one exception: they do not eat their dentist. And so you may see a crocodile squatting patiently in the mud of the Nile or the Ganges, with jaws wide; while in that place of death a small and tasty bird– whose name I forget – picks his teeth for him.

Sentimentalists look on and say, 'How beautiful! how wonderful!' So it is; but not in the way they see it. There. is no sentiment about it: it is merely the economy of life intelligently applied. The crocodile depends for his good digestion, and his ability to satisfy it, on the efficiency of his teeth; and as he cannot clean them himself he gets a small clean bird to do it for him.

Similarly when Mr. Trimblerigg opened his mouth to me, he was doing so for a genuine reason, as do most people: and why should I complain?

I get a meal – something that adds to my interest in life. Far more prayers mount up from the world below for selfish than for unselfish reasons (I have experience, and I know); and they are not the less sincere, or the less eloquent, or the less emotional, because they have a mundane and a self-centred object.

Now when I compare Mr. Trimblerigg to a crocodile, I hope nobody will suppose that I am taking the ordinary sentimental view of crocodiles, as of creatures more cruel than other creatures. A crocodile when it eats a human being is no more cruel than a thrush when it eats a worm; and if people could only get that well into their heads theology would have a better basis than it has at present. A crocodile only appears more cruel than nature's average because it is peculiarly efficient to its end, and makes a wider sweep. Being big, it requires a larger meal than others of the predatory species; also it happens to carry on its countenance an almost unchangeable expression of self-satisfaction, and so by appearing pleased it appears more callous. And the fact that it does not always wait for its offal to die is another point which the sentimentalists have against it.

In all these characteristic features – not to mention the tears, which are merely accidental – there was between Mr. Trimblerigg and the crocodile a resemblance. He was in his own line – the line of getting on at the expense of others –preternaturally efficient; and as his efficiency took a wider sweep, and required for the fulfilment of its plans a larger contribution of sacrifice from assistants and opponents alike, he appears in retrospect, even on the ministerial side of his career, more rapacious, more predatory, and more callous than others. This arose partly from the size, the necessary size of his meal, and partly from the satisfaction it gave him; and if, when all was done, that satisfaction did not break out in smiles, he would have been a hypocrite. Being surface-honest, he smiled, quite aware that his success was for ever being built up on the failure of others – failure which he sometimes forced on them, or more often into which he tricked them, when they themselves were reluctant to stand aside.

But was that a reason why his smile should diminish? His smile only diminished when his meal did not agree with him. There have been occasions when he did not devour soon enough, when the nuisance which was obstructing his path had time to turn and give him one in return before the happy despatch could be effected. Then and only then did Mr. Trimblerigg ever appear sore. He much preferred to swallow a nuisance before it could retaliate.

The Puto-Congo nuisance, which had now come to so large a head, had done so while his attention and energy had been turned elsewhere. The fight for Relative Truth in one direction is apt to give Relative Untruth its opportunity in another; for the good that man does, or intends to do, is never absolute and all-embracing; and if Relative Truth is only relatively successful, – the untruths incidental to its propagation come into undue prominence and take the shine out of it.

So it was now with Mr. Trimblerigg's evangelical war record; the recrudescence of the Puto-Congo trouble had begun to take the shine out of it; the nuisance had become monstrous and must be stopped.

For obviously what had happened was not fair to Mr. Trimblerigg. Years ago he had planned beneficently a working compact for the development of native races between Free Evangelicalism and Capital. By a lightning stroke of genius he had brought a business organization of vast proportions virtually, if not actually, under the control of the most active missionizing body in the whole world. It almost seemed as if the stainless record of the Quakers, whose peaceful but profitable contact with Red Indian scalp-hunters had extended over seventy-five years of the seventeenth and eighteenth centuries, might now repeat itself on a larger scale; and if Mr. Trimblerigg on the flush of that generous prospect, saw in vision his name pass down to posterity as the great Liberator, – saviour of an oppressed race, is he to be blamed for anything but a too sanguine temperament? Hitherto it was that very temperament which had brought to pass things almost

impossible; but now here, just once, because his attention
had been diverted, the scheme had gone wrong, so wrong
as to become unrecognizable; and since he could not
recognize its distorted features, he denied himself with a
clear conscience either the parentage or the responsibility
of it. A thing so remote from his intentions was necessarily the doing of others; and when crossing the sea for
the first time he set out on the adventure, he had no other
aim but to put it right and re-establish, on a sound basis,
the concordat between Christianity and Capitalism which
he had originally planned.

But when he got there he found things very much worse
than even his enemies and traducers had either discovered
or declared; for in the restoration of order the missionaries of Free Evangelicalism had become implicated; very
much as in former time they had become implicated on the
commercial and profit-making side; and the natives, to
whom sequences were the same as consequences, had
begun to turn on the missionaries.

And they also were hardly to blame; for wherever the
missionaries went before, order – or attempted order –
had come after. Submission had been preached till the
natives would no longer submit; civilization had been
painted in all the colours of the rainbow, till civilization
had come and bruised them black and blue, and tanned
their hides for them; or did so when it caught them. For
to begin with the natives had only rebelled by ceasing to
hew wood and draw water, or collect the rubber and other
commodities which the Chartered Company was out to
collect; and running away into the woods had hidden
themselves; only defensively setting traps and laying
ambushes, when the emissaries of the Chartered Company

came to fetch them back again. And because, in many cases, the missionaries were sent as fore-runners, they started to make examples of the missionaries; and when the missionaries came and opened deceiving mouths at them, they devised a sure method for keeping their mouths shut by burying them head downwards in the ground. And when the missionaries showed them those rainbows of promise, in which they no longer believed, they painted the missionaries in the truer colours of black and tan. And so it had come about that, when Mr. Trimblerigg got to the country, the mortality among the missionaries and their lay-followers was very nearly as high and very nearly as painful as the mortality had been among the natives of the Puto-Congo and Ray River Territory, till they had taken to the woods to save themselves.

I have little doubt that had Mr. Trimblerigg's diverted attention – diverted to the saving of democracy, the skinning of the scapegoat and the hewing of Agag, – had it been recalled a little earlier in the direction where it would have done more good, and had he promulgated his idea of a Free State Limited five years sooner, when the call first came for Puto-Congo to assist in the saving of civilization, I have very little doubt that he could have done what he now failed to do, by methods which would have left his reputation very much as they found it. But when he arrived upon the scene the natives had got to a state of mind in which they could see nothing with any appetite except blood, and hear nothing except the cries of their victims; and in spite of Mr. Trimblerigg's proclamations of peace and goodwill (under certain governing conditions) the burying habit, with its painted accompaniments, went on: got worse, in fact, instead of better.

No doubt had Mr. Trimblerigg been able to announce
to the natives, that the white race with its civilizing mission, its religious principles, its rubber interests, and its
shares, was prepared to clear out of the country, lock,
stock, and barrel, and restore them the crude indepen-
dence they had never willingly let go, – no doubt had he
begun withdrawing his missions to the coast, and made
the interior prohibited territory to his rubber-collectors, he
would have found fewer of his missionaries entered head-
downwards into future life as he advanced his armed
guards, his rescue-work, and his reforms. But so long as
the white missions and the traders remained active the
natives could not be convinced. Nor was Mr. Trimblerigg entirely a free agent, he still had the shareholders
behind him – albeit shareholders professing Christianity;
and these were people who believed in the civilizing mission not only of race but of organized capital. And because
native ways of shedding blood were a savagery which must
be put down, while civilized ways of restoring order were
a 'military necessity' and a 'moral obligation' combined;
and because if they did not get the rubber somebody else
would, and their civilizing trade would suffer, – therefore
they hung on, and would not let go. And though Mr.
Trimblerigg had full power given him, it was power that
must be used to a certain end; and the end, put briefly,
was that Christianity and Capital must continue their
civilizing mission in company, and win back Puto-Congo
to the ways of the world.

Having stated the moral obligation I draw as much of a
veil over it as I can, making history brief; for Mr. Trimblerigg, much against his will, was obliged to fulfil it in
terms of Relative Truth, such as the natives could under-

stand. In a crisis the Mosaic law is so much easier and quicker to explain to primitive races than the other law which came later. For these races stand at a stage of the world's history; and what the higher races went through, by way of judicial experiment, they must go through also. Even by Christians, when it comes to the point, Christianity has never been regarded as a short cut — not even among themselves. For them and for all the rest of the civilized world, Moses is still the law-giver, and there is no transfiguration yet for the thunders of Mount Sinai; its lightnings continue to strike under the New Dispensation as of old.

So it had to be now. The natives of Puto-Congo themselves indicated what form of instruction best suited them; and under Mr. Trimblerigg's dispensation it was no longer only the missionaries who were buried head-downwards and painted black-and-tan, to match the landscape with its foregrounds of burnt-out villages and long tracks of charred jungle wherein nothing lived or moved.

For this painful necessity Mr. Trimblerigg had good material provided him. Civilization had trained for war far more men than it could now employ in peace; and what, at the call to her children of a country in danger, had been an act of heroic sacrifice had degenerated in course of time into a confirmed habit, wherein fierce craving and dull routine were curiously mixed. And when peace supervened and became in the hands of diplomats a feverish and restless thing, almost as nerve-racking as war, then by many hundreds of warriors unwanted by the State and without employ, the dull routine was forgotten while the fierce craving remained. Thus, here and there, as luck would have it, in a still unsettled world, use was found for them, and governments to which they owed no allegiance and for which they had no affection, and as to whose rights and wrongs they knew nothing and cared less, sent and hired them as experts for the shedding of blood in quarrels not their own. And because governments, good or bad, are organized things, and because men are accustomed to have a government over them justifying them in what they do, therefore, without trouble of conscience, to these foreign governments they gave themselves, and shedding blood to order, on a contract which promised them good pay, were not regarded as murderers at all, but as men still honourably employed in the service of civilization.

And some of these having returned home in the nick of time from building castles in Spain, cheated of their pay, and very much disgusted with the camps and the food and the sanitary arrangement which had been provided for them, hearing that there was more employment of a similar kind to be had in Puto-Congo and Ray River Territory, went and offered themselves to the Chartered Company and found grateful acceptance. And when a thousand of them had been collected, they were sent out to the help of Mr. Trimblerigg, well supplied with arms and ammunition, also with spades and tar-brushes. And when they arrived Mr. Trimblerigg gave them their welcome instructions, plenty of work at blacking and tanning, one pound a day, and their keep.

CHAPTER TWENTY-SIX

Civilized and Simple

IT WAS UNFORTUNATE THAT MR. TRIMBLERIGG, AT THIS
crucial stage of his career, not having Davidina to worry
him, had no need to worry about Davidina. Some six
months earlier she had started upon a career of her own on
rather a big scale – a research expedition, which, though
merely an extension of that taste for travel in strange places
which she had already indulged, was now organized upon
such novel lines and to cover so far-stretched a route that
it had attracted public notice, and had won for her at the
moment of departure many send-off paragraphs in journals of science and in the daily press. It was still something
of a novelty for a lone woman to head an expedition into
tropical wilds south of the equator, for no other apparent
object than to collect botanical specimens, and incidentally study the habits of the native tribes encountered on
the way. In addition, Davidina admitted that she had a
theory which she wished to put to the test; for though not
a Christian Scientist, she was one of those curious people
who are without fear; and being without fear she believed
herself safe; and as she did not mind dying she did not
intend to carry fire-arms. The whole gist of the experiment lay in the fact that, disappearing from the eye of
civilization to the south-east of tracts which no white
woman had ever yet penetrated, she intended to re-emerge
2,500 miles to the north-west, an unharmed specimen of
that superior race-product which she believed herself to
be.

She and Jonathan had not been pleased with each other
during the War; and for the first time in his grown-up
life Mr. Trimblerigg had adopted toward his sister the

241   Q

superior moral tone which circumstances seemed to justify; for in this contention he had not only the world with him but all the Churches. He told Davidina that she was wrong. Davidina's reply was: 'Seeing is believing; and at present I don't see much except mess, nor do you. In war nobody can.' And having waited till travel by land and sea had once more become possible, Davidina sent him word of the object-lesson she was going to give him. 'And if,' she concluded, 'you don't see me again, you needn't believe in my method any more than I believe in yours. In any case, I shan't haunt you; and I've left you my love in my will.' And with that cryptic remark she took herself off, leaving no address.

It would be hard to say what exactly Mr. Trimblerigg wished, hoped, or expected to be the outcome of her attempt to give him the promised lesson. Probably he thought she would come back the way she had gone, with a good record of adventure to her credit, a safe failure; for he had great faith in Davidina's powers of survival. What he did not expect in the least was what actually happened. Mr. Trimblerigg was inattentive to maps and unattracted to geography; and when Davidina started on her adventure she was more than 2,000 miles away from any part of the world in which Mr. Trimblerigg had interests.

Miss Trimblerigg's travels have since been published in two large volumes, with photographs taken by herself of things never seen before, and of some, towards the end, which Mr. Trimblerigg would rather she had not seen. For the scientific side of her work, two rival societies awarded her their gold medal for the year – the first time these had ever been won by a woman; for the other and more adventurously experimental side, she received an address of commendation from certain philanthropical and humanitarian societies and other bodies with crank notions, whose zealous leaflets and public meetings give them an appearance of life, but whose influence in the world is negligible.

Davidina had as her companions two other whites, husband and wife, whom she chose for the curious reason that they were both deaf and dumb, – very insensitive therefore to shock, very uninterfering and very observant of the natural phenomena that lay around them. By this means she secured undisputed control of the expedition, and as much insulation for her moral experiment as was practically possible. The deaf-mutes were a great success with the natives whom she employed as carriers: they regarded them as holy mysteries, and held them in as much awe as they did Davidina herself. Another curious choice she made was to have in her following no native Christians. For this particular experiment she regarded the unspoiled pagan as the better material; and there was plain horse-sense in it, seeing that before long her following not only looked upon her as a goddess, but worshipped her as well. This great sin (though by some it might be regarded merely as an example of Relative Truth) Davidina committed for more than a year and over a space of 2,000 miles with great apparent success, and was not punished for it. It was not my affair: those who read this record will have discovered before now that I do not hold myself responsible for Davidina: she belonged, and belongs still, elsewhere; and what were her inner beliefs or her guiding authority I have never been able to discover. She never applied to me. And yet between us we shared, or divided the conscience of Mr. Trimblerigg. The phenomena of the spiritual world are strange, and many of them, to gods and mortals alike, still unexplained.

Davidina, then, went upon her travels unarmed – unarmed, that is to say, with civilized weapons of war, or even of the chase – but by no means unprovided for. Weapons of a certain kind she had, weapons of precision, very subtle and calculated in their effect. But these were aimed not at the bodies but at the minds of those denizens of the forest and swamp and high table-land whom she encountered in her march. Every member of the expedition carried a toy air-balloon: and they had mouth-organs and bird-warblers; and the two deaf-mutes carried concertinas on which they played with great effect tunes by no means in unison. Natives, chiefs and warriors, coaxed to the encounter – often with difficulty – wept and bowed down to their feet as they performed; also they blew soap-bubbles which had an even greater effect, so that word of them went far ahead and on all sides, and the route they followed became populous.

Upon Davidina's shoulder, for mascot, sat a small pet monkey in scarlet cap and coat; and he too, when the occasion fitted, carried a toy air-balloon. And as it went by land or by water, the expedition, instead of going secretively and silently, made music and song, and bird-warbled; and waving its toy air-balloons, and blowing its soap-bubbles – with nods, and wreathed smiles, and laughter, and hand-clappings – was safe by ways that never varied but never became dull.

Again and again, in the dense forest jungle, ambushers who had hung in wait for them, fled howling at their approach – first to report the heavenly wonder to the heads of their tribe, then returning as watchers from a dis-

tance to be won by the beauty of their sound and the delicacy of their going — the decorativeness, the ritual, the
blithe atmosphere of it all. And at the next settlement to
which they came, the natives in holiday attire would turn
out to greet them with propitiatory offerings, and songs
which had no tune in them, but which meant that all was
for the best in this best of all possible worlds.

Month after month, sometimes camping for weeks, sometimes marching in the track of rivers or skirting swamps,
the expedition wore its way steadily on, making for the
point of the compass to which it had set its face, north-
north-by-west. And still word went ahead, through a
thousand miles of virgin forest; and Davidina coming
after, continued — however bad her theology might be —
to prove the thesis she had set out to demonstrate; always
triumphal in her progress, successfully collecting botanical specimens, her course unpunctuated by gunfire and
unstained by blood. For when, in the languages of the
native tribes they became variously known as the Music-
makers, the Ball-bearers: the Breathers of the breath of
life, their way was not made merely safe but prepared
before them, and a choice of many roads was offered them.
Runners from a hundred miles distance to right and left
of their route would come entreating them to turn aside
and do honour to communities waiting to welcome them.

For food they depended entirely on the skill of the native
bow-men, slingers, trappers, and blowers of darts who
formed their company; for Davidina had quite correctly
calculated that if by this means the natives could support
themselves in life, they could also support an expedition
in which the whites were only as one to ten. Had these
followers deserted, she and her two companions would

speedily have starved. It was a risk – not greater, she maintained, than the carrying of fire-arms; and since some risk must be taken, that was the one she preferred.

In the end she had actually to face it and come through on her own; but the goal of her itinerary was then not far.

It happened one night, after a heavy march that, without knowing it, she had pitched her camp upon the confines of the Ray River Company's sphere of operations, – at the point, therefore, where civilization might be said to begin. When she turned in for the night all appeared to be well. Outside her tent the native guards sat motionless upon their haunches looking out into the black bush; the toy air-balloons floated dreamily on their pole in the centre of the camp, and about its base all the impedimenta of the expedition stood neatly piled: there was then neither sign of danger, nor prospect of alarm, for up to that time nobody knew that they had touched civilization.

But during the dead hours, some sense – sight, or sound – of peril lurking ahead: native runners, perhaps, from a distance, or hidden dwellers in the surrounding forest, had struck the hearts of her followers a blow. In the morning the camp was empty. The cases of botanical specimens lay undisturbed, but the toy air-balloons had vanished. The pipes, the soap, the bird-warblers, the monkey, and the two concertinas remained, also a small amount of food – rice, flour, extracts of meat, and other medicaments which white men think that they require when travelling. It was panic not the loot-instinct which had cleared the camp of its carriers.

But the cause of the trouble – the propinquity of civilized man – was also the way out of it. Shouldering what they could of the things most necessary to life, and striking the downward course of the Ray River – here a baby stream, shallow and fordable, – they headed toward civilization.

Toward the end of the second day they came upon the sun-dried bodies of six natives planted head-downwards in the soil: their withered limbs trained upright on stakes, their dark leathery trunks still showing the scores of stripes borne by the flesh.

Davidina had been, for over a year, so far removed from civilization, that she did not know the latest things that civilization in its military necessities had been doing; nor had she at that time any clue for connecting this unsightly object-lesson with the pacific and missionary efforts of her brother Jonathan. But that night, coming into a white camp, well fenced and armed – offshoot of the larger expedition now actively out to impose peace by reprisals – she got the situation fully explained.

On the same spot where she had seen the impaled natives, a lay-missioner a few weeks earlier had been found dead from the same causes.

'This time we only managed to catch six,' explained the commandant; 'our regulation number is twenty.'

'Regulation number is good,' was her tart comment. 'It suggests order and discipline. Do you reduce the number as you go on; or do you increase it?'

'Increasing isn't much good,' replied her informant. 'These beggars can only count up to ten. We chose twenty as a good working average: it's the number we can generally manage to bag if we butt in quick enough.'

'But a higher scale,' said Davidina, 'would give you a better clearance: rid you of more dangerous characters.'

'Not necessarily. The dangerous ones can run. We only get what's left.'

'You are acting strictly to order, I suppose? Whose?'

'Trimblerigg's,' said the man.

'I'm Trimblerigg's sister.'

After that he treated her as though she were royalty – a little puzzled, however, not quite understanding her. Her dry ironic commendations were thrown away on him; he was the plain blunt man, doing his job honestly according to the light or darkness with which others provided him.

The information she got from him decided Davidina not to stay the night. The natives, it appeared, had a wonderful faculty for moving invisibly and without sound in the darkness; so in that camp throats were sometimes found cut in the morning; and Davidina wished rather particularly not to come to that end before she had seen Jonathan.

She spent the rest of that night and the whole day following in a canoe rowed by picked Christian natives; the two other members of the expedition going back under an escort to recover what could be saved of the impedimenta and botanical specimens which they had been forced to abandon.

Late the next evening she arrived ahead of rumour at the armed camp of the central mission. Off the river's landing-stage she met some one she knew who directed her to Mr. Trimblerigg's quarters. 'I think he has turned in. Shall I call him?' he asked.

'I'll call him myself,' she replied, 'if you don't mind. It will be a nice little surprise for him.'

He gave her the necessary password through the lines, for the camp was well guarded, double sentries everywhere.

CHAPTER TWENTY-SIX

The coming of a white woman seemed to startle them, being so much less explainable than a ghost; but she and her monkey got through. Coming to a window covered by a chick-blind and showing no light, she lifted the blind and looked in.

CHAPTER TWENTY-SEVEN

A Night's Repose

MR. TRIMBLERIGG, LYING ON HIS WELL-EARNED BED, was looking out through the dark canes of the chick at the large-eyed tropical night, when an opaque and curiously crested form entered his square of vision. The chick lifted, to the flash of a torchlight the crest detached itself, and a small scarlet-coated monkey leapt down on to the bed. This incongruous combination scared his calculating wits out of him; snatching his revolver he fired without aim.

The monkey, chattering in alarm, skipped back to the shoulder it had sprung from. 'Missed again!' said a familiar voice. 'How do you do, Jonathan? May I come in?'

She clambered in as she spoke, and sat upon the bed, while Mr. Trimblerigg, exclamatory with anger and apology, lighted the lamp and stared at the unwelcome apparition. Met under such nightmare conditions, they did not stop to embrace.

'So that was your object-lesson, was it?' said Davidina. 'Bad shot. What made you do it?'

'*You* made me do it!' retorted Mr. Trimblerigg sharply. 'A fool's trick, coming like that! How could I tell it was you?'

'You couldn't. But what are your sentries for? Haven't you enough of them to feel safe?'

Mr. Trimblerigg, defending himself, gave away more of the situation than he intended. 'Why, it might have been a sentry himself!' he exclaimed. 'You can't trust one of them.'

'Not even your converted Christians?'

'Not as things are now. Christians? – scratch the surface, and you find they go pagan again.'

'So you've been scratching them?'

'No need. They scratch themselves; it's reversion to type; the commonest disease missions have to contend with.

'And catching to civilization,' remarked Davidina; 'A scratch lot, all of you.' Then, as Mr. Trimblerigg looked at her with furtive suspicion, 'I've been interviewing a specimen,' she said; 'one of yours.'

She named her man. 'He seemed honest enough,' she went on, 'but he's been scratched badly, acting (*he* says) under your orders.'

Mr. Trimblerigg bristled to the implied criticism. 'He has only done what was absolutely necessary.'

'Necessary, of course,' she returned. 'You can always make a thing necessary if you want to. If a man sets fire to the tail of his shirt, he has got to get out of it. But that doesn't make him look less of a fool, Jonathan. Necessary? It's necessary, I suppose, that you should shoot people at sight before you know who they are. But if you mean that for an object-lesson, I don't find it attractive.'

'Object lesson of what?' demanded Mr. Trimblerigg.

'Yes, of what?' she retorted. 'It's not Free Evangelicalism, it's not common sense, and I don't suppose *you* think it comic either.'

Her accent on the word enraged him, as she had expected. 'I was only asking,' she said. 'You've your sense of humour, and I've mine, and they don't always agree. A man who can never see a joke is a poor creature; but when he makes a joke of himself and can't see *that* – he's past praying for. Did you say your prayers to-night,

Jonathan? You did? Then better say 'em again backwards, and see if you can't get more sense out of them.'
'Thank you,' said Mr. Trimblerigg. 'You mean well;
but I don't need to be told how to pray: I pray as I feel.'
'You do,' she said comfortingly. 'D'you ever look at your
tongue first to see your symptoms? No? Well, you should
then. There's nothing in this world so dangerous as
prayer if you've fixed up the answer before you begin.
Forty years ago, Jonathan, you set that trap for yourself,
now it's a habit you can't get rid of. Let's look at your
tongue. It's my belief you've got an attack of it now, worse
than usual. Either pray backwards from the way you've
been doing – which means don't begin by giving yourself
the answer – or leave off.'

Mr. Trimblerigg, who during the past six months had
been through deep waters and in his own eyes had done
valiantly, sat up quivering with indignation.

'If I hadn't prayed,' he cried, 'prayed all I knew, prayed
without ceasing – and if I had not depended every instant
on my prayer being answered in ways beyond human
power to devise, before this I should have been dead.'

'Yes,' said Davidina, 'and if you had aimed your last
prayer a little straighter, so should I. It missed – like
some of the others, I'm thinking. Two days ago I met
six of your prayers, as you call 'em, striped like a barber's
pole, dead as door-nails, standing on their heads in native
earth. They weren't exactly addressed to me; but I've
come in answer to them; and if you don't think it's the
word of the Lord I'm telling you now, Jonathan, put up
another and have done with me!'

Mr. Trimblerigg's sense of lifelong grievances came to
a head, and he spoke plainly: 'I shall never have done with

you, Davidina, never, never! All my life you've hated me, persecuted me, wished me ill. Yes; you've been sorry whenever I succeeded, glad when I've failed; and if I were to fail now, you'd only say – "Serve him right! Serve him right!"'

'That's true,' said Davidina; 'the rest isn't. Hated you? Don't flatter yourself! You wouldn't so much mind me hating you; it's my seeing through you that you don't like. "O Lord, so look upon me from on high that You don't see me clear as Davidina sees me!" That has been your life-prayer, Jonathan, though you never put it into words. Yes, to you it may sound like blasphemy, but if you'd prayed a little less to yourself, and a little more to me, maybe, you might not have cut so famous a figure in the world – been such a firework, setting a spark to your own tail and running round after it (which is what you are doing here) but there'd have been more meat on you for one to cut and come again than there is now. It's my belief, Jonathan, you don't truly know where you begin and where you leave off. You've been standing in your own light so long, and walking in it, that you see yourself a child of light every time you look in the glass. I've only to switch this torch on' – she played it upon him as she spoke – 'and you look like a saint in a halo, waiting for the Kingdom of Heaven to come. Yes, that's what you are always giving yourself – a halo; you've only to pray and it comes – like hiccoughs, or housemaid's knee. You touch a button, you switch on the light, and you see yourself in a glory. Some day you'll get one in real earnest; and when you do, I wonder what you'll make of it, and what people will say? I think they'll laugh.'

Mr. Trimblerigg looked at her with that same sort of

253

uneasy awe which weak saints have for the Devil. Under
her penetrating gaze he sealed himself to secrecy. This,
that she was saying – so nearly true, yet treating it as a
joke – was not a thing about which even relatively the
truth could be told. Davidina had no sense of the mysterious, and very little of the divine; she lacked reverence;
but her uncanny way of touching the spot did rather
scare him. He changed the subject hastily. 'Where have
you been all this time?' he inquired. 'You've come a long
way. How did you get on?'

Davidina, accepting the diversion, gave him a sketch of
her travels. He heard of the toy air-balloons, the bird-
warblers, and the soap-bubbles; the singing, and the playing, and the worshipping deputations of natives. Nor did
Davidina disguise from him the fact that she had allowed
godlike honours to be paid to her.

Mr. Trimblerigg, though he had used Relative Truth
for his own ends, could not, as a Free Evangelical, think
that was right.

'I dare say it isn't,' said Davidina, 'not as we think it. But
if you start applying your own sense of what's right to
natives, they don't think you a god, they think you a
devil. That's what you've been doing, Jonathan; and
devil's the result. And for my part, I don't see that it's
any more against true religion to let yourself be worshipped as a god than to make yourself feared as a devil. Devil
or god, it's one or the other – you can't get out of it; and
to be thought a god and to act accordingly does less harm,
comes cheaper, and makes things easier for all concerned.

'Anyway here's your object-lesson and there's mine. I
could have soon enough made them think me a devil if
I'd taken your line, Jonathan. So now, unless it's against

your religion, you'd better try mine for a change. Be a god, Jonathan, be a god! It won't be true; but believe me — sing, glory hallelujah! it's the better hole to fall into. And now I'm going.' So saying, she started to climb out the way she had come.

'Where to?' inquired Mr. Trimblerigg, astounded at so abrupt a leave-taking.

'Anywhere, so long as it's away from civilization — and you!' she declared. 'I'll send my specimens down to the coast, then go back the way I've come. And, Jonathan, if you get beautifully burnt out by a bush-fire in the next day or two, don't think it's them; it'll be me.'

'What for?'

'For fun, or for a moral object-lesson, just as you like to take it: Davidina's dose — or jumps for Jonathan. Good-bye!'

She had escaped — had already gone a few paces, when Mr. Trimblerigg bethought him and called after her.

'Daffy!' It was the old abbreviated usage from days of childhood. She returned, and stood outside the chick without lifting it.

'Well, what?' she queried.

And Mr. Trimblerigg's voice came cooingly from within: 'You haven't kissed me, Daffy.'

'I have not,' she replied starkly.

'But we haven't quarrelled, have we?'

'Quarrelled? Have I ever quarrelled with you yet, Jonathan? No fear! I've been saying your prayers for you — right way up. Now you say "Amen"; kiss yourself your own way, and go to sleep!'

She heard him chuckle; then in a whinnying tone, as he

stretched himself: 'Oh, you *are* a comfortable person to talk to!'

'You've said that before.'

'It's true. I'm glad you came, Davidina. You've given me a new idea.'

'I generally do,' she replied.

'But this is my own,' he insisted.

'So is the stuffing of a goose, once it's inside him,' was her retort. And with that she was gone.

And Mr. Trimblerigg, with the feeling that something now remained to his credit, turned over and went blissfully to sleep. For having let Davidina know that she was 'comfortable to talk to,' he had turned the sharp points of her arrows, and so robbed them of venom that not a word she had said troubled him any more.

So he gave his beloved sleep; and into his dreams came hovering the crocean dawn of that new idea, so entirely his own, prompted by Davidina.

CHAPTER TWENTY-EIGHT

Practical Idealism

WHEN MR. TRIMBLERIGG AGAIN WOKE, HE WAS HAPPY; he had an idea, and the idea was entirely his own. It was not less his own because it had flashed into life during his talk with Davidina, or because it ran on diametrically opposite lines (up to a certain point, at least) from his previous policy of black-and-tan stripes and head-downward reprisals.

The thing which had been 'absolutely necessary' the day before and on those grounds had been justified, was now a discarded, if not a discredited device. He had found a better. It was inconsistent, no doubt; for if it could be put into practice now, it could have been put into practice earlier, and the tarrings and the featherings and the rest need never have happened. But it is no good condemning Mr. Trimblerigg for his inconsistencies; they were as much a part of that strangely divided unity, his character, as the extreme notes which give the range of a singer's voice; and even when he had a divided mind, it served like the divided hoof of the mountain goat which gives nimbleness and elasticity to the tread. Often and often, because of his divided mind, his enemies did not know where to have him, nor sometimes where he would have them.

In these see-saw gymnastics his doctrine of Relative Truth helped him not a little. Mr. Trimblerigg never worried about methods; he judged himself only by results, and expected the world to have as short a memory as his own and to do likewise.

And I cannot deny that if results are a justification for doubtful faith and slippery dealings, results often did justify him; and many of his flashlight successes were won entirely because he had a mind of two parts diametrically opposed, which he never troubled to reconcile. They were there for alternate use and combined effect, just as oil and vinegar are used by a maker of salads – opposites resulting in a balance of flavour.

And undoubtedly, though they produced a mixed record, the tactical advantage was great. For what enemy of sane mind could anticipate attack from such opposite quarters as those chosen by Mr. Trimblerigg when he found himself in a tight place? It was not the simple strategy of a general whose armies came into action simultaneously from north and south; it was rather the conjuration of a wizard able to summon to his aid at the same moment and for a common end the hosts of Heaven and the powers of Hell – or of one who came offering peace, with a dove in one hand and a vulture in the other, undecided up to the last moment which of the two he intended to let go.

So it was when, in all the freshness of his new idea, Mr. Trimblerigg set out to play the god – the god of peace, mercy, and reconciliation to the expropriated natives of Puto-Congo; not because he regarded it as specially true to his character, or as the better hole to fall into – for to fall he did not intend; but because the coming of Davidina had made him realize that a sporting alternative to reprisals did actually exist; and being a sportsman by instinct, where matters of principle were concerned, he saw it adventurously as the obvious game to play.

Having made up his mind to it, he played it with a swift hand, and three days later set off unattended for the upper wilds of Ray River Territory (into which the elusive natives had gradually retired) with nothing to protect him but the safe conduct of one of their chiefs whom he had made captive, and whom he now released handsomely on parole to be his fore-runner and messenger.

And who, seeing him thus set forth, his feet shod with the preparation of the gospel of peace, his loins girt with truth, and having on the shield of faith, and the sword of the spirit, who, seeing him so arrayed, could ever have supposed that at the same time he had planned, swiftly and covertly, a forced march of armed missionaries by night to secure at dawn the ratification of an imposed treaty; and that the signal of their presence was to be – not indeed the dropping of bombs and the rattle of machine-guns (though the bombs and machine-guns were to be all there, primed and ready to let go), but a strain of holy voices setting forth the alternative thus presented, threat and persuasion combined, to the tune of the Puto-Congo love-chant, which from time immemorial the young warriors had sung in spring outside the wigwams of their beloved ones.

It was possible to suppose one or other of two such courses of action: but to imagine them inextricably combined as the single homogeneous plan of a sane mind was altogether beyond reckoning; only Mr. Trimblerigg could have thought of it, only Mr. Trimblerigg could have asked a blessing for it – as he confidently did, in his prayers, and have gone forth to the experiment assured that he had not only the bombs and the machine-guns with him, but the favour of Heaven as well. And though a word from Davidina had prompted it, he was quite right in saying that the idea was entirely his own.

And so at dawn of the third day his idea came to fruition, and Mr. Trimblerigg saw the desire of his soul and was satisfied. He had laboured for long hours in the rough

259

council-chamber of the tribe, and his efforts still hovered between success and failure, when the wailing sound of the love-chant arose in the woods without; and all the warriors, struck mute by the wonder of it, stiffened and sat up on their haunches. And as they listened they joined hands, and their faces softened as the growing light of day crept in through the wattled walls. Then Mr. Trimblerigg took up a banjo which he had brought with him, and though no expert as a musician, played his country's national anthem upon one note; and then 'Rock of Ages'; and then, in alternate phrases (*'Nothing in my hand I bring, God save our gracious King'*), the two tunes combined: a symbolic performance emblematic of the Treaty of Peace which he now called on them to sign. And there he was, still in their hands, confident, resourceful, self-assured, with nothing to save him from death but his calculative understanding of human nature, and the soft drift of the love-chant coming like bird-song from the wood.

Then, through his interpreter, he spoke the final word, in so persuasive a voice and with so smiling a face, that they could not but feel that all was now well; and with nod and grunt, and soft patting of palm on thigh, and slow swayings to and fro, they glimmered back at him, suspicious no more of one so equal and fearless, and confiding, sitting peacefully in their midst.

'Brothers,' he said, 'these are your white friends, who have come, feeling their way through the dark night with hands eager for the dawn, to know whether we have indeed made peace. We have, have we not? I told them that I should be here sowing seed fit for fruit-bearing, and that in the night it would take root, and grow, and become a tree wherein the love-singers would nest: I told them to wait and hope. But their hope was so great that they could wait no more; therefore have they come. Their eager hearts have led them through the blackness and terror of night to behold the glad faces of their dark brothers shining to welcome them. O Brothers, what matters a little giving and taking on this side or on that, if only we can be at peace, and share together the heat and light of the sun which are, indeed, so abundant that if we each take half it will be better for us. Hark! they have learned your song of love, and you shall learn ours; let us go out and meet them!'

He rose and led the dazed and awe-struck natives to the gate of their stockade; then, as it opened, skipped nimbly across to the shelter of that happy band of pilgrims, who, wearing white robes and carrying guns concealed under palm-branches, stood and smiled amicably upon the situation which Mr. Trimblerigg had prepared for them.

The faces of the chiefs fell; without a word they stepped back into the council-chamber where lay the drafted treaty, cut each a small wrist-vein and signed it in his blood. 'Our tribe will kill us for this,' said one chief as he affixed his mark. And two months later he was dead.

And Mr. Trimblerigg, having successfully won his point, by a judicious mixture of incompatible principles, was quite pleased with himself – and me. For while he took over most of the credit, he did not forget his stars for having made him the man he was. Grateful as well as gratified, and very tired after all his efforts, he fell asleep without having risen from his knees. And as ·in that attitude he slept the sleep of the just, with just a suspicion of the crocean dawn once more illuminating the pillow on which at sideway turn his head so confidingly rested, I felt once again that curious sense of helplessness which his achievement of a good conscience always imposed on me; and the old doubt recurred – difficult to put into words, but virtually to this effect: was the relation between us a reality or only a dream; did he belong to me, or did I belong to him? Was I using him, or was he using me? Ought I to consider myself anything more than a rather shining reflector of his brain?

All through the world's history there have been men doubtful of their makers, honestly incredulous of the source from which they sprung – infidels, sceptics, atheists – of lives too short to mark the changes, vicissitudes and final disappearance of the creeds they would not hold. Many such have I known with sympathy and with understanding; but Mr. Trimblerigg, so far as my experience goes, is the unique instance of that process reversed – one who has raised a like doubt in the mind of his creator. Was he really mine, or did I only dream of him as fantastically as he so often dreamed of me? Now he has gone from me, and I do not know: perhaps I never shall. But if in that other region to which he has now passed he has at last found not me but himself – and in that image has satisfied the requirements of his soul – can it be called a lost one – so far as he is concerned?

His work accomplished, he returned home. Incidentally the ship which bore him and his fortunes back to the old world encountered storm almost the whole way. But Mr. Trimblerigg's conscience was at peace, and he was not afraid. For myself I own that I was anxious; I never quite know how storms are going to end; and I did not wish, at this juncture, to lose Mr. Trimblerigg merely by accident.

Second Wind

M R. TRIMBLERIGG'S HOME-COMING, IN SPITE OF THE triumphal note sedulously given to it by his out-and-out supporters, was a sad one. He found Free Evangelicalism divided against him. His results had not wiped out the memory of his methods; and as there had been loud protest while these were still going on, there was now controversy as to whether they had in the least helped to the more peaceful *dénouement* which had followed. In the main his only backers among the Free Evangelicals were the armed missionaries who had carried out his policy, and the shareholders whose investments he had saved from ruin. And though True Belief had rallied whole-heartedly to the support of his more than Mosaic discipline – finding for it the warrant of Scripture – True Belief, in spite of the new importance thus given to it, was not the mould into which he could pour himself at this advanced stage of his career upon his return to civilization. Except in the mission-field, where he had used it to meet an emergency, its die-hard tenets were incompatible with Relative Truth; yet though some of its followers still held that the world was flat, and others that it did not go round, in a matter of religious war against the barbarism of savage tribes he could work with them, and in their eye-for-an-eye and tooth-for-a-tooth standpoint find the Relative Truth which served his need. But they, for their part, would not doctrinally budge an inch to come to him.

So when the main body of Free Evangelicalism turned against him, intimacy with True Belief stood rather as a liability than as an asset; though for a time it was a

question whether he had anywhere else to turn – whether
any religious connection large and lively enough to serve
his purpose was willing to have him except on terms into
which even his diversified record could not fit without
foolishness.

With the ruddy honours of Puto-Congo fresh upon
him, he stood for re-election to the Presidency of the
Free Evangelical Union, and got turned down. The blow
was a shrewd one, though he met it with a smiling face.
But when, following upon that, after long and heated discussion an adverse motion was carried by the executive
of the Free Evangelical Missions, whose organization
on its present vast scale owed its prosperity mainly to
him, then indeed he felt as though the bottom was being
knocked out of his ministerial career; and was almost
of a mind – of two minds, that is to say – to turn from
divinity to politics.

For in politics at that time events were moving fast,
creating for adaptable men opportunities of a new kind.
If, as seemed likely, the old two-party system was about
to give place to group-formations, whose tenure of life
must necessarily be more of a negotiable than a fixed
quantity, and if for the manipulation of democratic
government to a safe middling course, opportunism must
henceforth take a higher place than principle, could anyone be found with a more instinctive touch for the job
than Mr. Trimblerigg?

In the political world the situation was there waiting
for him: in the religious world, on the other hand, where
for the time being movement seemed retrograde rather
than forward, the situation would have to be made. It
was the tougher job.

264

CHAPTER TWENTY-NINE

To give Mr. Trimblerigg his due, that – if only he could find for it the right environment – would be but an added attraction. A tough job always delighted him; so much so that, setting his teeth to the toughness of it, he thenceforth forgot everything but appetite; and as his appetite always grew with what it fed on – given a proposition of sufficient toughness, his appetite was apt to go strange lengths. So it had been when he set out to hew Agag, and skin the scapegoat, giving to the fantasy that air of probability which it needed in order to make it popular; so likewise when he had to find moral excuse for standing Christianity upon its head in the burnt-out cinders of native villages, with the compulsorily converted Free State of Puto-Congo as his reward. In each case the toughness of the job and the moral difficulties it presented took the place of conviction, supplied the necessary enthusiasm, and jogged him on to his goal.

So it was to be now. All that he lacked for the moment was the necessary environment, the atmosphere into which a new spiritual movement could be born. In politics it existed; in religion it had still to be found. Mr. Trimblerigg hesitated; and while he hesitated the call came, the spark of inspiration descended from on high, and what thereafter was saved to religion in a revivalism which swept the world, was lost to politics.

Two events, small in themselves, gave to his mind the impetus and direction it required. The first was the death of the harmless, unnecessary Caroline, the wife whose previous uneventfulness had given to his career the only ballast it had ever known; the other was the recrudescence of Isabel Sparling, manufacturing for herself in the spiritual and religious world a success which arrested his

265

TRIMBLERIGG

attention, and awoke in his breast first a small spark of jealousy, then emulation and the determination, doing likewise, to make a bigger thing of it.

Caroline's death was due to obscure causes for which the doctor found a scientific name that satisfied all legal requirements; but if I have any qualification for diagnosing mortality in the human race, I should be inclined to say that she died of a gradual and cumulative attack of fright. Mr. Trimblerigg had once made her doubt the evidence of her senses — and not only of her own but of the children she had borne to him; and though she had acquiesced submissively at the time — having the negative proof always before her that the glory with which her imagination had surrounded him was departed, that he was in truth no saint, and had not after all taken his baths in cold weather — she was never the same woman again. That she should have imagined so difficult a thing, only to be told that it was a delusion after all, caused a shock to her system. Her breathing became asthmatic, she coughed with nothing to cough for, had flutterings of the heart, and began to wear shawls even when the weather was warm. And waking one night, [shortly after Mr. Trimblerigg's return from Puto-Congo had made them bed-fellows again, she saw or thought she saw upon the pillow beside her a recrudescence of her fear — the thing which could be seen but was not to be believed. Faint, very faint — the product only of a dream — it flushed feebly and passed away. But that single sight, or the mere suspicion of it, gave her a habit of wakefulness which grew on the apprehension that lay at the back of it; and just as people who see spots crossing the field of vision damage their eyesight by pursuing them, or as

266

others who have a singing in their ears go mad in trying to be quit of it; so did Caroline in trying both to realize and get rid of the suspicion she wished to avoid, reduce herself to a nervous wreck; and day by day, eyeing Mr. Trimblerigg with looks whose meaning she would not explain, sank into a despondency which by destroying her domestic efficiency robbed life of its remaining *raison d'être*.

And so one morning, after an ecstatic dream of more than usual vividness, Mr. Trimblerigg woke to find her lying very quiet and open-eyed beside him; and though the expression was not peaceful, Caroline had nevertheless found peace; and Mr. Trimblerigg with curiously mixed feelings, yet with a decent modicum of grief which was quite genuine, saw that he had become a widower.

Among the letters of condolence which reached him after the sad event — not immediately but a few months later — was one of peculiar interest from Sir Roland Skoyle, conveying not merely sympathy, but news. For it now appeared that Caroline was not as lacking in spirit as her life had made out; rather had she reserved it for future use. Caroline, in fact, had suddenly become interesting; and if she had not quite found herself again in the old world where her real interests lay, she had found her medium; she was there, waiting for her credentials to be put to the test, and asking for him with such urgency that Mr. Trimblerigg had a doubt whether he was yet free to consider himself a complete widower.

If, on that matter, he felt that his liberty was less than he could have wished, there was nevertheless a compensating interest; for here, in germ, was the idea he had been waiting for: if he could convince himself that

267

spiritualism was really true – his previous experience, though momentarily impressive had finally disappointed him – he would go on and convince the world. It was some such conviction that the religious world was now needing to spring it into fresh life; and he himself only needed confidence in the case to be presented, in order to become the man to do it. And so, at this point of his career, when he least expected it, Caroline became an important character.

It was a strange apotheosis; and the realization of its truth came to him in strange words at the first interview which Sir Roland Skoyle arranged for them. The medium, sitting entranced, was not in the least like her; but no matter. She breathed asthmatically, coughed, and holding hand to heart hugged an imaginary shawl. Taking her disengaged hand tenderly, he asked: 'Caroline, my dear, is that you?' And the voice of Caroline answered: 'I did see it, Jonathan; I really did! And I can see it now. You look beautiful.' Then, after a pause, 'Who have you got to mend your socks for you?'[1]

That was Caroline all over; and as conviction settled into his brain, her importance established itself. The conversation that ensued was trivial and domestic in character; it was, nevertheless, a world-moving event.

And the second was like unto it – in this at least, that a woman whom he had come to regard as of no importance assumed all upon a sudden a new significance and took her place once more in the shaping of his career.

Isabel Sparling, failing to find lodgment for her preaching powers in any home-grown community among the Free Churches, had passed on to America, where strange faiths and novel methods have always a better chance.

CHAPTER TWENTY-NINE

A stray paragraph in a newspaper gave him the news that among the Blue Ridge and Alleghany mountains she had achieved a startling success in the propaganda of Second Adventism. The rural population of Virginia, Tennessee, and North Carolina had begun robing itself in white; drawn by the spirit, thousands upon thousands of Last Day saints made periodical pilgrimages to the tops of the high mountains, and there picnicked for whole weeks at a time waiting for an Event which, though it failed to show visibly, always sent them back to their homes spiritually refreshed. Rain-baptisms — by preference in a thunder-storm — were another manifestation of the new faith. There were startling cases when a date had been fixed weeks beforehand; torrential rains had descended in answer to prayer and washed into renewed sanctity five thousand converts at a time.

Mr. Trimblerigg had always had a modernist's doubt about the efficacy of prayer either for fine weather or wet. But supposing these accounts to be true, Isabel Sparling was a water-finder of no uncertain power. If she had ever failed, the papers made no report of it; at any rate, in States where the rainfall was generally less than could be desired, the average was going steadily up, and conversion to Second Adventism had in consequence become popular. Manifestly she had got her stick by the right end; in this practical age a combination between revealed religion and good business was the one thing needful, and as the increased rainfall was welcome to a large agricultural interest, so also were the pilgrimages and the picnics to the retail traders. Pious people, who had hitherto been frugal stay-at-homes, were now spending a great deal upon white linen sunshades, Panama hats, shoe leather, thermos

269

flasks, mineral waters, cooked food of a portable kind and all other necessary accompaniments for outings conducted on a large scale. In a quite important slice of the States religion had once more become not merely popular but vibrant and all-embracing in its character. An 'urge' for righteousness had taken hold of whole districts where no 'urge' of any kind had been felt before; and what at first had only occurred in rural districts was now rapidly assuming a civic, a municipal, and a territorial character. It was announced that one State Governor at least, and the whole population of a large penal settlement were waiting to receive rain-baptism on the earliest date that Isabel Sparling's engagements with Heaven would allow.

Mr. Trimblerigg read and was impressed. He went further; he took steps to have the matter investigated, and while awaiting a further report he thought much. Over there something was moving which had affinity to the motions of his own brain; a sense of opportunity and of environment began to stir in the inner recesses of his soul. And when the report came – favourable in its main facts – he found all at once that he had recovered his spiritual appetite. The world was the right world after all; there was something in it waiting for him to do.

Nevertheless, for a man of his modern tendencies, Second Adventism was a big pill to swallow; he did not quite see how he was going to believe in it – sufficiently to make it a popular success, and for a while wondered whether he could not run spiritualism alone, with Second Adventism left out.

He consulted Caroline; she was stimulating, but rather vague. 'Oh, if you only knew, if you only knew, you could do anything!' she told him. 'Let your light shine, Jonathan! It's there, though you don't see it. If you did, you'd know the way. If you don't, it may go again, like it did before.'

That little imperfection of grammar, uncorrected in the spirit-world, gave Mr. Trimblerigg a fresh thrill of conviction that this was the real Caroline. How often, as they climbed the social ladder, had he corrected, a little impatiently, those symptoms of a lowly origin. But now it rejoiced his heart to hear her recount the beatific vision she had of him with homely incorrected speech 'like' she might have done before.

Yes, it sounded encouraging, but it still left him in doubt; there was too much 'if' about it. He wanted to be quite sure, without any 'ifs', before he began.

It was at five o'clock one morning, after a sleepless night, that the spark of inspiration swam into Mr. Trimblerigg's brain, and though it was not my sending — being entirely his own — I saw it come.

He was lying with his head on one side sucking a cough lozenge, when, with a sudden jerk of astonishment, first his eyes opened, then his mouth. The cough lozenge fell out, staining the pillow: he turned his head sharply, eyes front, and sat up.

The conception which had got hold of him was large but quite simple; he saw that Second Adventism depended for its success on one thing and one thing alone. If what he was pleased to regard as Christendom — that is to say, Free Evangelicalism and its dependent relatives among the Free Churches — if Free Evangelicalism could but be persuaded to believe in a Second Advent, and to desire it wilfully, whole-heartedly, passionately — then by the law of spiritual gravity, the Second Advent would come.

It was a great idea; Pragmatism, a thing he had only half-believed in before, would thus be given a test worthy of its powers – would, he believed, win through and make the world what it ought to be – theologically up to date. The saints under the Throne crying 'How long?' would suddenly change their tune, take up the initiative, and with spiritual Coué-ings themselves fix the date.

It was a bold democratic conception, and since he had always been a whole-hearted democrat there was no inconsistency – though he now thought of it for the first time – in applying it to things doctrinal. Man had his spiritual destiny – including dates – in his own hands; all he needed was unanimity or, failing that, a commanding majority. He had never had it, had never applied it till now. Had he done so the millennium would already have bloomed into being.

And the means to this spiritual unanimity, or commanding majority, by which the race was to be won? In the moment of inspiration that also had been flashed into his brain, and Civilization stood explained. The conquests of science were to become the weapons of faith, and publicity the final expression of religious art. What countless missionaries could not have done in a previous age a single voice would do now. All that was required was a world-wide audience of converts to Second Adventism, a voice going out into all lands, a trumpet signal, and a shout, and at that shout the walls of Jericho would fall flat:

> Faith would vanish into sight,
> Hope be emptied in delight,

and every man would go up straight before him and possess the city of his inheritance.

CHAPTER TWENTY-NINE

Nor had Mr. Trimblerigg any doubt – in that first flush of inspiration – whose the voice was to be. As for the trumpet whose blast was to rend the veil of a new world, science had providentially supplied the instrument. It would be a big business to get possession of it; but once done, it would be Big Business indeed. At the stroke of a wizard's wand – or call it Aaron's rod – trade and commerce were to become spiritualized, and the fiery chariot of Elijah would be found among men once more, conveying the voice of prophecy to the far ends of earth – in that moment, that division of a breath, that twinkling of an eye of which older prophecy had spoken. Or to put the matter quite prosaically – on that business footing which was to prove the secret of its success – a monopoly of Broadcasting throughout the English-speaking world was revealed to him as the means for the coming of the Kingdom on Earth.

'The coming of the Kingdom'? The phrase was picturesque; but it was old and obsolete. 'Making Heaven safe for Democracy' was better. That was what Mr. Trimblerigg intended to do.

S

CHAPTER THIRTY

' *Arise, Shine !* '

MR. TRIMBLERIGG'S ACCEPTANCE OF THE PHENOMENA
of spiritualism, though it drew mass-meetings to
hear him, gave a bad jolt to Free Evangelical unity.
Thenceforth pulpits were divided; and Mr. Trimblerigg
had the run of only half of them. But when, following
upon that, he announced his conversion to Second Adventism, a special conference of the connection was called, and
secession followed. Mr. Trimblerigg went out hopefully
into the wilderness, drawing a tail of all the Free Churches
after him; and though for a time they lacked funds, and
found many doors closed against them, they had not to be
long in doubt that theirs was the winning cause.

What the world wanted – the religious even more than
the secular – was a real bird-in-the-hand; proof positive,
quick results, practice not theory, ocular demonstration,
moral certainty, wheels which actually went round,
whose buzz could be heard to the far ends of earth. A
race for Heaven without obstacles, and a goal visibly to be
won were the materials to make religion once more popular. Spiritualism and Second Adventism run together
seemed to meet the demand. The Free Churches Militant began, in an expressive American phrase, 'to palp
with emotion'; and as the new spiritual Combine devised
by Mr. Trimblerigg, with joined effects of dark séance
and lurid anticipation of coming events, filled its hired
halls to overflowing with suffocating converts, the churches
grew empty.

With the sword of his spirit unsheathed and high uplifted, Mr. Trimblerigg did not spare his old associates
who hung back in this day of battle for the new birth of

spiritual democracy; and, to ears which had drunk in the sound of it, the old gang's trumpetings ceased henceforth to avail or mean anything. Starting upon his fiery crusade to the sound of a hundred drums hired for the occasion, he stood at the door of his Pulman car, in the special that had been provided for him, and flourished defiance to all opposers over the heads of the seething multitude which filled the terminus, frantic with joy at having found a leader whose single aim was to keep things on the run.

He stood there at the crowning point of his career; for here at last he had created his own atmosphere; at the touch of his magician's wand a new and densely populated environment had sprung up to spread itself round him. Power had been given him, vision, and the gift of tongues; the future of revealed religion in the Free Churches hung trembling in the balances of his mind.

But though it trembled (as it might well), he himself did not. From all over the world he felt a responsive rush of wings to meet him; the right button had been touched, his call to make Heaven safe for Democracy had come at last and the means to it had been found. All the rest had been but a preparation; this was the real thing.

The first sure proof of it was the readjustment of the news-headings in the daily press; Religion began to take a front place. In the beginning this perhaps was merely due to the novelty of the thing, with its attendant features of controversy and secession upon a large scale. But when weekly meetings all over the country, in the largest halls that towns or cities could provide, became an established feature of the new movement, it acquired not only a popular but a commercial importance as well; and when presently Mr. Trimblerigg did his first great stroke of business

– combining the earthly with the heavenly on a scale that
had never been attempted before – Big Business itself sat
up and began to pay attention. In less than six months,
for reasons soon to be explained, the Stock Exchange, for
the first time in its existence, became sensitive to the call
of Religion; and before the finish even the Bank-rate had
become affected by the vast scale of reinvestments in
other worldliness engineered by Mr. Trimblerigg. For
it was quite natural, was it not? – if the world was coming
to an end – that people should want to take their money
to Heaven with them. Mr. Trimblerigg obligingly provided them with a way, and even coined a new form of
currency to give it better effect, image and superscription
no longer Cæsar's.

But this is to anticipate. Before these things happened,
Mr. Trimblerigg's faith in himself had reached an in-
tensity which, except for outside assistance, it could hardly
have achieved. The impetus had come from an unexpected quarter, and at first had not been welcome.

It was characteristic of Mr. Trimblerigg, when he took
up with Second Adventism, to do so without acknowledging or even recognizing the source of his inspiration; for
it is safe to say that within twenty-four hours of making
it his own he had, by an acrobatic feat of mental detachment, put Isabel Sparling entirely out of his mind as having anything to do with it; and had almost forgotten her
existence in the whirl of his own discovery, when among
the rushing wings that flew to meet him from the far parts
of the earth, came first a message from Isabel, couched in
tactful terms, hailing him not as her follower but as her
leader, and then Isabel herself. Nor did she come with her
hands empty; she brought with her the proffered allegi-

ance of her own vigorous following, already some fifty thousand strong and going stronger every day; Rain-Baptists, Seals of Solomon, First Resurrectionists, Second Adventists, Last Day Disciples, New Jerusalemites – all these, so little known in their separate capacities, now joined together under her leadership in a common bond were a force no longer to be despised. And however little Mr. Trimblerigg might welcome the reminder that his inspiration was shared by another, he was too practical to reject the material thus offered him. Even though at home the movement was going ahead by leaps and bounds, a nucleus of fifty thousand souls in a country so impressionable as America was worth having: it meant at least a year to the good in solid spade-work; in publicity it meant even more.

But Isabel had something else to give beside adherents; something very unique and wonderful and precious –so, displaying it, she told him; nor was it the first time he had heard of it.

It was not much to look at: a small wooden box with a domed lid, and a cover of mildewed paper in an old-fashioned diaper; and around its rim were seven seals, chipped and blackened with age, two of them already hanging loose where the covering paper had detached itself. But though a poor thing to look at, it had of late years acquired fame, or at least notoriety; and the Press had made copy of it. For this was the box of the American prophetess, Susannah Walcot, dead now for over a hundred years but having followers still – the box concerning which she had said that it must wait till one wearing a crown should open it, and reveal to the world its prophecies concerning the last things. And because all the

crowned heads approached had refused to open it, and had
been much abused by the faithful remnant of her followers
for so doing, therefore it had remained sealed; till, coming
into the hands of Isabel Sparling, upon the adherence to
her teaching of the dwindling group which held it, it
brought to mind a bright particular head she had once
seen, which, though in no earthly or material sense, had
indubitably been crowned in a glory of its own, so fulfilling
the condition which the prophetess had laid down.

And that memory being in her mind when the treasure
came into her keeping, it may be guessed with what joy-
ous confirmation of hope she heard presently that the
once-crowned head had itself become a sudden convert to
Second Adventism. No sooner did the news reach her
than she felt that he was already hers; and having first sped
a message, a week later she was upon the high seas, on her
way to meet him, and the box with its seven seals, bore
her company.

At the Customs she expensively saved its sacred contents from profane scrutiny by declaring it to be a special
brand of tea hermetically sealed from sea-air. And as nothing of that weight could have cost her more, officials
with uncrowned heads took her word for it, and passed
into the country a prophecy destined to make its mark in
history, besides giving a neat finish to the career of Mr.
Trimblerigg.

What happened next must be briefly told; for I do not
quite know all the circumstances that lay behind it. With
the soul of Isabel Sparling I have had so little acquaintance
that I do not make myself responsible for it; only as she
came within range of Mr. Trimblerigg, and affected his
career, did she interest me. For which reason I must leave

unsolved the problem of the seven seals and what they con
tained at different dates, more especially whether they
contained different things before and after the day when
she actually took charge of them. I will only say this, that
Isabel Sparling was by the look of her an astute, a daring,
and a resolute character; nor do I think that for good and
great ends she would stick at trifles or have more scruple
than Mr. Trimblerigg himself. Also I have reason to believe that she knew her man; and it may well be that in the
gyrations of her emotional career, on which Mr. Trimblerigg's own orbit had had its gravitating effect, she may
have assimilated the doctrine of Relative Truth more than
one knows. And so whether it was genuine prophecy,
coincidence, or only Relative Truth which brought the
thing to pass, I leave each reader to decide according to his
own taste or credulity.

The initial fact is that when Isabel Sparling, obliterating
a disputatious past, again met Mr. Trimblerigg, in order
to make him the instrument of her vision for the Millennium that was to be, she did not find his head visibly
crowned. Nor had she expected it; yet she was puzzled
that it was not so. Such self-abnegation, to the foregoing
of a gift so uplifting and spiritual, though admirable as a
mere act of humility was not to be encouraged when a
world in flux was waiting to be saved not so much by
knowledge in things spiritual as by novelty, and when, in
consequence, anything in the way of signs and wonders
might be of so much help.

Miss Sparling had seen the manifestation, and had believed in it; believed therefore that what had been once
could be again. The circumstances under which she had
seen it, gave her grounds for suspecting that Mr. Trim-

blerigg had not then borne witness valiantly to the light which was in him, had in consequence lost it, and needed perhaps to be encouraged in order to find it again. She recalled also the case of Jonah: prophets were sometimes reluctant and had to be pushed. All that I have now to record is the pushing.

Outwardly it was very gently applied: Miss Sparling merely placed the box in Mr. Trimblerigg's hands for safe-keeping, and there left it. Inwardly? There after stating the facts, I can only leave others to guess. But be it noted that when she left it in his hands she did not ask him to open it; she even told him that only a crowned head could qualify for that purpose; and at that time at all events Mr. Trimblerigg was wearing no crown. Nevertheless – she having asked him to use his influence and persuade a crowned head to open it – the box lay in his undisputed possession. And, as I have said before, I think that Miss Sparling knew her man, and how best to have him.

And so it came about that, finding himself alone with it, though by no means yet convinced of its importance or the truth of its credentials, he became interested in it. The mere fact that a box has been shut up for nearly a hundred and fifty years makes it interesting – at least until it has been opened again: and this was a box claiming to contain prophecy.

Mr. Trimblerigg was no longer of a mind to reject anything which might bring grist to his mill. His discovery of Publicity as the wide gate and the broad road leading to eternal life, forbade him to dismiss as common or unclean anything which might seize the public interest. And his public was now in a mood to seize anything: a whirl of excitement had caught hold of the great semi-detached unsectarian forces of this transitional age; and the fact that he was emptying the Churches was sufficient proof that what the public wanted was something it did not get there. The Churches had ceased to prophesy; prophecy, therefore, might be the right card to play. Second Adventism was based on it: if anticipation was to be raised and seals opened, any old box might help; and this one had already attained publicity though not of a very serious kind. 'Can any real prophecy come from America?' had been the depreciatory attitude with which the religious communities of the Old World met its claims; and if from America, why this demand for a crowned head to open it? Why not a President, or a millionaire?

Mr. Trimblerigg himself, though doubting the extreme claims made for it, had never entirely rejected prophecy. Even when, for a brief spell, he had counted himself a modernist, the better to escape from the trammels of True Belief, he had still found a rhetorical use for it; and the Land of Promise with its flowings of milk and honey had oftentimes evoked soul-stirring utterances from his tongue which, when they failed to materialize, became mere figures of speech. But he would much rather that they had materialized; and had they done so would have claimed the credit for it. That precisely was, and always had been his attitude toward prophecy; if he could give its fulfilment he would claim credit for it; if not he would treat it as a figure of speech.

It was in that same attitude, tentatively, that he laid his hand on the box. It might be a good egg; but he did not want to commit himself publicly to anything that would let him down. He would like first to know more of the contents. Prophecy might be what his public required to complete the spell he had begun to lay on it; but the extant writings of Susannah Walcot, obscure, diffuse, and ungrammatical, together with the diminished number of her followers, did not inspire him with confidence; and so for the present his attitude toward prophecy, as he laid his hand on a box said to be full of it, remained unchanged, – he was only prepared to accept it conditionally – in his own time and in his own way; that is, if it suited him.

But as he stooped and examined the box, its structure as well as its possibilities began to interest him; for he noticed that though it had many seals at the top its bottom was quite removable; long rusty nails sticking out a little where the dried wood had shrunk, and at one point a gap where cautious leverage might be possible, suggested a way which in the interests of Relative Truth one might adopt. From one aspect – the one which practically did not matter – it was an equivocal and surreptitious deed; but as over everything else which might have held others in doubt, having quite made up his mind to it, he prayed long and fervently that he might be guided aright in what he did, and also that he might have sufficient skill in carpentry to cover up his tracks when the will of Heaven was done.

He worked at it very patiently for three hours, when the rest of his household was a-bed, till with gathered experience he acquired a standard which, if not skilled, allowed him to feel safe.

It was not hard work so much as delicate; the wood was tender and worm-eaten, the old-fashioned nails with screw-heads came out quite easily – too easily in fact, at first; bits of the wood came with them. This frightened him, he went more slowly. After a tedious period of minute labour the wood was ready to come away in his hand. With his attitude to prophecy still unchanged he lifted it away, and out of the box like a pudding from its mould came a compact mass of very yellow stained paper slightly stuck together by mildew, and dampness that had dried.

Mr. Trimblerigg saw at once that a long task was before him. The prophecies were in a small cramped hand with numerous contractions, and many words badly spelt.

Here and there the ink had gone faint; in other parts time and moisture had made whole passages undecipherable; portions of the prophecy had indubitably passed into oblivion; but far larger portions remained.

With the help of headings – titles symbolic in character – Mr. Trimblerigg began skimming. At first sceptical and a little bored, he presently grew interested; and though not yet convinced, he saw that from the publicity point of view the thing had possibilities. This, for instance, he regarded as an arresting passage:

'And lo, when the Cock, stricken by the double-pated Eagle, draws in its claws, causing the Scarlet Parrot to fall from its perch, then shall a city fall and a people go free, and the mark of the Beast that was on it shall be blotted out.'

Mr. Trimblerigg, questing this way and that, searched his history; and when presently his mind lighted on a likely spot, he found there an astonishingly close parallel; for this, clearly, was – or could be taken as – a reference, couched in unfriendly terms, to the Papacy's loss of Temporal Power in the year 1870, owing to the withdrawal of the French troops which protected it.

283

Presently he began to feel that he was missing things through not knowing as much about modern history as he ought to do; and that a great deal that he was reading might possibly be true could he but discover the application.

Presuming that the prophecies followed a chronological order, he turned on, and before long had struck substance. Here he was no longer out of his depth.

'When the Bear and the Lion and the Cock shall rise up and stand together in a heap, and become as one for the defence of a Lamb that was without blame –' This clearly was modern history, and though not quite true history it was the kind of history that was still being swallowed by the Public for which Mr. Trimblerigg had to cater. This at all events was the sort of thing that would go down; there was, in the journalistic sense, good copy in it.

At first Mr. Trimblerigg had inclined to suppose that 'the Lamb' had a scriptural significance; he soon decided, however, that it was better for it to mean Belgium; without making the prophecy more true it made it more obvious.

This wresting of the text to suit his possible requirements was a sufficient indication that now Mr. Trimblerigg's interest had become active. His attitude to prophecy had not exactly changed, but it was being accentuated. He was beginning to see Opportunity upon a large scale; in fact he was not far off from becoming a Susannah Walcotite. With hope mounting to enthusiasm he read on.

Startling analogies began to come thick and fast; with a whirring of wings like coveys put up from fields of unreaped harvest – invisible at one moment, at the next dominating the whole landscape, they flew over his head making a plumed darkness on the bright heavens beyond. From this strange scripture, diffuse, chaotic, with pages not numbered, he began to take notes. Amid much that he did not understand and a good deal which might mean anything, certain figures leapt into definite significance, capable of meaning but one thing only.

'When the Striped Eagle is seen walking upon the waters with his face to the sun,' was the entry of America into the War. It is true that, in the first instance, he read the third word as 'stupid'; but on consideration of the facts and the post-war susceptibilities of America, he decided that 'striped' was better. And there was more like unto it.

Then, turning for awhile from its theme of nations at War, the prophecy became personal and particular.

'And in that day behold a man shall arise and become a beacon; in him a candle shall be set up, and its wick shall be kindled, so that the four corners of the earth shall know of it. His light shall shine; yea, men shall see it and be amazed. Honour shall be upon his head; and whatsoever he sayeth shall come to pass; his hand shall prosper it. My "yea" shall be upon his lips, and my yolk upon his shoulders; to his voice the "yea, yea" of the nations shall answer: they shall be all yolked together because of him.'

Susannah's spelling was often queer; but as I read this, looking over Mr. Trimblerigg's shoulder to do it, I began to think that her spelling was sometimes inspired; for I saw now what was coming.

Turning a page, – a page which stood somehow by itself, mildewed like the rest, but with most of its script obliterated – Mr. Trimblerigg read on:

'He is my prophet, my messenger; unto Nineveh have I

called him; yea, I have given him a name that he may be known, that he may be called the second Jonah. Than him none shall be more exalted; and of all feet that run no feet shall run faster.'

Jonathan sat up; his name almost *was* Jonah; and with the word that followed, dropping only an H, the anagram was perfect. Uplifted and entranced, he read on:
'When I call him, he shall be afraid; but though he fears me I will run after him. Yea, I will run while I wait; and though I bide my time yet will I catch him. When I make my light shine on him he shall be in doubt; I will withdraw my light from him, so that in darkness he may learn and know. I will put my hook in his mouth and lead him; yea, I will bait his breath so that he may become a catcher of men. He shall travel west, but east he shall return: he shall go far, but I will make him come again. Yea, the ship whereon he goes shall be shaken because of him; the rigging thereof shall tremble. Have I not given him a name?'

Mr. Trimblerigg no longer merely sat up, he skipped to his feet. Only one letter – the letter 'i' was missing to make the prophecy absolute. But proper names, he remembered, were very seldom correctly spelt in old days; and it had ever been a source of pride to him to know that upon his father's side, far back, the family had been illiterate for generations.

'Trimblerigg!' 'And the rigging thereof shall tremble. Have I not given him a name?' What could be plainer than that?

He continued to pore over the quaint crabbed writing, with its misspellings and its occasional misconstructions, – a style of grammar belonging to the half-educated of a century ago, but not much worse on the whole than the bad Greek of the New Testament. Was bad grammar and bad spelling a reason for rejecting a message so high? In the world's eyes he feared it would be. In the worldly sense this Susannah was but a half-educated person; sometimes she made prophecies which he not only failed to identify, but which even seemed contradictory, in a wrong tone, out of place. This, for instance, presented a meaning less doubtful than undesirable; he had no use for it:

'In that day the Lion and the Ass will lie down together; they will share a bed, they will eat hay together, and the heart of the Lion shall wax faint, and his thoughts grow foolish. And the Lion shall listen to the voice of the Ass, and shall think it wisdom. For the Ass shall bray and speak, saying, "It is going to rain"; and immediately it shall do so. Then shall the Ass say, "Come into my stable; for there I have a place prepared for thee, where it does not rain." So shall they rise up and go, the Lion and the Ass together; and in the stable they shall find one waiting for them with his tackle prepared; and he shall let down his tackle upon their backs and harness the two of them, the Lion with the Ass, and the Ass with the Lion, making them to be a pair under one yolk. And all their apples shall be in one cart; and the man, the owner of the Ass shall drive them whither they know not.'

Mr. Trimblerigg read the passage twice; he did not like it, it perturbed him. Assuming the Lion to mean what he thought it to mean, this was an event which no reading of history could justify: it never had been true, it never would be true. In the other prophecies it was quite evident that the Lion was the chosen beast, well-pleasing to the Lord; how, then, did it come into this forecast of divine dispensation that the Lion should go so far astray?

And who the dickens was the Ass? He looked ahead wherever he saw Ass and Lion figuring together; and the obscurities and perversities of the prophecy became more confounding. The Lion was clearly not doing the right thing; it was following the Ass into a course of action which was leading to no good, which was, in fact, morally wrong; and so far as he could place the prophecies in their chronological sequence, these misdoings must some of them be quite recent, and some actually taking place now. Unedified, he began turning the pages in haste, to find something better; and so doing – it was a pity! – managed to miss this, which caught my quicker eye:

'And the Ass said to the Lion, "Let us drive the scapegoat into the wilderness and there skin it; and from the skin of the scapegoat let us make coats for ourselves and for our children." And the Lion said, "Will it be enough?" And the Ass answered, "It shall be enough; for we will stretch it this way and that and make it enough; or if so it be not enough, then we will wait till a second skin be grown, and will take that also; and after that another, and another, till we be satisfied." Then said the Lion, "But if he die of it, how shall we be satisfied?" And the Ass answered, "We will not let him die, till we be satisfied." So together they drove the scapegoat into the wilderness, and there they lost him. And the Lion reproached the Ass saying, "Where is the skin of the scapegoat that you promised me?" And the Ass answered, "A proposal is not a promise, neither is a promise a performance. Let it suffice that we have driven the scapegoat into the wilderness, and that he will presently die there. What matter how he dies, so long as he does die?" But the Lion said, "I have no coats for my children, and I am not satisfied."'

Had Mr. Trimblerigg read that, I wonder what he would have made of it? Had he done so his attitude toward prophecy might have altered. He might have given the box back to Isabel Sparling 'unopened,' without having found what followed.

This was a separate enclosure of folded tissue paper, spotted and yellow with age, broken at the folds, and very frail to the touch. It was sealed with the seal of the prophetess; but a single seal on paper presented little difficulty to Mr. Trimblerigg. With great circumspection and delicacy of handling he applied the hot blade of a knife, lifted the seal away, and laid open the contents. A wash-drawing in sepia on mildewed paper was what met his eye. From the artistic point of view it was very poor and amateurish; but to say that it interested him were to put the matter very mildly indeed. It represented a man with rather short legs, middle-aged, somewhat full in the body, and clad in a full-skirted coat. As a forecast of present-day fashions it was not very good; but the legs were in trousers, not knee-breeches, and the head did not wear a wig.

It was the head that most interested him; a large spot of mildew had partly obliterated the features, but not enough to obscure the type. The face was broad, the cheeks were smooth-shaven, the forehead was noble, the hair rather long, and curled up at the ends like the hair of the knave of hearts in a pack of cards; a large bow-tie sat under the chin, – the black tie of a Free Church minister. Underneath were the words, 'Behold the Fore-runner!' And again, underneath that, were these words of Scripture:

'Arise, shine, for thy light has come, and the glory of the Lord is risen upon thee!' Around the head was an indubitable halo; and faint, very faint, upon the blank space of it to right and left, the initials 'J' and 'T.'

CHAPTER THIRTY-ONE

The Procession of a Flea

MR. TRIMBLERIGG STOPPED TO BREATHE; AND WHILE
he did so I made a psychological examination of
that poor work of art which was yet, in its way, so perfect
a masterpiece. Had Mr. Trimblerigg been more of an
expert in old wash-drawings and brushwork, had he been
gifted with a more sceptical turn of mind than that which
had fitted his views to such differing situations, he might
have examined those initials, and that spot of mildew
defacing the supposititious features, more minutely,
analytically and chemically than he actually did. That the
wash-drawing as a whole was well over a hundred years
old any expert would probably have agreed; whether he
would have given the same date to the initials, and a few
other salient touches I had my doubt, and the doubt
remains unresolved; no expert has ever been called in to
decide the matter. If Miss Sparling herself limed that
snare, she certainly did it well; the obliteration of the face,
with just the suggestion of a likeness left, was finely controlled; and yet the control may have only been Father
Time's; and whether it was luck, or whether Susannah
Walcot was in truth a prophetess of penetrating power,
who is now to say? The lengths to which the human
faculties can go have often filled me with astonishment;
Mr. Trimblerigg was only one instance among many. On
this occasion, however, he did not astonish me in the
least; he did what I expected him to do.

Before that culminating piece of evidence – that silent
but resounding call – he sank upon his knees, and remained on them for a long time.

I watched the motions of his mind; they were very

interesting; but they had not really to go far. That he
was called to be a shining light to the whole civilized
world did not at this stage of things surprise him. As a
probability he had thought so ever since he could remember; recently he had been made sure of it. It was only the
strange manner of this final call, and its clearly miraculous
accompaniments that did a little stagger him. It also
caused a definite shift – a shift to the right – in his always
adjustable theology. It drew him definitely from modernism back toward True Belief. For this was something
with which modernism could not be reconciled; it was
primitive, apocalyptic, ultra-evangelical, it made, amongst
other things, for the literal interpretation of Scripture: if
this was true, the other was not.

And so it became clear that in accepting the call from
such a source, his own cast of faith must be simplified
once and for all, – that he must revert to the earlier faith
of his Uncle Phineas.

Uncle Phineas was right. It might still be true that the
sun did not actually go round the earth, that the earth
was not literally fixed, or flat, as Uncle Phineas had wished
him to believe; but there was nevertheless a principle of
fixture in eternal truth, fixture rather than evolution or
motion, going much deeper into the nature of things than
he had supposed. He became, all at once, curiously doubtful of his doctrine of Relative Truth, for he saw that to his
exposition of this more divine and direct dispensation it
might prove a hindrance.

It was for his followers he was now troubled. As regards
himself he had no difficulty in getting rid of it. For the
recovery of that purer faith his early training now stood
him in good stead, and Uncle Phineas became a rock in

whose shadow he could hide. What he had trained himself to believe in his 'teens, what he had broken away from in his early twenties, what he had exploitively used for opportunist purposes in the propaganda of war and of Mosaic reprisals on savages who could not otherwise be taught better, was still in his blood – waiting to give him the upward push. In his new childlikeness he thanked whatever gods there be that he had always treated with tender allowance and regard the primitive views of Caroline, both as wife and mother; and that he had never allowed the scepticism of Davidina – Davidina, who had now found a new sphere for her dispensing powers in the exploration and humane taming of savage tribes – to discolour the rainbow gradients of his mind. The theological problems she had maliciously presented to him in old days, he had happily ignored: they had at least done him no permanent harm. Reversion to type, in his case at all events, was not difficult. In a certain sense Relative Truth helped him; for even if the simpler faith were not as absolutely true as it now seemed to him, it was true relatively to the immediate purpose in hand. And so still, as one might say, upon two legs – one numbed and quiescent but the other lithe and active – he entered confidently and with singleness of purpose into the Kingdom that had been prepared for him.

Going up to bed in the small hours he was very tired, and did not stop to look in the glass, did not stop to do anything. He switched out the light and got into bed. Only then did the great recovery he had made dawn on him.

Turning his head sideways in comfortable adjustment for slumber, he saw upon the pillow a patch of yellow light, faint, but for small immediate use efficient. In the centre of its radiance marched a flea.

Mr. Trimblerigg did not like fleas; he made an instinctive pounce, and the flea died the death. Then the wonder of it occurred to him. He sat up, he got out of bed, he went to the glass. In the darkness he could see himself: Crocean dawn was round him once more. His surreptitious action of the last few hours, Heaven had now justified. He had no longer any doubts, any fears; he did not even see difficulties, for now the world was running to meet him, and millions of his fellow-creatures were prepared to take without question anything he offered them.

Faint with bliss, he tottered back to bed, laid his crowned head upon the pillow, and slept.

CHAPTER THIRTY-TWO

The Procession Continues

THE NEXT MORNING THERE WAS A SMALL FLY IN THE ointment of his bliss; a letter from Davidina. Thousands of miles away, among the swamps of the Amazon, news had apparently reached her of her brother's marvellous doings; and of course, as he might have expected, her comment sounded the note of criticism.

'My dear Jonathan,' ran the letter, 'if you go on like that, you will burst.

'Yours affectionate,

'D. T.'

The letter came too late. Mr. Trimblerigg no longer cared what the far-removed Davidina thought of him. Her long-distance pin-pricks had lost their medicinal virtue. 'Puff!' he remarked airily; and as he flipped the letter into the waste-paper basket, his fate resumed the jiggety tenor of its way, and the bursting process went on. For in the last few hours Mr. Trimblerigg had greatly fortified himself by prayer, so that his good opinion of himself was now undeflectable; and the old helpless feeling, which his attacks of prayer so often gave me, had come upon me once more. But this time I was rather enjoying it, and was very much interested, wondering how far – left to himself – Mr. Trimblerigg would go.

If ever the human race comes to read its own history, without prejudice, or blindness, or superstition, it will discover as never before what a tremendous part answer to prayer has played in man's making. As never before: for the strangest part of that discovery will be from which end the answer to prayer has come. Man claims many virtues which he does not possess; but he has also a few which he does not know; and if my materials have sometimes disappointed me, and inclined me to think that, on the whole, the making of man was a mistake, I have only had to turn and watch him in his marvellous manufacture of answers to his own prayers, to feel afresh the encouragement and diversion with which the work of creation has provided me.

Under the auspices of a thousand religions, which cannot possibly all of them be true, operated in the interests of gods who are, or who were some of them, no better than they should be, prayer has always been answered. And the more firmly man has held to that faith bowing before the dark altars of his strange and shifting creeds, the more surely and swiftly has he evolved and made for himself a life worth living, and for me a spectacle worth contemplating.

Had all those Heavens to which he addressed his prayer really sent back the answer, bobbing it like a cherry to the open mouth of the supplicant, what a poor effete parasitic thing he would have become! But because the Heavens were more aloof and the gods much harder of hearing than he knew, or because a wise silence was the true air from which his spirit drew breath of life, therefore has man, left to answer himself from that Kingdom of Heaven which is within him, become the overruling factor of his still changing and troubled world; possessing himself of the lies wherewith priestcraft has so generously provided him, he takes and turns them into truth.

And so, by prayer, he has made history. But, though he has told many tales to the contrary for the bettering of his faith, has anything ever really happened in his contact with wind or weather, seed-time or harvest, storm, earthquake, eclipse, course of sun and moon, that he has not brought about himself? He still talks of the evidence of his senses: but there the evidence of his senses stands immemorially before him, and he still does not believe them! In spite of all the Bank-holidays and National Fêtes that wet weather has spoiled for him, inflicting disappointment and misery upon millions of his fellows out for a snack of holiday whose date cannot possibly be changed — in spite of that evidence staring him in the face, he still thinks that I am the clerk of the weather, and prays to me about it, and still likes me; and does not think me cross-grained, or spiteful, or revengeful, because I have spoiled so many of his holidays! Truly, with all his faults, man is the most marvellously forgiving creature that was ever made — or else the most inconsequent in all those matters which are called matters of faith.

Often and often have I had cause to wonder at the things which man found possible to believe: his queer creeds, his superstitions, his transference of justice from this world to the next, his appetite for making his gods like himself in their bad as well as in their good qualities; and then for making them unlike himself, with miraculous powers, attended by signs and wonders, and visitations, and unexpected happenings, which even in his insurance policies he calls 'acts of God.' All these things fill me with amazement that any man should believe in them as having any spiritual significance whatsoever. But when I consider how many believe that I provide the weather for Bank-holiday and harvest, and can change it at will, then I have to admit that man can make himself believe anything if once he starts praying about it. And so it was quite natural that having prayed about himself so long and

297

earnestly, Mr. Trimblerigg should also believe in himself as much as he did.

And so upon its second advent, Mr. Trimblerigg's halo was a great success. It did not have to appear unexplained; a public meeting was arranged for it. And there with due solemnity for the strengthening of faith the box of Susannah Walcot was brought forth like a new ark of the covenant; and a crowned head, having first prayed to be guided aright, broke the seals, drew out the contents, and read extracts, and coming upon an illustrated page was for putting it modestly aside, when his hand was stayed by the vigilance of Isabel Sparling. After that the success of Susannah's prophecies was assured. Judiciously edited they caused a tremendous sensation, arousing also, in the episcopal churches, derision and furious opposition.

It was the finishing touch requisite for full success. With that final push Second Adventism, under the ban of the older theology, moved on from strength to strength. In the Free Churches it swept the board, and not many months later candidates for holy orders, in all congregations where the incumbents were democratically chosen, had little chance of selection unless they came as certified converts to Spiritualism, Second Adventism, and the prophetic writings of Susannah Walcot. The organ of the movement, *The Last Trump*, displaying on its cover an ace of hearts with rays emanating, ran into a circulation of millions. And though its opponents might call it 'The Artful Card,' and its radiant editor 'The Artful Dodger,' and publish parodies of the prophecies as they appeared in weekly instalments, its scope and influence became more and more irresistible. In the price and extent of its advertisement columns alone it was only beaten by that most popular of all ladies' journals *The Toilet Table*. And even *The Toilet Table* in its editorials was kind to the movement, and gave prominent reports of its preachers and the smartness of its congregations.

Indeed before long there were scarcely any other congregations worth talking about outside the high and dry pale of Episcopacy. And then, against that also, Mr. Trimblerigg struck his blow. A brief announcement without boast or comment, in *The Last Trump*, told that exclusive arrangements had been made by Second Adventism for the broadcasting of Mr. Trimblerigg's orations, every Sunday, morning and evening, at the competitive hours of divine service.

At that scrapping of its preachers, Episcopacy became active, appealed to public opinion for its protection, and found that it was too late. Within a month informal disestablishment had become its lot; and though with its endowments and its powers of preferment left, it remained rich, and in its own narrow circle influential; it ceased to count as an organization of national importance. And meanwhile, in surreptitious driblets, adherents of the Free Church rump – Baptists, Congregationalists, Methodists, Free Evangelicals were passing over to the ranks of Second Adventism.

How, indeed, could any who did not accuse Mr. Trimblerigg of demoniacal possession – which was the cry of the 'Scarlet Parrot' – do otherwise? For here, undeniably, was a light that shone, which only spiritual agencies could explain; and, good or bad, the world must make its choice, and camp accordingly. For the most part it camped where the extraordinary phenomenon could best be seen

– that is to say among Mr. Trimblerigg's audiences, which now – aided by loud speakers – had become vast, occupying almost daily a deserted stadium, where an ephemeral exhibition, having burned out its six-months' popularity, still stood with only its shell of lath, plaster, and paint, awaiting the dissolution of time. Into that vast auditorium, in all weathers, wet or dry, special trains, running to the exhibition terminus, poured their thousands day after day. And day by day the world's conviction that it was coming to a speedy and a prosperous end, increased and became a fever raging through the body politic, unstabilizing the currency, doing certain vested interests much harm, but others much more good.

When it was announced that Second Adventism had become a co-operative company for the conversion of Commerce to the reception of the New Jerusalem, presently to appear upon earth in concrete form, and when Mr. Trimblerigg promulgated a great building scheme – mainly of the said concrete – by which the vision was to materialize on the ground where the derelict Exhibition with its plaster palaces stood awaiting decay, then began ugly rushes on the Stock Exchange, a sharp shifting of investments; and between Big Finance, Episcopacy, and the Liquor Trade a desperate alliance was formed – quite as in the old days of Mr. Trimblerigg's early career – sign that at last the real issue was to be joined, and that there were interests in the world – and powerful ones – which Second Adventism did not suit.

Mr. Trimblerigg, though it often annoyed him, was not the kind of man to fear opposition when it came. He did not avoid the challenge, he went out to meet it. But he saw that the tussle was coming, and in order to gain access of strength as expeditiously as possible for the ordeal that lay ahead he decided that the psychological moment had come for him to visit America.

Offers of a sensational character had, of course, already reached him. One Lecture Agency had assured him that if his halo would stand the change of climate, a scientific investigation, and the nervous strain incidental to a daily appearance before mammoth audiences, it could guarantee that thousands should be turned away in every city, and no seats sold to the public under five dollars a head.

Mr. Trimblerigg, when the time came, decided otherwise. He announced that admission was to be free. When America heard that, it first fell down and worshipped him, then in panic began to mobilize its army, double its police force, set up steel barricades and enlarge its cemeteries in order to cope with the record crowds and the ensuing mortality which would result. The problem of how to deal with countless multitudes all ruthlessly set at whatever expense to life and limb, on seeing a real halo alive on a man's head, and hearing the man's head speak from the midst of it, occupied the head-lines of the newspapers for weeks, even before Mr. Trimblerigg started on his voyage. And when he had started, then all the reporters of the American press chartered a ship and went out to meet him.

It was then that Mr. Trimblerigg was asked the historic question what it felt like to be the greatest man in the world. And Mr. Trimblerigg answered that it made him feel shy; and the next moment could have bitten his tongue out for having fallen so easily into the first trap which an expert in publicity had set for him.

It did not in the least really matter. It made good copy;

and though it also made the judicious smile, the judicious
– always an insignificant minority – in an affair conducted
on so vast a scale did not count.

'Trimblerigg charges that he is the greatest man alive,'
was an unfair way of putting it; but it could not be described as untrue. And so he just had to live it down.

He did so without any difficulty. He was in a country
where only the statue of Liberty shared the distinction
that he carried about with him; and while her halo only
shot out in separate rays from perforations concealed under
her crown, his was a perfect round, it went out everywhere; it was also alight continuously day and night.
The torchlight procession organized up Fifth Avenue to
greet its arrival was thrown into the shade by its ever-
increasing vitality. The torches were a foolish excres-
cence, they interested nobody; and though five miles of
them impeded the distant view, the one central fact out-
shone them all.

The reporters, dealing with that central fact, after a brief
attempt to be facetious had become hushed and awe-
struck. Their public would not allow them to be otherwise; America, having gotten a live halo to its shores, was
not in a mood to have its genuineness questioned, the
mystery of its origin derided, or any other slight put upon
its dignity. It became a thing inviolate, sacred as 'Old
Glory ' herself; and when an unfortunate youth, unim-
pressed by the beauty of its holiness, shouted a derisive
remark at its passing, the crowd lynched him for it. After
that minority opinion became as terrorized from expressing
itself as it had been while the 'Liberty Loan' was voluntar-
ily subscribing for America's entry into the war. There
was no half-way safety point left: those who doubted the

divine origin of Mr. Trimblerigg's luminosity were regarded as Satanists; and when here, as in the old world, Episcopacy persisted in holding out, the genuineness of its Orders began for the first time to be generally doubted, and the numbers of its adherents seriously diminished. No wonder that even the 'Movies' became afraid of him, and offered him fabulous sums to turn film-artist, on the single condition that during his term of contract he would keep himself hid from the public eye.

And so, if anybody had laughed at Mr. Trimblerigg's ingenuous answer on the question of his greatness, the laugh speedily died down, having left nothing to feed on. For if Mr. Trimblerigg was not the greatest man in the world, he was, at all events, the greatest success. In a single week he had made America believe in miracle; after which, from such a source, America was ready to believe almost anything.

His first message was delivered from the plinth of the Statue of Liberty in New York Harbour, to an arrangement of loud-speakers which enabled him to be heard from Newark round by Staten Island to Brooklyn; thence, to a yet wider circle – embracing the greater part of the western hemisphere – broadcasting took up the tale, and if not quite making the world one, making Mr. Trimblerigg its sole topic of conversation.

Record crowds attended the performance; two ferryboats capsized under the one-sided weight of the thousands who jammed the upper decks. The churches, smarter in the uptake than those of his own country, were satisfactorily filled; for there also loud-speakers adorned the vacant pulpits, and congregations of a hundred denominations hung upon his lips.

In that there was a danger, since verbal inspiration was now generally ascribed to him: and Mr. Trimblerigg being one of those orators who, when they let themselves go, are never quite sure what they may say, – or, afterwards, what they actually have said, – found it very hard to keep within safe bounds, or to withhold certain inspiring facts which he believed himself to possess.

He knew, for instance, the day on which the world, as regards its present dispensation, was to end. Susannah Walcot had given her word for it; but hitherto the Council of the Second Adventists had decided not to publish it, – to keep it till their position had become more absolutely assured, and the world psychologically ready to receive it.

But it was very difficult for Mr. Trimblerigg, when a whole continent was rushing into a state of conversion, and millions listening fervently to his daily orations, it was very difficult to keep back, in moments of inspired utterance, a declaration which would give the *clou* to the whole movement, letting organized society know in definite terms how brief, how startlingly brief, was its time-limit, before that great cataclysmic change which would take and turn it upside down.

And so one day, in a moment of effervescence, Mr. Trimblerigg let it out. And having done so, there was no going back on it.

With many millions already declared converts, and at least as many more hovering upon the brink, waiting for the deciding push, Second Adventism in that act of inspired indiscretion revealed its weakness and its strength. Western civilization (the East staying strangely unmoved, sceptical, slightly amused) received a shock comparable to a renewed outbreak of war. It was as though a half of the world had leapt to its feet in startled amaze, then staggered and plunged. For then on all the stock exchanges the wildest rush for reinvestments began that had ever been known, and mainly for shares in the vast co-operative concerns of New Jerusalem Ltd. which had been set going before his departure to America by Mr. Trimblerigg. A city designed to hold a million souls – self-governing, self-supporting, with its own trade-tokens for currency, and closely encircled by an agricultural combine exclusively supplying its needs from day to day – was now being rushed into being before the astonished eyes of a metropolis which had hitherto regarded itself as the biggest thing of its kind in the world.

But if, in less than a year, such a city could spring up mushroom-like from the soil, with a mere used-up playground set about with toy palaces as its nucleus, what might it not do within a decade under a new dispensation? Its huge neighbour, unplanned, haphazard, fortuitous in the slow growth through which it had attained its present dimensions, and replete with vested interests opposed to so dislocating a change, paled at the mere thought of it. But the plan was already in operation, building was going on; and half the farmers and dairymen of the surrounding counties had signed contracts of future service entirely subversive to the supply-system of a city ten times its size. The trade-interests tried to get an act through Parliament, but the electoral power of Second Adventism was too strong. They tried to engineer a strike in the building trade, but Second Adventism was paying its workers too well. In every department there was prosperity and contentment; and when the Trade Unions and their leaders themselves became converts to Second Adventism, what

more could the enemy do? They tried to get Mr. Trimblerigg's co-operative currency prohibited as a base imitation of the coin of the realm; but Mr. Trimblerigg's currency had been designed with holes through it – haloes
with the heads missing – so that it could deceive nobody;
and the Courts ruled that as a trade-token for convenience
in commerce, it was allowable. Then they tried to swamp
out its value by forging it; but as it had its full worth of
silver in the world's exchange, forgeries did not matter.
Of course no bank would handle it; but that also did not
matter. The New Jerusalem was going to have a bank of
its own; and when the present state of things came to an
end, it might well be the only bank that would count.

For Second Adventism did not teach that the world was
going to end in fire, and earthquake, and physical over-
throw; but that a new spirit would come hovering, responsive to the call of its worshippers; and entering into the
place prepared for it, there set up a light; and all the world
would see a working object-lesson of the new society that
was soon to be; co-operation would take the place of competition; a reorganization of industry would make strikes
superfluous; internationalism would arise, not from the
adjustment of racial differences but from religious unity.
And out of that would come Peace.

The originality of Mr. Trimblerigg's idea had been this
– first to make religion irresistibly popular, by running it
as a kind of 'stunt' – big business and beatific vision combined – and then having made piety prosperous, to sub-
stitute, for the solution of the world's ills, the religious
organization for the political.

Mr. Trimblerigg had seen that habit – habit of mind as
well as body – is the dead weight in the world's affairs

which separates man from faith, and prevents mountains from being moved. And so with Second Adventism, backed by spiritualism and prophecy, he had routed men's minds out of their groove, simply by convincing them that on a given date, willy-nilly, the groove was coming to an end. Mr. Trimblerigg's greatest exploit was not in building a city capable of containing a million souls, but in finding a million souls ready to flock to it. And he had done so, in the main, by convincing them that the New Jerusalem meant good business. 'Homes for Haloes,' the motto he had chosen for his scheme, did not really mean much when you came to examine it, for though the homes were fast taking shape, the haloes were still to seek. But 'Homes for Heroes' or 'Homes for Haloes', have an encouraging sound about them, and each, on different occasions, have served their turn, helping publicists out for popular applause to rouse a fictitious enthusiasm in their followers, till cold fact came after and snuffed it out.

CHAPTER THIRTY-THREE

The Procession Ends

HAVING ANNOUNCED A DATE FOR THE END OF THE world — the old world with its troublous record, its damaged reputation, its useless strivings after success, — an end which was to be brought about not by the death and destruction of the wicked, but by a new birth unto righteousness upon an unprecedented scale, — having so definitely announced the spiritual transformation which was about to take place before the eyes of all, the Second Adventists had to live up to it.

And to their credit, be it said, they did so without a qualm of doubt. Mr. Trimblerigg's experience since his adoption of Second Adventism had convinced him that if only it were well organized for a fixed purpose, prayer could get itself answered; and that given a commanding majority and a united aim, the human race was master of the Event. He had backed his country through war with prayerful conviction, had even prayed that it might go on an extra eighteen months so as to avoid a negotiated peace, and secure the dictated one which was to be so much better; and then, because hearts and aims were divided, had seen the dictated peace lost and become very much worse than a negotiated one; and though he did not for a moment consider that his own prayers and strivings for a dictated peace made him in the least responsible for its bad results, he had an uneasy suspicion that the world, and even his own country, might have done better for itself by letting the war end sooner than it did, for the simple reason that though it could agree about fighting it could not agree about peace.

But about making the bad old world come to an end on

a given date, Second Adventists were all enthusiastically agreed; and when Mr. Trimblerigg returned from America he found the building of the New Jerusalem so well advanced that though it might not be entirely habitable on the day, externally it looked habitable; and though a good many scaffolding poles still had to remain, they would serve to hang bunting on, and so enhance the welcoming effect when Heaven sent down its new spirit to take possession.

For that something auspicious and visible would take place was the general belief; the writings of Susannah Walcot suggested it, and though the idea had not been officially endorsed, yet, since it helped publicity, nothing had been said to discourage it. It might be prophecy, or it might only be figure of speech; but in a very literal sense the faith of millions did undoubtedly look skywards expecting a sign to be given it. For it must be remembered that always now before men's eyes one sign stood conspicuous; and if upon one eminent head glory had so forecast itself, might it not be possible when the Day came that Heaven would rain haloes by the million upon those found faithfully waiting to receive them?

For that given date the railway companies had already arranged to run special excursions from all parts of the country, timed to arrive at latest before the stroke of midnight signalled the beginning of the new Day. Behind the railways were the caterers, all ready to link up the meat and the fish markets, the dairies, the greengrocers, and the provision-dealers, with the demanding appetite of the new-born and spiritualized world.

It was computed that not less than a million prospective inhabitants of the New Jerusalem would be there all ready and waiting in wedding garments for the hour when Heaven should declare itself.

All were to come dressed in white; and a city dressed in white stood prepared to receive them. A little garish by day, the New Jerusalem looked very beautiful by moonlight; then, with its white walls, and pearly windows, and blue-grey roofs, crowned fantastically by the points and perforated pinnacles of its toy-palaces, it seemed like a city of silver. In the midst of it – the great co-operative shopping-centre – were buildings composed entirely of glass, with covered streets where the weather would no longer count for anything; and on the outskirts, separated from the residential quarters by parks and public gardens and ornamental lakes, stood the power-stations, and watertowers, and above all these, in noble battlemented walls, like a mediæval castle converted to spiritual ends, the gasometers had concealed themselves. It was all very expansive and opulent, and self-complacent, and plausible, and what perhaps in an earlier age might have been called genteel; but what to my mind it resembled most was the character – the public character, I mean – of Mr. Trimblerigg as it appeared when things went well with him. In this 'Home for Haloes' he had finally and magnificently expressed himself as he wished he might be. 'Si monumentum requiris, circumspice' was the motto with which, after looking out of his Presidential window on that last happy night of his career, he closed his eyes in postprandial repose, so as to be up blithe and fresh for 'the Great Watch' which at midnight was to begin. In all the streets that lay before his gaze orderly crowds, clothed in white and carrying lanterns and palm-branches in their hands, paraded with happy unanimity, all marching one

way as the traffic signals directed, and singing as they
went. It was a marvel of organization; as a human demonstration – the expression of a commanding majority
devoting itself for the first time to one single spiritual end
– it was still more wonderful.

And so with a happy smile upon his illuminated face Mr.
Trimblerigg lay down in his Presidential robe, and slept
like a child.

He was awakened at about half-past ten by a terrific ex-
plosion. Fragments of plaster battlements were falling
into the street and against his front-door as he opened the
window and looked out. Hurriedly he drew his head in
again; but what had sent him back was not the falling
fragments but the despairing ululations of the crowd,
which, dropping its hymn-singing parade was now rushing hither and thither frantic for shelter from showering
rubble and glass which filled the air. Under the calm
blaze of the full moon, queening it in a cloudless heaven,
a ragged scud of black dust jagged its way from roof to
roof, obliterating the distant view; in its rear, at a more
ponderous gallop, came a hunch of smoke, which as it
advanced billowed and spread, and became huge; swal-
lowing up the clear air as it advanced, it left in its track a
pallid haze which went everywhere. The New Jerusalem
became a ghost, vague of form, clad no longer in white,
but in a dun grey streaked by scarves of black lined with
colours of fire. In this settling obscurity the sound of
human woe went on increasing, enlivened now and again
by cries of rage. The crowd, cumbered by its wedding
raiment, was fighting confusedly for priority of place;
the terminus was being rushed, empty excursion trains
boarded. A faint-hearted exodus from the New Jerusalem

had already begun: the world was not coming to an end in the peaceful way that had been foretold.

A ring-up on Mr. Trimblerigg's telephone gave him the news. His castle of gasometers had been blown up; as to the cause, inquiry was being made; incendiarism was suspected. Following upon that came other news of a similar kind. Something had gone wrong with the power-stations; wires fused and lights went out; after that went the water-supply; about midnight to the sound of bombs, three water-towers cascaded to earth; and when, here, there, and everywhere, fainting people turned taps to get water, none came. Presently in various parts of the city fires began; and as there was no water to put them out, they spread. Before morning the New Jerusalem had had several bits taken out of it, and many of its prospective inhabitants were left homeless. About dawn a covey of aeroplanes let down a discharge of sticky-gas — the latest military invention for the humane dispersal of unarmed crowds. It had adhesive properties of an extraordinary effectiveness; the New Jerusalem became like well-spread fly-paper, and all humans with whom it established contact walked thereafter as though they had been anointed with treacle, or honey, or preserved-ginger, or turpentine; and having no water in which to wash themselves, their misery became greater than they could bear; and from all that crowd of souls which had come together with such singleness of purpose, and confidence, and goodwill, the social sense was cast violently out, so that they all hated the sight and the touch and the sound of each other.

Now all this, it must be understood, was not the operation of Heaven, but only of Big Finance, and certain other vested interests which did not wish the old ways of the

312

world to end, or competitive society to become co-operative, or religion in any form to have control over economics and politics, or Mr. Trimblerigg to go any farther than they considered safe for the well-being of the country. And as Second Adventism had in these respects become a peril, quite as formidable in its way as foreign invasion, therefore an underground organization had been formed, which, calling itself 'Red Knights of the Fiery Cross', had designed for itself a costume, and a secret ritual, and an oath which could not be broken; and had laid up store of military preparation, and with prayer and fasting and genuflections, had practised bomb-throwing and incendiarism and the casting down of sticky gas in solitary places where a Duke preserved pheasants, and where, therefore, no members of the outer public were allowed to intrude. And having become experts in the game, upon the advertised day they made a match of it, and in this, the first round, had apparently won hands down. For the New Jerusalem had become a sticky object, coated with dust and very offensive to the smell: and the Second Adventists sharply divided into two bodies of an unequal size: the larger fugitive and dispersive in tendency, no longer wishing for the end of the world, but only for the excursion trains to start upon their return journeys: the other comparatively small, but vigorous, vocal and tending to direct action: truculent, abusive, full of grievance, clamorous for the return of its deposits in a co-operative scheme which no longer seemed safe, and with regard to which, in certain important respects, the undertakings, as per contract, were not being carried out.

It was this section which presented itself at an early hour outside the Presidency, and howled to be received in deputation by Mr. Trimblerigg. For three hours they howled, while Mr. Trimblerigg, in order to give confidence to his frightened followers, had his breakfast and his bath (for which sufficient water remained in the cistern) and dealt with certain arrears of correspondence.

At ten o'clock punctually, he looked at his watch, and said to his secretary, 'Now I will go out and speak to them.'

The secretary said, 'I think, sir, you had better not. If I know anything of crowds, that crowd is dangerous.'

Mr. Trimblerigg said, 'I hope it is. I shall do my best to make it so.'

The light of battle was in his eye. He said to his secretary, 'You must dress yourself up; you are a Knight of the Fiery Cross whom we have taken prisoner. You must be shown to the people, with your hands bound and your face stained with blood. It will only be for a moment; but it will satisfy them. I will do the rest.'

But before he had finished, he spoke to emptiness: the secretary had fled. He looked out into the ante-chamber. All the others had fled with him. Outside the crowd was howling like a pack of wolves.

Mr. Trimblerigg sighed: 'Then I must do it all by myself,' he concluded thoughtfully. 'Deserted of my followers, I stand alone. No matter; they shall see!' He felt that he was a great man, and this a great occasion for making the fact known.

He went out from his study into the Council Chamber, a handsome apartment hung with mirrors. It had four windows overlooking the street, windows that went down to the ground and opened upon a balcony supported by a

colonnade extending from the entrance-porch to right and
left.

I have never admired Mr. Trimblerigg more than I did
at that moment; as he crossed the open space before him
he paused to glance at himself in one of the mirrors: his
light had not failed him; its radiance was undiminished;
in the midst of it his countenance shone cherubic and
hopeful. He was going to enjoy himself; for of all whose
fortunes depended on the breath of popular applause there
was no one who understood a crowd as he did.

That this one was now hostile only added to the zest
with which he faced the task that lay before him. Standing back in the deep interior of the room and where he
could not be seen, he studied its physiognomy – a sea of
faces in storm, multitudinous but yet one. He looked at
it with affection and pride; for in another minute he was
going to take and turn it round his finger, and make it
into a new instrument to suit his need.

Suddenly, while he so stood, the very window-pane
through which he looked fell into splinters; from the
crystal chandelier above his head came a rain of shattered
glass. That was the prelude; he stepped back, and skirting the wall, while all the other panes flew into fragments,
reached the far window, in which by that time not a pane
remained unbroken. He only paused to fasten the last
button of the morning coat into which he had tactfully
changed; and then, lightly embraced by the civilization he
had come to save, he opened the window and stepped out.

For one moment the crowd, shocked into mute amaze,
stood and gaped; then a roar of execration filled the air.
Even the bright manifestation of his mission, which had
once awed and delighted, failed to placate them now. Mr.

Trimblerigg knew enough of crowds to admit that his secretary was right; this crowd was dangerous; but he knew also that he had only to get them to listen, to hear his opening words, for his spell to be on them. He could trust the inspiration of the moment to do the rest.

And so, with exactly the right emotional expression upon his face, he leaned out from the stone balustrade, and over the heads of the crowd pointed into the distance.

The gesture had its calculated effect: heads turned, necks were craned; the roar died down to a confused murmur. Presently they would turn back to him and seek to have the thing explained; then would come silence and they would hear what he had to say; and though that was not going to make them less dangerous, it would no longer be danger for him, but for others.

Now it so happened that in the direction where he pointed there was, by fate or by chance, something which on being pointed at, did excite the curiosity of the crowd. On its far outskirts a lone taxi with persistent wrigglings was trying to get through; an attempt which, until the attention of the crowd had been directed towards it, would have been absolutely hopeless. But now, as if by the manipulation of an invisible police, a way grew open before it, and the taxi triumphantly advanced.

As it did so it became – though nobody could guess why – a thing of extraordinary importance; people began climbing on each other's backs to look at it. Even Mr. Trimblerigg became interested; for this – though an interruption – was also a diversion; it meant safety. A crowd which could focus its interest on a taxi-cab, could focus it also upon him; nor had he now the slightest doubt that when he spoke to it the crowd would prove amenable.

Folding his arms on the balustrade, and playing with his eyeglasses, he was the very picture of confidence and hope and courage and resourcefulness, and all the other things which, in their leaders, men admire. How could people look at him without liking him? How could they hear him without trusting him? How could there be any danger for a man who stood up to face it with such an air of high spirits and genial acceptance of a situation which seemed awkward. He felt with a sure instinct that the crowd was coming his way, that in another moment it would be cheering him.

The taxi was coming his way also. It stopped. Davidina put out her head. Over the hushed murmurs of the crowd, clear and incisive her voice reached him:

'Jonathan, take that off!'

If the end of Mr. Trimblerigg's world could have come then in whatever other form it chose to take, it might have been said of him thereafter that he died happy, died believing in himself, and believed in by others even though the immediate circumstances spelt failure.

But when he felt the probing eye of Davidina, and heard the challenge of her voice, 'Take that off!'—then all his sense of spiritual nakedness returned; and the power over his soul which she had been used to exercise reinstated itself in all its potency. In a moment, in the twinkling of an eye, and in the presence of all that people whose mood towards him was on the very point of ceasing to be dangerous, and whose hearts in another minute he would have won to the fulfilling of vengeance due – in a space of time too brief for breath to be taken, she had spiritually scalped him. With his head shorn of glory he stood and looked at

317

her; and fleeing suddenly to the domestic note as his last
chance of refuge from the storm which was about to burst,
'How do you do, Davidina?' he said.

It was magnificent, but it was no good. The crowd's yell
of derision told him that it had failed. Suddenly the taxi
disappeared from view; ten, twenty, thirty human atoms,
excited, gesticulating, were up and were over it. He saw
Davidina fighting her way out of the collapsed frame-
work; saw her in imminent danger, saw her emerge safe
and unharmed. With no use or duty to stay him, conscious that all was lost, he turned to flee. It was too late.
Active members of the crowd pushed from below swarmed
up the colonnades; faster than the eye could count, heads
appeared on a level with his waist, – hands, feet, fiery eyes,
fierce mouths showing teeth; he became one of a confused
group, felt his legs carrying much more than his own
weight, his buttons bursting to a rending strain – from
behind. Collared, surrounded, forced to the balcony's
edge, he looked down into a sea of eyes; and heard dimly,
in the background of his dream, Davidina knocking for
admission at the door under his feet; a door which nobody
would answer.

'Up, up!' came the cry of the crowd. He was hoisted,
stood giddily on the stone ledge; swayed, tottered, but
hands still held him. Everything then seemed very near
and immediate and objective: individual faces, blemishes,
blackened eyes, the very cut and colour of men's clothes, a
broken watch-chain, the taxi-driver trying to recover possession of a cab that had become a wreck. Fifty yards
away an arc-lamp high aloft on a street refuge for some
unexplainable reason spat itself into light. That attracted
him, only to remind him with a pang of despair that he

could no longer do the same. Light and hope and faith had all gone out of him.

'Down! Down!' the crowd's cry had changed: but its intention was the same. A thousand hands reached up, opening and shutting like mouths, hungry to have hold of him. The hands from behind gave a jerk, then tossed and let go. He felt himself falling, but of that was not afraid. A real fall was impossible; of that the thousand hands made him feel safe. They caught him, forced him down, and set him upon his feet. A voice at his back cried: 'Stand clear! Give him a run!'

Magically a way cleared for him: a long stretch of pavement, then a road: in the middle of the road, aloft on its iron standard, spluttered the arc-lamp, very wan and pale against the healthier light of day.

Propelled from behind he began running towards it, with an agility which for a moment, in his responsive mind, wakened an absurd hope.

But a moment later, under the lamp-post, he was off his feet again. Up in front of him swarmed a man-monkey of the sailor-breed trailing a rope. The crowd roared gloriously, its rage changing to delight.

Clasping the iron standard despairingly with legs and arms in a last embrace, he felt hands below pushing him, making him go higher. Then suddenly there came a wrench; the hands loosed him, but his feet did not touch ground. And as his agitated body sought this way and that for the hand-hold or foot-hold it had lost never to find again, I, reading for the last time the scrip of his brain, found the truth fairly lodged there at last:

'O, you fool! O, you damned fool! O, you silly, damned fool, look what you have done to yourself now!'

And then something happened: something quite unexpected, for which I cannot account; though I have a sort of a fear that I know in what direction the account may hereafter be found.

I followed him into those last moments – for his last moments they proved to be – with a breathless interest, which at least told me that though he had tried me much, I was not as tired of him as, for my own peace, I would have liked to be. And up to the last hitch, I still wondered whether so agile an executant of quick turns would not manage even then to escape from his enemies. His enemies, I say. But my wonder now is whether his last escape has not been made from one who, like Davidina, was his faithful though discriminating friend. For when, after the rope had done its work, I looked for him on the spiritual plane, it was to find that he had vanished. And if I, too, must own the truth – I do not know what has become of him.